Strong for Service

Minister of Civil Aviation in 1946

H. Montgomery Hyde

Strong for Service

The Life of
Lord Nathan of Churt

W. H. ALLEN
LONDON
1968

© ELEANOR LADY NATHAN

PRINTED AND BOUND IN GREAT BRITAIN BY

BUTLER AND TANNER LTD, FROME AND LONDON

FOR THE PUBLISHERS

W. H. ALLEN AND CO LTD

ESSEX STREET, LONDON WC2

491 00471 0

Contents

Illustrations

Acknowledgements

ALTHOUGH I was personally acquainted with the subject of this book during his lifetime and had the advantage of his friendly advice on a number of occasions, my meetings with him were relatively few and mainly confined to professional business affairs. Consequently in writing the book I have had to depend in great measure upon those who knew him much better and more intimately than I did. My debt to them is considerable.

First of all, I must thank Eleanor Lady Nathan for putting her husband's private papers unreservedly at my disposal, and for answering my numerous questions with unwearying patience. Other members of Lord Nathan's family have likewise been most helpful, notably her son Roger, the present Lord Nathan; his daughter Joyce, the Hon. Lady Waley-Cohen; his brother, Major Cyril Nathan; his nephew, Mr Peter Nathan; and his cousin, Mr Leonard Stein.

The Earl of Longford, who suggested that I should undertake this work in the first place, has been good enough to contribute a Foreword to it, besides showing a kindly interest in its composition throughout.

I am grateful to Mr T. E. B. Howarth, High Master of St Paul's School, and to Mr A. N. Y. Richards, the school archivist, for making available the records for the period that Lord Nathan was a pupil.

My thanks are also due to the following for their help and interest: Professor John Burnaby, Mr Graham Carritt, Mr Frank Cobb, Miss Marjorie Dyce, Mr Morris Ernst, Mr Herbert Garfield, Mr L. P. Kirwan, Major J. G. Martin, Mr Peter G. Masefield, Sir Clement Price Thomas, and Mr Donald Tyerman.

For the background to an interesting and important episode in Lord Nathan's career as a solicitor, I am indebted to *Given to Salt*, by M. A. Novomeysky, published by Max Parrish Ltd, in 1938.

H.M.H.

Foreword

by the Rt Hon. the Earl of Longford, P.C.

IT is for me a privilege and joy to write a Foreword for Mr Montgomery Hyde's life of Lord Nathan. The biographer seems to me to have performed his task splendidly, and if I add anything it is a small tribute of friendship rather than any attempt to rectify omissions. During the last eighteen years of his life I worked closely with Harry Nathan in many fields, but I had barely met him until I entered the House of Lords in 1945 and became his junior colleague in the Attlee Government.

His earlier life, as set out here, was only dimly known to me. I knew, for example, of his long-standing interest in social work, in which his wife played so notable a part, but I had never realized before quite how profound and constructive that interest was. I was well aware of his undying concern for the fighting Services. I can well remember a defence debate in the last years of his life when he was the only man taking part among many famous Service leaders who was actually going into camp that year with his Territorial Regiment. He had been in the habit of doing this for many years, and it was a practice he kept up until the end. He was then over 70, and indeed had been dieting conscientiously with the exercise in mind. But again, until I read Mr Montgomery Hyde's account, I had not fully appreciated the full gallantry of his First War achievement. And so with many other aspects of his earlier life.

There is much that is new to me here, yet it all fits in with Harry Nathan as I came to know him so well. I suppose that anyone like myself, who became his friend during his latter years, would single out his kindness as his outstanding quality. There was a general benevolence which showed itself in handsome but unobtrusive donations to all good causes and much labour on behalf of them.

There was, however, in addition, a personal warmth. It started, of course, with a family life of beautiful devotion and wonderful partnership. It spread through a circle of friends of all types and ages who will mourn him as long as they themselves are living.

It has been suggested to me, by someone who knew him most intimately, that perhaps his second most outstanding quality was a kind of practical creativeness. Whether in Civil Aviation, where his full achievement has not yet, I think, been appreciated; in his work for the Services; in business; in his hospital and other charitable work, including his report on the whole future of charities; he was always the same, thorough, patient, apparently rather slow-moving, and yet coming out at the end with bold and far-reaching proposals.

One of his qualities which went closely no doubt with these achievements was a fundamental approach. Victor Gollancz told me once that on returning from Russia he was asked by Harry Nathan to lunch. After the preliminaries had been concluded—'It will occur to you, Victor,' said Harry deliberately, 'that I did not ask you here to talk about the weather. Tell me, Victor, what is Stalin up to?' Curiously, his son Roger (the present Lord Nathan) recalls a similar formula being applied to the Japanese Ambassador before the War. 'You must not think me discourteous, Mr Ambassador,' said Harry, 'if I ask you bluntly *what are you up to?*' Harry Nathan, for all his deliberate manner, liked to get to the bottom of things and get there quickly.

I end by wondering whether he was at all different in the years of our friendship from his earlier self. I doubt if he was quite so combative in the latter period. Nothing, I gather, gave him greater pleasure in earlier days than a good stand-up election fight or any kind of political rough and tumble. In our time together I must think that he had mellowed a good deal as the years passed. I should describe him as sensitive, kindly to others and hoping to meet a reasonable degree of civilized behaviour in return. He was still the same fighter as in the far-off days of Gallipoli, but he was, by this time, seeking the result rather than the combat and extreme partisanship I felt had come to bore him.

I don't know anybody whom I have ever consulted with such absolute confidence that he would bring complete knowledge and selfless dedication to bear on one's problem. To have been counselled by him was a great experience. To have enjoyed his friendship and trust is one which is still richer and more lasting.

But strong for service, and unimpair'd.

WILLIAM COWPER
The Task

CHAPTER ONE

Early Years

IN 1795, THE FORCES OF REVOLUTIONARY FRANCE SWEPT THROUGH the Netherlands, and the French set up the Batavian Republic, later to be incorporated in Napoleon's Empire. Among the Dutch families who followed the ruling Prince of Orange in his flight to England at this time was one of Jewish origin called Van Noorden. On their arrival in England, the various members of the Van Noorden family adopted an English style of nomenclature. One took the name of Clifford, another that of Eskell, and a third that of Nathan. In deciding to call himself Nathan, the latter may merely have reverted to the name borne by his ancestors. Meaning literally 'the given one', Nathan is a name distinguished in Hebrew history, its best known bearer being the Old Testament prophet, who rebuked King David and, along with Zadok the priest, proclaimed and anointed Solomon as David's successor.

Michael Nathan, otherwise Van Noorden, great-grandfather of the first Lord Nathan, was born in Holland about 1782 and was probably a youth still in his teens when he came to England. He had a son named Henry, who was born in 1812, and he is known to have been in business as a general dealer in Birmingham, where he lived at 18 Pershore Street, dying there in 1842 from the effects of 'inflammation in the bowels', no doubt typhoid fever. Among his co-religionists with whom he appears to have done business was one Joseph Jacobs, a general dealer in Manchester. At some date, possibly after his father's death, Henry Nathan moved from Birmingham to Manchester where he lodged in the same house as Joseph Jacobs, with whose daughter Matilda he fell in love. By this time Henry Nathan had gone into business for himself in Manchester as a stationer, a term which then included the sale of books and journals as well as writing materials. On September 2, 1846, he and Matilda Jacobs were married according to the rites of the Hebrew religion in the house at 55 Water Street, Manchester, where both the bridegroom and bride were then living.

It is likely that Henry Nathan and his wife's family both lived 'over the shop' and that the two businesses were carried on from these premises. Also it was probably through the help of his father-in-law that, shortly after his marriage, Henry Nathan branched out as a manufacturer of artists' brushes and painting materials. The business prospered, and he and his wife moved to a larger house at 10 Back King Street, Deansgate. Here their son Michael Henry was born in 1852. There were two daughters and two more sons of the marriage. The youngest brother Joseph, who married Minna Possenniskie, emigrated to New Zealand, where their descendants are still living.

Michael Henry Nathan left school at the age of thirteen to join the family business in Manchester, owing to his father's comparatively early death. To make himself look older, he wore a top-hat to the office. He worked hard since he had to keep his mother and sisters and he also had to help his brothers, so that it was not until he was in his middle thirties that he could afford to get married. By this time he had extended the business to include the manufacture and publishing of Christmas and Valentine cards and other coloured greeting cards and prints which were so popular with the Victorians. He had then concentrated more and more on the fine art publishing side of the business and, leaving his youngest brother Maurice in charge of the Manchester office, had eventually moved to London, prompted by the success of Raphael Tuck and his son Adolph (later Sir Adolph Tuck, Bart.), who had inaugurated a series of original Christmas Card Designs Exhibitions at the

Dudley Gallery, with such distinguished artists as Sir John Millais and Sir Coutts Lindsay as judges.

Michael Henry Nathan's wife was born Constance Beaver, the ninth and youngest child of Louis Beaver, jeweller and silversmith of Manchester, by his wife Rachel née Mayer of Hanley, Staffordshire. Louis Beaver, whose surname was originally Bibergeil, had come to England about 1838 from near Bromberg, then in East Prussia, where his father Abraham Bibergeil was a surgeon. He seems to have been accompanied by an elder brother Hirsch (Henry), who had recently qualified as a physician in Berlin and came to continue his medical studies in Glasgow. Both brothers changed their surname to Beaver, Louis doing so before his marriage to Rachel Mayer in 1846. The elder brother eventually emigrated to New Zealand, where he died in 1865. Other brothers went to Australia and Russia and another settled in Berlin as a banker. All did well, particularly Adolph Bibergeil, the eldest, an orthopaedic surgeon, who became a medical adviser to the Czar Nicholas I, and Louis, who founded what was eventually to become the leading firm of jewellers and silversmiths in Manchester. Louis Beaver died in 1879, leaving the business to be carried on by his son Marcus under the style of M. Beaver & Co. Mrs Rachel Beaver had died some years before her husband.*

Their youngest child Constance, left an orphan at the age of fifteen, went to live with her elder sister Matilda, who was married to a Manchester shipping broker named Philip Stein. Four years later the Steins moved to London, taking Constance Beaver with them, by which date her future husband had also transferred his business to the City.

Michael Henry Nathan remembered Constance and her sister from their Manchester days, and it was natural that the acquaintance

* Mrs Rachel Beaver, Lord Nathan's maternal grandmother, who died in Manchester at the comparatively early age of 37, appears to have been a woman of outstanding character. 'Seldom, if ever, was there such a large funeral procession of sympathizing friends witnessed in this city, all bent upon paying their respects to the memory of that "true woman in Israel" ': *Jewish Chronicle*, December 15, 1865.

should be renewed when they went to London. At this time Michael Henry was living with his mother in Porchester Gardens, Paddington, and from time to time he would visit the Stein household in Ladbroke Grove. There he became engaged to Constance Beaver. They were married on July 14, 1887, in the Marlborough Rooms, Regent Street, by the Rabbi of the West London Synagogue, the official witnesses being the bride's uncle Marcus Beaver and her brother-in-law Philip Stein.

The Nathans' first home, which they set up on getting married and where they were to remain for the next thirty years, was at 36 Bassett Road, an impressive stucco-fronted detached house of three storeys in one of the thoroughfares leading off Ladbroke Grove. For this desirable residence, which was large enough to accommodate his mother and one of his unmarried sisters as well as his wife and any children they might have, Michael Henry Nathan paid £90 a year rent. Although the young breadwinner could have afforded to buy a house, he preferred a rented dwelling. 'Fools build houses for wise men to live in,' he used to say. Indeed few people outside the aristocracy and wealthy classes owned the houses they lived in in those days and when they did so it was usually as the result of inheritance.

Matilda Nathan, née Jacobs, only survived her son's marriage by a few months. A diabetic and already in failing health when she came to Bassett Road, she died there early in 1888. Thus she did not live to see the birth of her grandson Harry, who was born in the house in the following year. She was buried in London and her son Michael Henry had an appropriate tombstone erected over her grave with an inscription recording her womanly virtues in a sentimental verse under the heading 'Gone but not forgotten.'

> Loving mother and devoted wife
> Thine, Earth's anguish nevermore,
> Pattern in thy path through life,
> Peaceful rest thou evermore.

Michael Henry Nathan also had a photograph taken of the grave, which he later passed on to his son Harry. The latter treasured this

memory of the grandmother he had never seen, carefully preserving
the faded photograph which was found among his papers after his
death three-quarters of a century later. Harry's mother, on the other
hand, was to live to see him become a peer of the realm and a
Minister of the Crown.

2

Harry Louis Nathan, elder son of Michael Henry and Constance
Nathan, was born at 36 Bassett Road, North Kensington, on Feb-
ruary 2, 1889. He was followed two years later by another son,
Cyril. The two boys were their parents' only children.

The home was a happy one for both boys, and their parents
were as devoted to them as they were to each other. 'If I should
not survive,' Harry was to write on his way to Gallipoli in 1915,
'my last thoughts will be of them, who have ever been loving,
helpful, forgiving and kind.' While there was no extravagance,
there was no shortage of money in the Nathan home, and with the
Christmas card trade increasing the family lived comfortably.

Michael Henry Nathan was a genial and warm-hearted man, an
excellent host, who liked entertaining his friends, to whom he was
always most loyal. Every morning he travelled by horse-drawn bus
to Aldersgate, and the driver would always keep a special seat for
him next to his own. Occasionally the boys would be taken by
their mother to call for him at Australia House in Aldersgate, where
his office was. Once Harry went to the City with his mother to have
his photograph taken by a professional photographer; the pleasing
likeness of the child, his hair in curls and wearing a wide-brimmed
straw hat, was subsequently used by Michael Henry Nathan for one
of his Christmas cards.

There were plenty of other domestic diversions to keep the boys
occupied. Their mother played the piano and their father was a
passable singer, so that there was plenty of musical entertainment
in the house in which the boys joined. It was a good middle-class

neighbourhood with a fair sprinkling of carriage folk. Food and domestic servants were cheap and income tax was just over a shilling in the pound. The family's closest friends and neighbours were their cousins the Steins, and Harry and Cyril would play with the two Stein children Leonard and Agatha. There was a spacious nursery on the third floor with the window well protected by stout iron bars on the outside to prevent the more venturesome from jumping out. They also saw a good deal of a family called Guedalla who lived in nearby Maida Vale. David Guedalla was an almond broker in Mincing Lane, while his wife Louise was Constance Nathan's closest friend. Their son Philip, the future historian and master of epigram, had been born a few weeks after Harry Nathan. 'He was my earliest friend,' Harry was to recall at the time of Philip Guedalla's premature death in 1944, 'because his mother and mine had been friends since girlhood and as youngsters we used to play in our respective nurseries together.' The two families sometimes spent holidays together at Folkestone and other seaside towns in the summer.

As a young boy Harry was sent to two private schools in the district, one a convent school and the other a dame school kept by a Miss Finzi, a relative of the composer Gerald Finzi. Harry's schooldays were as happy as his home life. He was in no sense a withdrawn boy; he got on well with other boys of his age and enjoyed playing games with them. Indeed he was quick to organize games himself. For instance, he and Leonard Stein, who was two years older, formed a cricket club called the Audax. They secured a pitch near the prison at Wormwood Scrubs, and the necessary funds to keep the club going were raised by amateur theatricals in the drawing-room at Bassett Road.

When Harry was about ten years old, his father suffered some kind of nervous breakdown, which determined him on medical advice to retire from business, although he was not yet fifty. He had managed over the years to accumulate about £30,000, which when carefully invested in gilt-edged and other sound stocks could be relied upon to bring in a steady income of £1,500 a year. Now, although he no longer made the daily journey to the City, he had plenty to do. He had been appointed a Justice of the Peace, so that his attendances in court, together with prison visiting at Wormwood Scrubs, kept him fairly busy. Then he had always been a keen Liberal in politics and a strong supporter of Mr Gladstone. He had been a member of the National Liberal Club and now sat on its committees. He would take his lunch there two or three times a week, after which he would adjourn to the card room for a game of bridge. Twice a week he would play golf at Neasden. If the political horizon was temporarily clouded by the South African War which broke out at this time, for a moderately well-off family like the Nathans' life was pleasant enough and largely free from anxieties, public and private, as the long Victorian sunset gave way to the brief but rosy Edwardian dawn.

When he was about eight, Harry was sent as a day boy to Colet Court, the preparatory school for St Paul's, there to be followed a year or two later by his younger brother Cyril. One Whitsun holiday, their parents went away on a ship's cruise, and Harry sent them a daily account of his doings. As the following extracts show, their main preoccupations were cricket and meals.

36 Basset Road, W. June 5th 1900. . . . This evening we played cricket. We both practised over and round arm and got Cyril out twice with it.

We had steak and liver for dinner and blancmange with strawberry jam. For supper we had boiled plaice and stewed gooseberries and ginger beer.

I got a history of Greece, by Smith.

June 6th. . . . We had tea at Kew amongst the grass under a tree yesterday. This morning we had a game of cricket with Leonard and Haines and some boys who challenged us to a match. They won by 2 runs because they had 1 more boy than we.

June 7th. . . . Yesterday we had roast mutton, jam tart and soda water for dinner. For supper we had a sole and soda water and biscuit and cheese.

June 11th. . . . The weather is abominable here, it is so beastly hot $79\frac{1}{2}$ degrees in the shade. I am going to the baths when I have finished my lessons. I am 8th in Classics, 6 higher

than last time. I am feeling pretty well. I've got neuralgia but
don't trouble about that.
It is so hot I have not the patience to write any more.

However, he added a postscript that 'Middlesex won by 209
runs' in a county cricket match, and, thinking his parents had not
heard the latest news from the Boer battle front, 'More fighting,
Roberts cut off'.

Shortly before his twelfth birthday, Harry Nathan competed for
an entrance Exhibition to St Paul's School; it was the only formal
academic distinction, as it turned out, that he ever won. For the past
sixteen years the school had been established in the familiar neo-
Gothic buildings of red brick on the Hammersmith Road under the
legendary rule of the High Master Frederick William Walker, who
had been appointed when the school was still in the City. In the
Easter Term of 1901, Harry Nathan joined as a Capitation Scholar,
as the fee-paying pupils were called, to distinguish them from the
Foundation Scholars whose tuition was free. He was placed in the
Upper Fourth, where he was taught Latin, Greek, French, English,
Mathematics and Drawing. As a practising Jew, he was excused
Divinity. But his religious education was not overlooked; he
regularly attended classes in the West London Synagogue under
the instruction of Katie Magnus, wife of Sir Philip Magnus, Bart.,
and a well-known authoress of Bible stories for the young. Besides
his brother Cyril and his cousin Leonard Stein, Harry's Jewish con-
temporaries at the school included Cyril Picciotto, who later wrote
a history of St Paul's, and Victor Gollancz, whose subsequent
successful career as a publisher was to owe something to Harry
Nathan's encouragement, professional as well as moral.

Harry and his young brother would travel daily from West-
bourne Park or Notting Hill station on the Metropolitan Railway
to Hammersmith, usually running the last part of the way so as to
be in time for morning prayers in the School Hall. Besides their
train fares they were given a shilling each to spend on their lunches.
Although Harry was to end up in Upper Eighth, a School Prefect,
an officer in the Cadet Corps, and Vice-President and Treasurer of

the Union Debating Society, his academic career had its ups and downs and his school reports varied considerably. 'Has worked very well and made good progress,' his form master wrote at the end of his first year. 'Greek and French are his weakest points. But he is still young.' His half-yearly reports for 1902 were discouraging. ('Is too careless and inattentive to do good work.' 'Forgetful and not industrious.') But he picked up in the following year, when he was chosen by written examination to fill one of the twenty or so vacancies on the Foundation, thereby relieving his father of paying any further tuition fees on his behalf. Two years later he was re-elected a Foundation Scholar, which he remained for the rest of his time at St Paul's.

In the summer term of 1904, he entered History Eighth, a comparatively new type of senior form created to cater for boys who were considered to have somewhat unusual or unconventional talents. Harry remained there for the next eighteen months. At this period the History Eighth consisted of eight boys under the charge of Mr R. F. Cholmeley. To this master's teaching Harry Nathan probably owed more than to any other teacher in the school. 'Shows promise,' was Mr Cholmeley's initial impression. 'As yet is inclined to write without thinking.' Six months later the same master remarked: 'Works well. Knows very little and has a great deal of bad style and rubbish of all sorts to get rid of, but has brains and means to use them.' His first half-yearly report in 1905 read: 'Works very hard and shows some originality of thought beneath a good deal of imitative writing; needs a thorough training in facts.'

No Pauline could escape some contact with the formidable and awe-inspiring High Master. The son of a hatter from Tullamore in Ireland, Dr Walker, after carrying off a host of academic prizes at Oxford, refused the Corpus Professorship of Latin at that university to become one of the most celebrated headmasters in English public school history. Sir Compton Mackenzie, a Pauline who left the school several terms before Harry Nathan entered it, has described Walker in language which most readers of his novel *Sinister Street* will readily recall. Walker resembled Dr Johnson not a little in his ungainly figure, his bellowing voice and his tendency to explode over apparent trifles, just as quickly recovering his equanimity.

Frederick William Walker was to a small boy the personification of majesty, dominion, ferocity and awe. He seemed huge of build with a long grey beard to which adhered stale morsels of food and the acrid scent of strong cigars. His face was ploughed and fretted with indentations volcanic: scoria torrents flowed from his eyes, his forehead was seared and cleft with frowning crevasses and wrinkled with chasms. His clothes were stained with soup and rank with tobacco-smoke but over them he wore a full and swishing gown of silk. When he spoke his voice rumbled in the titanic deeps of his body, or if he were angry, it burst forth in a roar that seemed to shake the great Hall.

Walker possessed a profound and almost uncanny insight into the characters and capacities of small boys. He would often take a boy whose talents were as yet unrecognized out of his class and send him through the swing doors into the Hall, where he would be received by Mr W. E. P. Pantin, the author of *Pantin's Introduction to Latin Elegiacs*. Here Mr Pantin, whom Sir Compton Mackenzie remembered as a kindly man with a perpetual cold in the head, presided over the Special Class, 'where boys picked out by the High Master himself underwent for days or weeks as the case might be a period of intensive culture, after which they were planted out in a higher form beyond the ordinary mechanics of promotion'. This was the experience which befell Harry Nathan between leaving Upper Fifth A and joining the History Eighth. Much of the period of incubation under Mr Pantin consisted of turning conditional sentences into imperfect Greek.

While these exacting exercises were proceeding, the High Master would frequently indulge in his favourite practice of 'going into Hall' to satisfy himself as to the progress being made by the select pupils. To quote Sir Compton Mackenzie again:

His method of approach was appalling to the young, for he would swing along up the aisle and suddenly plunge into a seat beside the chosen boy, pushing himself inward along the form with his black bulk. He would seize the boy's pen and after scratching his own head with the end of the holder he would follow word by word the conditional sentences, tapping the paper between the lines as he read each sentence, so that at the end of his examination the page was peppered with dots of ink. . . . If a boy confused the Present Particular with a Present General the Old Man would glare at him and roar and thunder and peal his execration and contempt. Then suddenly his fury would be relieved by this eruption and he would affix his initials to the bottom of the page—F. W. W.—after which endorsement he would pat the boy's head, mumble an unintelligible joke and plunge down beside another victim.

If the mistakes were those which a clever boy could quite well make, the lad usually got off with a tweak of the ear and a rumbled 'You goose.' On the other hand, if the exercise was thoroughly bad, the High Master would let himself go with an agonized roar, 'Mr Pantin, we'll have to send this boy to Science!' The sight of the majestic bearded figure in Hall on these occasions remained with Harry Nathan as an imperishable memory.

Nor was the boy ever likely to forget another occasion in the great school Hall in 1905 when at Apposition, as the annual speech day and prize giving was known at St Paul's, Dr. Walker addressed his pupils and their parents for the last time. He was then 75, he had been High Master for nearly thirty years, and the time had come for him to make way for a younger man. His final words, which embodied his profession of faith, were intoned with the slightest sarcastic inflection, which he habitually used in speaking to the School.

We do not presume to rival the great public schools of which Eton is the perfect type. We do not try—the attempt would be in vain—to impart that charming manner, that social attractiveness, that splendid *esprit de corps*, and many other precious things which make the domestic incidents of one individual school matters of national concern, which raise the election of a Head Master and the fate of a cricket match between Eton and Harrow into questions of almost Imperial

importance. Our work lies in a far lower sphere. But we remember the proverb, *Spartam nactus es, hanc exorna*. We
strive, not without success to make our boys intellectually
strong, industrious, loyal, and as far as we can do, morally
upright. The rest we are forced to leave, and I do not regret it,
to fathers and mothers and the influence of the home.*

3

Walker's successor as High Master, the Reverend Albert Ernest
Hillard, D.D., not yet forty, was cast more in the conventional
mould of school head. A learned theologian, he was the author of a
life of Christ and numerous Bible studies and had also produced,
along with a colleague named North at Clifton College, where
they had both been assistant masters, the well-known textbooks
of Latin and Greek composition which have been used by successive
generations of schoolboys. By nature a reserved and shy man, he
always wore clerical clothes and was not easy to approach, at least
in his early days at St Paul's. On the other hand, he exuded an air
of mild benignity, which contrasted strongly with Walker's Jovian
thunder, and as time went on he developed a deep-rooted affection
for the school and its interests. One of his innovations, from which
Harry Nathan among others was to benefit, was the restoration of
the prefectorial system which had been abolished by Walker, of
whom the story used to be told that, when it was pointed out to
him that monitors (as the prefects were then called) helped to preserve a healthy school democracy, he observed, 'There shall be no
democracy where I rule.' Dr Hillard, on the other hand, lost no
time in choosing prefects from among the leading boys in the
School, who for reasons of character and personality he considered
were likely to be best suited for exercising authority over the rest
of their school fellows. For his last term, Harry Nathan was nomin-
ated one of the eight school prefects in September, 1907.

But that honour was still two years away when Dr Hillard first

* Cyril Picciotto. *St Paul's School* (1939), at p. 96.

took up residence in the High Master's house. Meanwhile Harry Nathan progressed through the various divisions of the Eighth Form. When he left History Eighth at the end of 1905, Mr Cholmeley wrote with some enthusiasm of him in his half-yearly report:

> Has improved more than anyone in the form; shows remarkable keenness and energy, and though his work is often rough it is never thin. Ought to do very well if he doesn't give way early to a journalistic way of writing.

His progress can be followed from the 'General Remarks' in his remaining school reports, which contain some acute comments:

> *Lower Eighth. July, 1906.* He has much ability and usually works well in all subjects. He is, however, capable of elementary mistakes and writes in an untidy manner.
> *Lower Middle Eighth. December, 1906.* An able and promising boy. His work is often good and sometimes wilful. He does not take enough trouble with French.
> *Upper Middle Eighth. July, 1907.* Shows taste and appreciation in his Classical work.
> *Upper Eighth. December, 1907.* Has done some good work, but not nearly as good as it might have been if he could ever have stuck to one line: he shows intelligence and interest, but is always ready to be distracted from the point, and is too easily discouraged when things are not arranged to his liking.

His best subjects were Classics and History, followed by English. 'Has improved in style,' wrote his English master in his final term, 'still very apt to get off the point. A desultory though interested reader.' Outside the classroom his favourite school activities were the debating society and the cadet corps. He also showed some interest in natural history, being elected Treasurer of the Field Club, an appointment which he appropriately marked by reading a paper on 'Darwinism'.

His school reports indicate that he was absent from class from time to time, apparently through illness. Besides the usual school boy complaints such as mumps, which kept him away for several weeks at a time, he went down one summer term with diphtheria. This complaint was fairly frequent in those days with a relatively high mortality rate, particularly among children and babies. Relief was obtained by the lumbar puncture treatment. 'I never knew diptheria was such a brutal thing,' a school friend called Arthur Bolter wrote to him at the time. 'However it is over now and so the best thing is to try and forget all about it—but I suppose it's rather hard to do that in a hurry.'

Arthur Bolter, it may be remarked here, was perhaps Harry Nathan's closest friend throughout his time at St Paul's, and their friendship lasted into later life. The son of the Assistant Secretary of the Great Western Railway, Bolter was a good-looking but delicate athlete, who was often on the sick list. Harry formed a strong sentimental attachment to this boy. They were in the same form, played cricket, visited each other in their respective homes, and used to go to the theatre together. They also figured prominently in the activities of the Union

Sometimes Harry would go to the theatre with his parents. 'We are taking you to see Adeline Genée,' his father told him on one of these occasions. 'It is something you will never forget.' Nor did he. At that time the popular Danish danseuse was performing to crowded houses in the old Empire in Leicester Square. Half a century later Harry was to recall the occasion, when he found himself at dinner beside an unknown lady, who turned out to be Dame Adeline Genée-Isitt, as the dancer had by then become. 'As the talk moved from the present into the past, that is from Margot Fonteyn backwards,' he reminded her afterwards, 'I asked you if you had ever seen Adeline Genée. I was altogether staggered when you announced to my astonished ear that you were she. . . . I can see you now, as in my recollection, a slight slender figure looking indeed rather tiny from the place where we were seated in the auditorium, and how captivated I was by the grace and perfection of movement of that one small figure on the stage—movement, the precision of which I watched with admiration with an attentive and astonished eye. This first occasion I have never forgotten, or others after it. Now an ageing man, I reflect on how wise my father was.'

The Union had been in existence as the St Paul's school debating society for more than half a century. It met once a week or fortnight during the winter terms and cherished a tradition of complete freedom of discussion with no outside interference of any kind. Membership was confined to boys in the various divisions of the Eighth Form and was by election. According to Cyril Picciotto, the school's historian, the Golden Age of the Union occurred perhaps during the fifteen years prior to the outbreak of the First World War, when a number of really first-rate speakers took part in the debates and attained office. Although this statement may to some extent be coloured by the fact that Picciotto himself was a member and office-holder during this period, the fact remains that there were some outstanding performers, of whom one of the most brilliant who competed with Harry Nathan was G. D. H. Cole, the Fabian socialist and future Chichele Professor of Social and Political Theory at Oxford, whose publications were to become so numerous that their titles eventually filled over a column of close print in *Who's Who*.

Mr Cholmeley, the History Eighth Master, took an active interest in the Union, of which he was an honorary member, and it seems to have been largely due to him that Harry Nathan was elected to this society at the beginning of the Michaelmas Term, 1905. A fortnight after joining, he made his maiden speech when he spoke against a motion condemning the policy pursued by the London County Council. To condemn the L.C.C., which had returned Progressives with increased majorities, he pointed out with patent logic, was to condemn public opinion. He went on to say that in his opinion, its members were not corrupt, but on the contrary. Then he somewhat surprisingly proceeded to enumerate the advantages of high taxes. However, these arguments failed to convince the majority who carried the motion by 39 votes to 36.

A few weeks later, he seconded the motion 'That this House regrets the existence of the House of Lords.' The following account of his speech on this occasion was recorded by the Secretary in the society's Minute Book.

> Since the Education Act [of 1870] men admired brains, not wealth or birth. The disadvantages of one House [i.e. the Lords] was the feeling that it possessed absolute power. It was essential to all forms of government that no body should be able to do what it liked. But assemblies without popular support were bound to fall. It was indeed stated by Mill that a centre of resistance to the dominant power was necessary; but the House of Lords was a bad centre of resistance. It could hardly be called a check. The best system was for the majority in the country to have a majority in Parliament, letting resistance be supplied by the minority.
>
> Further, the House of Lords was hereditary, that is it contained men eminent in certain paths of life. Thackeray had said wittily that when a man became rich or achieved success as a lawyer or a minister, the country gave, on those remarkable merits, the privilege of governing to him and his heirs.

But Harry's arguments failed to win the day, the motion again being rejected by three votes. Viewed in the light of hindsight, it was an interesting exercise, for the motion's seconder can scarcely even have dreamed that almost exactly forty years later he would himself join the ranks of the hereditary legislators, whom he had once so roundly denounced.

At this time he had an unforgettable experience for any schoolboy when he saw and heard all the Liberal party leaders on one election platform. On December 21, 1905, his father took him to the mass meeting in the Albert Hall, when Sir Henry Campbell-Bannerman, who had succeeded the Conservative Mr Balfour who had resigned as Prime Minister a fortnight previously, now asked the electorate to return him to power at the head of a strong Liberal Government. The young boy listened enraptured as the elderly 'C.-B.' proclaimed as a trumpet call that the Liberal policy was to make the country less of a playground for the rich and more of a treasure house for the nation. It was a convenient occasion for the new Premier to introduce his team, who included H. H. Asquith,

Sir Edward Grey, R. B. Haldane, John Burns and Lloyd George in the Cabinet and a fair-haired youngster in his first junior ministerial post, Winston Churchill. But most of all Harry Nathan recalled in later years the slim, youthful figure of the newly appointed President of the Board of Trade, with his pleasing smile and flashing eye—David Lloyd George. Years later they were to become close political friends and neighbours.

The sweeping Liberal victory at the General Election in January, 1906, led the Union to stage a two-day debate on a vote of confidence in the new Government. On this occasion, according to the school magazine, *The Pauline*, the two best speeches were those of Mr Cholmeley and H. L. Nathan in favour of the motion. The magazine added: 'Decided promise is shown by H. L. Nathan, who, however, suffers from a rather ponderous style.' At the same time the Secretary remarked in the Minutes: 'Mr Nathan was fluent and convincing.' In his opening speech against the motion, the Librarian had attacked Mr John Burns, the President of the Local Government Board and the first working man to reach Cabinet rank, as 'an indecent and scurrilous noisy windbag'. Harry Nathan immediately leaped to the Minister's defence. The Librarian's attack on Mr Burns, he said, was based on nothing but his (Mr Burns') grammar and his desire to end or mend the House of Lords. 'The Liberals are emphatically not divided, while the Conservatives have not even a leader.' (This was a reference to the fact that Mr Balfour, the former Conservative Prime Minister, had lost his seat at the Election.) 'Man for man,' he concluded, 'the Liberals are intellectually superior.'

But the House did not agree and rejected the motion of confidence by 20 votes to 9, the result perhaps reflecting the politics of the members' male parents.

Later in that term Harry Nathan proposed another interesting motion: 'That this House welcomes the increased representation of Labour in the House of Commons.' Labour had 53 seats in the 1906 Parliament and for the first time had become a cohesive parliamentary party. This gave the proposer his cue, when at the outset he confessed his rashness 'in asking the House to change its political perspective'.

> A new power had arisen and must be considered as such [he said]. Its influence was decidedly beneficial. It had no connection with any other party as was proved by the Labour member's oath.
> It was an outrage that men should starve in the midst of plenty. Such was the case which the Labour Party would remedy by their policy of social reform. Other reforms were the graduation of income tax, the enfranchisement of women, the amendment of the licensing laws, the strengthening of Trades Unionism, and municipal enterprise. . . . Socialism should find an outlet such as this, and no Party understood so well the needs of the public, nor were so earnest or useful.

This time the motion, proposed by a future Labour M.P. and peer, was rejected by 20 votes to 6.

The schoolboy politician had acquitted himself so well during his first year in the Union that at the election of office-holders for the ensuing year (1906–7), held at the end of the summer term, he was induced to put himself forward for the office of Secretary. In the result he was elected, although an attempt was afterwards made to have his election declared invalid on the ground of canvassing. Perhaps it was not entirely without significance that this move should have been made by a fellow member, Cyril Picciotto, who was also Vice-President and Treasurer.

Apparently there was a rule, or at least a tradition, that members seeking election to office in the Union should not canvass support of their candidatures. In ignorance of this convention (so he said) Harry Nathan wrote several letters to friends soliciting their votes. At the next meeting the Treasurer accordingly moved 'that the election of Mr Nathan be declared invalid,' although in doing so he was obliged to admit that he (the Treasurer) was in some degree responsible for what had happened since 'he had not given sufficient publicity to the laws concerning canvassing'. The peccant candidate was then heard in his own defence, when in what was described in

18

the Minutes as 'a grave and complimentary speech' he declared that he did not know of the canvassing rule nor why it was in force. Even his accusers recognized that it was insufficiently known, he argued, urging that it should be incorporated in the printed laws of the Society and posted on the notice board. He finally appealed to 'the supreme authority' of the President, who thereupon added his voice on behalf of the Secretary-elect. The motion was then put to the House and rejected by a majority of 17, the voting being Ayes 9 and Noes 26.

The new Secretary threw himself into his duties with enthusiasm and at the end of his year of office *The Pauline* paid tribute in its columns to the 'untiring energy' of 'an indefatigable worker in the Society's cause'. One of his first innovations was to procure a notice board detailing the Society's activities which he placed in a prominent position near the School entrance. ('The advantages of bringing the Union into closer touch with the School are manifest and need not be commented on here.') It was also largely due to his initiative that the room in which the debates were held was redecorated, 'the walls being painted in two shades of green, and the general effect is excellent'. He also attended to the type of magazines and journals supplied for the use of the members. At his first committee meeting he proposed 'that *The Spectator* be not taken in'. Another member had advocated a similar fate for the *Daily Graphic*, and after a spirited discussion in which the contrary argument was advanced that one could not thrive on *The Strand* and such like, the motion to throw out *The Spectator* and the *Daily Graphic* was carried by the President's casting vote.

Besides keeping the Minutes, he spoke on a variety of subjects during his year of office. These included Home Rule for Ireland, Imperial Federation, the need for the Channel Tunnel, and the increasing sale of magazines. He again defended the Progressives on the L.C.C. ('It was true that the rates had risen by 2d in the last ten years, but in return the people of London had got seventy more parks than when the L.C.C. was established, better sanitation, a more efficient fire brigade, a splendidly organized Board of Works and a system of tramways.') He also contributed to the annual anniversary meeting at which the High Master and about ninety others were present. Among the speakers on this occasion was an eighteen-year-old boy whose nickname was 'Monkey'; he was the future Field Marshal Viscount Montgomery of Alamein, whose path was destined more than once to cross Harry Nathan's.

Although he shone at games, becoming Captain of the Rugby XV, where he gained the reputation of being a ferocious tackler, as well as a member of the Cricket XI, Bernard Montgomery's reports on the scholastic side were at first considerably worse than Harry Nathan's. Yet like Harry, Montgomery was on the whole very happy at the school. 'St Paul's is a very good school for work as long as you want to learn,' he was afterwards to write in his *Memoirs*; 'in my case, once the intention and the urge was clear, the masters did the rest and for this I shall always be grateful.'

Both Bernard Montgomery and Harry Nathan were the subjects of sketches in 'Our Unnatural History Column' in *The Octopus*, a less conventional school publication than *The Pauline*, Montgomery figuring as 'The Monkey'* and Nathan as 'The Secretary Bird'. The latter, which was almost certainly written by G. D. H. Cole read as follows:

This animal belongs to the thick feathered class of winged vertebrates, and is noted for its imposing crest, and the facility and dignity with which it stands on one leg. From a projection in its crest like a quill pen it has been likened to a secretary. But in other respects it is entirely different. There is, if I may so put it, no union between the bird and a secretary.

This astonishing bird partakes of the characteristics of several mammals, e.g., of the hippopotamus, in the matter of skin, and of the domestic cat in the matter of plumage. Its chief traits are an unflagging energy, and a limitless fund of chatty conversation, by no means pompous or boring. It apparently lives on 'Union' notepaper, and its chief occupation is in the duties of the amiable official whose name it bears. Though not a big bird it is very strong, and the amount of 'shove' it

* Reprinted in Montgomery's *Memoirs* (1958) at p. 21.

20

can on occasion put on would undoubtedly earn it a place as an English forward—*ceteris paribus*. The cheerfulness and easy gaiety of its disposition are proverbial, as is shown by its motto:

'Hostili nostrum nulla victum arte cadet cor.'

The last two words of the Latin tag were a typical schoolboy pun on Nathan's other main extra-mural interest, the Cadet Corps, later known as the Officers' Training Corps, an activity in which 'Monkey' Montgomery enthusiastically shared before passing in to Sandhurst. Harry Nathan worked hard at drills and parades, military tactics and the rest, and went to Aldershot in the summer holidays for the annual fortnight's camp, the Corps for this purpose being integrated with the 2nd South Middlesex Volunteers. On August 2, 1907, his closest friend at St Paul's, Arthur Bolter, wrote to him in a tone of slightly patronizing banter: 'You seem to be having a good time down at Camp, going your rounds, giving your little orders and performing your duties etc.'

Once, in the early days of his rule as High Master, Dr Hillard was discussing the two most eminent Old Paulines. 'A second Milton is unthinkable,' he remarked; 'a second Marlborough is, I trust, unnecessary.' Unfortunately the second Marlborough was to be rendered necessary by two gigantic military conflicts. He appeared in the person of Bernard Montgomery, who returned to St Paul's in the Second World War to establish his headquarters as Commander-in-Chief of the 21st Army Group in preparation for the liberation of Europe. A dozen years later a panel in the school Board Room marking the occasion was unveiled by the Field-Marshal himself.

'IN THIS ROOM his personal office,' it read in part, 'he put the final touches to his plan for the Normandy landing of June 1944. IN THIS BUILDING he conducted on 15th May 1944 his final briefing Conference for the Senior Allied Commanders of the Sea, Land and Air Forces in the presence of His Majesty, King George VI, the Prime Minister, the Right Honourable Sir Winston Spencer Churchill, K.G., and the

Supreme Allied Commander, General of the Army, DWIGHT
D. EISENHOWER.'

It was appropriate that the panel recording these events should
have been presented to St Paul's by the Field Marshal's old school
mate and life-long admirer, Harry Nathan.

4

After the summer holidays in 1907, Harry Nathan went back
to school for what turned out to be his last term, although he did
not know it at the time. Brief as they were, these days were probably the most satisfying, if not the happiest, at St Paul's, for he
was in a position to exercise more authority and influence than at
any time in the past. He was in the Upper Eighth, a School Prefect,
a Cadet Lieutenant in the Corps, Vice-President and Treasurer of
the Union Society, Treasurer of the Field Club, besides which he
represented the school at water-polo. Indeed, he was an excellent
swimmer, and he won several silver cups for diving at this time.
Perhaps his favourite interest was the Union. *The Pauline*, which
described his rhetorical efforts as 'a well of English undefiled',
noted approvingly that 'in his new position as Vice-President [he]
displays the same indefatigable energy which, as Secretary, he
invariably fulfilled his duties'.

The last occasion on which he spoke at the Union was early in
December when he seconded a motion, proposed by Arthur Bolter,
'That this House considers the office of censorship of plays unnecessary and unwarrantable.' How this debate terminated is not
known, since it was adjourned to the following term and there is
no further reference to it in the Minutes. The reason for such a long
adjournment was at the time the next meeting would normally have
been held so many of the members, including the President
(G. D. H. Cole) and the Vice-President, would be sitting for
scholarship examinations at Oxford and Cambridge.

Along with G. D. H. Cole and other Paulines, Harry Nathan

spent a week writing papers in the college hall at Balliol, trying for one of the scholarships or exhibitions in History, of which the Brackenbury was the principal prize. When the results were posted up on the college notice board, it was seen that Cole had been awarded a major exhibition, but Nathan's name did not appear in the list of successful candidates.

Harry's cousin Leonard Stein had already gone up to Balliol, and Michael Nathan could quite easily have afforded to send his son there as a commoner, had he so wished. But Harry had made up his mind that he would not go on to the university unless he won a scholarship or exhibition. Now that he was rising nineteen, he felt the desire to earn his own livelihood and that the sooner arrangements could be made for him to start the better. A family conference was held at Bassett Road, and it was decided that Harry should become a lawyer. One of Michael Nathan's fellow justices on the magistrates' bench was a solicitor named Leopold Goldberg, senior partner in the firm of Goldberg, Barrett and Newell of 2 and 3 West Street, Finsbury Circus, E.C. Mr Goldberg agreed to accept Harry as an articled clerk and the necessary arrangements were quickly made so that the boy could begin work early in the New Year, 1908.

It was a pity in some ways that Harry did not go on from St Paul's to Oxford, since with the possession of a university degree he could have qualified as a solicitor in three years instead of the five in fact he had to serve in his articles. He was often to regret in later life that he had not enjoyed the additional advantages of a university education.

On the day Harry joined Goldberg, Barrett & Newell, his father took him to lunch at the National Liberal Club. In the Smoking Room afterwards, among the members taking coffee, was one in particular who attracted the eye. Looking back half a century later, Harry Nathan clearly recalled the appearance of this individual. 'He was elegant though not dapper, distinguished without ostentation, his attire was careful but not smart. His was a noticeable figure, slight in physique, the hair a glistening white and the moustache grey rather than white; the demeanour was firm of one accustomed to attention for his words; he was gentle in aspect, and he smiled with his eyes, eyes crinkled at the corners: for he was old.'

Michael Henry Nathan led his son towards him. Harry had no idea who he was, 'though clearly someone very special'. The father then presented his son to him as the latest recruit to their profession. 'I recall, and renew as I write, the tingle of excitement and the thrill of something like awe with which I heard the name. For this was the most famous solicitor of his age, indeed the most famous I suppose on all the lengthening roll: this was the legendary, the fabulous Sir George Lewis.'

Legendary and fabulous indeed George Henry Lewis was. For many years he had the practical monopoly of those cases where the seamy side of 'Society' was unveiled, and where the sins and follies of the wealthy classes threatened exposure and disaster. His reputation for settling awkward society cases out of court was unrivalled, and numerous scandals had been hushed up as a result of his adroit handling of the parties concerned. Among his most exalted clients was the sovereign himself, who as Edward VII and previously as Prince of Wales had had occasion to consult him more than once. It was through Edward VII's influence that the solicitor had been knighted, and had subsequently been created a baronet and made a Companion of the Royal Victorian Order.

The veteran solicitor rose to greet the newly articled clerk. Harry felt his congratulatory hand patting his shoulder, as he welcomed him to the honourable profession in which he had won name and fame. In introducing his son, the elder Nathan had suggested that Sir George might care to give him a few words of advice, since Harry was now on the threshold of his professional career.

'My boy,' said Sir George Lewis, 'my boy, there's only one piece of advice I can give you. Never write a letter if you can help it— and if you have to—make it a short one!'

As his own career as a solicitor was drawing to a close, Harry Nathan recorded the final impression which this chance encounter made upon him: 'During all the long years between, I have never

forgotten the occasion, the man, or the shrewd advice. I have practised it and preached it. It has stood me and my clients in good
stead.'

For the next five years Harry Nathan toiled away in the offices of
Goldberg, Barrett & Newall, attended the Law Society's lectures on
such subjects as criminal law, the laws of contract and tort, real
property and conveyancing, equity and trusts all of which he seems
to have had no difficulty in mastering. 'Congratulations on passing
first shot—splendid!' Arthur Bolter wrote to him in April, 1909,
on hearing that he had got through Part I of the qualifying
examinations.

In the spring of 1911, as a break from his law studies, Michael
Nathan took his elder son on a month's Mediterranean cruise. They
travelled overland to Marseilles, where they embarked on the
Peninsular and Oriental Company's excursion steamer *Vectis*,
which called at Ajaccio and a number of Italian, Greek and Turkish
ports. Judging by a letter which Harry wrote to his mother, who
was left behind with Cyril in Bassett Road, cruises would appear to
have changed little with the passing of the years.

16 March 1911. We are on our way from Palermo to
Nauplia, where we arrive tomorrow evening. Today has been
glorious; a perfect smooth blue sea, and gorgeous sunshine.
We have felt life worth living.

I am writing this just before dressing for dinner, with the
promise of a squally evening before us, so I am told. We have
already had one bad evening, when the dining saloon was
more than half empty: I hope the experience will not be repeated today. Both Father and I bore up well.

The crowd on board is rather odd: not too sociable, and
certainly not aristocratic. However, we have got on speaking
terms with one or two decent people.

Yesterday we spent at Palermo, which is a large and important town, far contrary to our expectations. We saw so many
Churches that my mind is in a maze when I try to remember
which is which.

Sports and competitions have been organized: Father has
not seen fit to enter for any, but I have put my name down for

several. Last evening there was a Progressive Whist evening: I received—and may be gave!—a good many lessons in how not to play. Tonight there is bridge and during the day there has been quoits, etc. It is rather a good thing, as otherwise we should probably find difficulty in scraping acquaintance with people.

'Tomorrow there is a dance again,' Michael Nathan wrote to his wife by the same mail. 'I could not get Harry to join the last one. He seems very nervous about it. He looks very well but has been very wakeful the last couple of nights. Tonight I am going to try him with hot milk and whisky.' This remedy apparently worked, as his father reported that Harry had had a better night and seemed 'quite chirpy' next day. 'His reserve is wearing off and I think he will be much happier.' Soon he was playing deck games with the other passengers and was 'now much more at his ease and quite happy'. He went on all the shore excursions and, according to his father, was 'quite excited' by the Greek antiquities they saw at Mycenae and Athens. After the Aegean islands, the *Vectis* touched briefly at Smyrna, where the elder Nathan noted the Bazaars teeming with life ('All so different to what we are accustomed to'), and the picturesque costumes of the Turkish men and the veiled women. The voyage continued to Constantinople. It was daylight as they entered the Dardanelles, passing the rocky Southern Gallipoli Peninsula on their left, where less than five years later young Harry Nathan was to find himself fighting against the Turks, and commanding a battalion in one of the most terrible military campaigns in modern history. But the thoughts of the passengers on board the *Vectis* that March day were far from the subject of trenches and bully beef, as they lay in their deck chairs and sipped their mid-morning bouillon.

Whilst reading for his 'Final', Harry Nathan was concerned in a noteworthy criminal case, which earned him the thanks of the authorities. Goldberg, Barrett & Newall had several German clients, one of whom was a Stuttgart merchant named Gustav Bender. It appeared that Herr Bender had read an advertisement in a German newspaper in which a London firm of stock and share dealers trading under the name of Brown Savile & Brother in New Oxford Street offered to buy shares on the London Stock Exchange for interested customers on margin, and holding out the prospect of profits ranging from 100 to 500 per cent. Herr Bender sent the firm 1,000 marks as 'cover' for a block of Canadian Pacific Railway shares. He subsequently received a letter from the firm saying that in consequence of 'disappointing traffic returns' the cover had run out and the only way to prevent loss was to provide additional money for cover. As a result Herr Bender sent the firm two further sums of 1,000 marks each. He afterwards stated that, since the firm had headed notepaper with 'German Department' at the top and used a telegraphic code, he thought that it was in a good way of business.

The truth was that the premises in New Oxford Street, which were run by a man named Edward Donallon with the help of his clerk, Eugene Beck, were what was commonly known as a bucket-shop, that is an unauthorized office employed for speculating in stocks and shares and other forms of gambling. Complaints had been made by the German Government about the numbers of Germans who had been similarly victimized; indeed subsequent police inquiries revealed that nearly £20,000 had been forwarded by 'customers'. However, it was only after a detailed statement had been obtained from Herr Bender and forwarded to the Department of Public Prosecutions that the authorities had sufficient evidence to take action. Donallon and Beck were accordingly arrested on a charge of obtaining money by false pretences from Herr Bender. They were then brought up before the magistrate at Bow Street and in due course committed for trial at the Old Bailey.

Both men pleaded not guilty and both were convicted by the jury. Donallon, who had a previous conviction for a similar fraud, was sentenced to two years' imprisonment with hard labour and ordered to pay £70 towards the costs of the prosecution. Beck got twenty months with hard labour.

When the case was over, Sir Charles Mathews, the Director of Public Prosecutions, wrote the following personal lettter of thanks to Goldberg, Barrett & Newall.

> *Director of Public Prosecutions Department*
> *Whitehall,*
> *S.W.*
> *31st July, 1912*

Dear Sirs,

REX V. DONALLON AND ANOTHER

I desire to thank the members of your firm, individually and collectively, for the great assistance which they rendered to me in the course of the prosecution of the above-named, and in this expression of thanks I desire to include Mr H. L. Nathan, who, by personally attending the different stages of the proceedings was able to give, and in fact did give, help of so valuable a character as to call for some reward, and I enclose a payable order for 10 guineas, in the hope thar you will assent to his receiving that sum of money.

> I am, dear Sirs,
> Faithfully yours,
> CHARLES W. MATHEWS

It was indeed rare, if not unprecedented, for a solicitor's articled clerk to receive such a tribute from the Director of Public Prosecutions. Mr Goldberg duly passed on the letter with its welcome enclosure to his industrious apprentice, who carefully preserved this remarkable testimonial.

5

After passing his Final and completing his articles, Harry Nathan was duly admitted to the roll of Solicitors of the Supreme Court in April, 1913. At first his father seems to have hoped that his satisfactory record of work with Goldberg, Barrett & Newall would lead to his being asked to stay on with this firm with the prospect of a partnership in due course. But such an invitation was not forthcoming or, if it was, the assurance about a possible partnership did not satisfy his father. Fortunately a solicitor named Herbert Oppenheimer with an office in nearby Finsbury Square and a rapidly increasing practice was looking round for a young partner who had recently qualified. It is likely that Oppenheimer, who had been practising on his own for the past twelve years, had already come across young Nathan in the courts and had been favourably impressed by him. At all events, when he was approached, Oppenheimer agreed to take in Harry as his junior partner as from August 1, 1913, the price paid for the partnership being £3,000, which was put up by Harry's father. So a new nameplate appeared outside the office at 1 Finsbury Square, proclaiming the existence of Herbert Oppenheimer & Nathan, Solicitors. Eighteen months later the style underwent a further change when Mr Arthur Vandyk, a son of the well-known London photographer of that name, also became a partner.

A lean-looking man in his late thirties with a bright eye and a sharp temper, Herbert Oppenheimer spoke with a strong Teutonic accent, having been born in Frankfurt of German parents who brought him with them to England at a fairly early age. Had he remained in Germany, Oppenheimer might well have become a professional pianist, since he had studied the pianoforte under Clara Schumann, the composer Robert's widow, and had shown himself to be a most promising pupil. Indeed, in his retirement he went back to his first love and took to composing, a number of his pieces being performed in public by Myra Hess. No doubt he decided to follow the law as a career, since in the England of the times it offered considerably more attractive prospects than a musical career. As a lawyer, he soon showed exceptional ability, combining an incisive mind with a shrewd and practical knowledge of commercial and financial business. By the date Nathan joined him, he had built up a good commercial practice including taxation, and he now needed help particularly on the litigation side, which his new partner was quickly able to supply. He was undoubtedly a remarkable character, both in the office and outside it, where his principal interest was the cultivation of roses. (For many years he was President of the Rose Society.) 'Clients often went in terror of him,' the present Lord Nathan has recalled, 'because he had an extremely fierce temper to which he gave vent to his client if in his opinion he was acting foolishly. He was, on the other hand, a man of complete loyalty and integrity and a wonderful partner.'

However Oppenheimer may have become enraged from time to time by his clients' stupidity, it was quite otherwise in his relations with the firm's junior partner. Nathan, by contrast, never got angry with clients, at any rate outwardly, and he was known for his exemplary patience in dealing with them. He once described himself in the early days of his professional career as 'a business man with a specialist training'. According to his son, this was perhaps an ambition rather than a statement of fact, since, apart from being indeed a good man of business, he had a knowledge of and 'feel' for the law which made him an outstanding practitioner of it. During his half-century of practice, the firm was to grow from two partners with a couple of clerks and a typist to one of sixteen partners and a total staff of 150.

But in 1913 this expansion was as yet a considerable time away. When he joined Oppenheimer in Finsbury Square, Nathan had barely twelve months of his career as a solicitor before him when it was to be drastically interrupted by the outbreak of the First World War. His immediate call-up for military duty at the beginning of August, 1914, was the result of his service as a volunteer officer with the 2nd South Middlesex Volunteers, of which the St Paul's School Cadet Corps had formed a part.

Nathan's other interest outside the office, which gave scope for his qualities of leadership and organization, was the Brady Street Club for Working Lads in Whitechapel, the oldest and largest of the London Jewish boys' clubs. He became one of the club managers and also acted as the club's Honorary Secretary, spending several evenings a week with the boys in the East End, when he was not out with the Volunteers or Territorials. These were some of the happiest days of his life, he noted some years later, looking back from the trenches in Gallipoli. 'I should like to be remembered by them as one who tried to teach a sense of duty and obligation to the British Crown.'

At the time he was not much given to other spare-time activities, such as dancing, though he used to accept dance invitations. 'Looking back,' he was again to write from Gallipoli, 'I realize that some of the evenings which I used to dread in anticipation and not, most of them, to enjoy overmuch at the time, had their good points. At all events, I would give a good deal now to hear light music, to meet clean and decently dressed men and to listen to the silly chatter and, most valuable of all, light-hearted laugh of some carefree girl.'

After the South African War at the turn of the century, there was a real fear that Great Britain might sooner or later become engaged in a major European conflict and that the enemy would attempt an invasion of the British Isles. A Royal Commission in 1904 had reported that the military forces supplementary to the regular army, namely the militia and the volunteers, which provided the second and third lines respectively, were not qualified by reason of defects of education and training to take the field against the troops of a continental army. The consequent reorganization, which included the regular army, was initiated by the War Minister, Lord Haldane, and carried through in 1908. The militia was changed into the special reserve with the duty of finding and training drafts for the first line, while the second line consisting of the volunteer (infantry) and yeomanry (cavalry) regiments became the second line and known as the Territorial Forces. The T.F. was organized on a county basis, and additional units were raised to complete the new arms or services, whilst other units, particularly infantry, were either disbanded or reconstituted into units of a different arm. In this process the 2nd South Middlesex Volunteers, with which the St Paul's Cadet Corps was connected, lost its separate identity. On leaving school Nathan had been gazetted to the old volunteer force as 2nd Lieutenant in the 1st Volunteer Battalion, Royal Fusiliers (City of London Regiment), and he thus became one of the original officers of the T.F. on its formation in April, 1908. The raising, equipment and accommodation of the new force became the responsibility of specially constituted county territorial force associations under the presidency of the Lord Lieutenant of each county and county borough, the membership of the associations including local government representatives and others as well as the territorial units themselves. Training remained the responsibility of the military authorities. The T.F. was earmarked primarily for home defence in the event of war breaking out. Liability to overseas service was not insisted upon, but personnel could volunteer for this service in the event of an Expeditionary Force being despatched abroad. Six months of additional training were considered necessary after mobilization before the force could take the field overseas.

This was the position in which Harry Nathan found himself as an original officer of the territorial army when he was ordered to report for duty with his unit on August 4, 1914.

As it turned out, this summons was to save him from having a complete nervous breakdown. 'I don't believe you ever knew how really ill from overwork I was in June and July,' he told his parents afterwards: 'sometimes I used to be prostrate and almost speechless before the day was over. When I look back, I don't know how I ever used to get through at all.'

CHAPTER TWO

Gallipoli and France

AT THE OUTBREAK OF THE GREAT WAR, THE TERRITORIAL ARMY
consisted of fourteen Divisions and thirteen mounted Brigades, to
which the defence of Britain was initially entrusted. On reporting
for duty with the Royal Fusiliers, Lieutenant Nathan was instructed
to take charge of a platoon and immediately proceed to Three
Bridges Station on what was then the London, Brighton and South
Coast Railway, there to patrol a stretch of the railway line and guard
the bridges. Before entraining with his men, Harry Nathan paid a
visit to the Wilkinson Sword Company in Pall Mall, where he
equipped himself with field glasses and a magnetic compass and
other articles which he needed and which territorial officers were
expected to provide for themselves.

On his first patrol, Nathan found that Leopold Goldberg, the
solicitor, to whose firm he had been articled, had a house in the
neighbourhood and he called to pay his respects. His first letter was
to his mother:

> *Three Bridges Station,*
> *L.B. & S.C.R.*
> *13 August 1914*

This is a very quiet place and consists of little but the station
and a public-house. Goldberg's place is not far away, and the
other day he sent me a van load of green vegetables, marrows,

tomatoes, etc., and Sir Francis Montefiore,* who has a large place in the neighbourhood, has sent a hamper of cabbages and apples. It is very important that the men should have green vegetables, but they are not provided by the Government.

I have charge of a section of the line about 5 miles in length, and have forty men and any number of boy scouts, cadets and police constables. Our chief anxiety is to prevent bridges being blown up, or obstructions being placed on the rails. That means patrolling the line day and night, and also having a sentry in each signal box.

I myself have my quarters in the Ladies' Waiting Room, which is not so uncomfortable as you might perhaps imagine. I sleep on one of the forms, which is rather narrow and hard. However, there it is. For the greater part of each night and for the whole of some nights I am out on the line, but I manage to get a few hours' rest during the day time.

Yesterday I was joined by Major Taylor, who now shares the Ladies' Waiting Room with me!

There is really very little to report. We are keeping our eyes skinned for spies, of whom there seem to be many round here. One or two of our people have been fired at, but I am glad to say without casualties so far. . . .

I don't suppose any of you have had much experience of walking considerable distances along railway lines; but I can assure you it is quite exceptionally tiring, and very wearing both to boots and feet. . . .

I hear from Oppenheimer that there is no work in the office save for applications for naturalization, and, as I gather from what appears in the papers that they are not likely to be granted, it looks to me as if we shall have a very lean year.

Three days later he wrote to his father:

It is very hot here, and I suppose it is the same in London. We are living a very simple life here; and I am writing this having just finished a lunch of soda and milk, bread and butter, a couple of tomatoes and a peach. Sir Francis Montefiore yesterday sent me a second hamper of vegetables, etc., and I also received from a local squire, in addition to a large quantity of

---

* Sir Francis Montefiore, Baronet, belonged to a well-known Jewish family of scholars and philanthropists.

vegetables and fruit for the men, a basket of the most gorgeous grapes and a couple of dozen first-rate peaches. Apart from luxuries in the way of fruit, Major Taylor and I are having the same food as the men. . . .

Until Major Taylor joined me here three or four days ago, I had not seen an officer to speak to for some days and was quite isolated. I have seen the Colonel once or twice and also several of the other officers, but some I have not seen at all.

The only real excitement here (and that is wearing off) is when a number of German prisoners of war pass through the station, as about 300 have done, on their way to Christ's Hospital at Horsham, which is being used temporarily as a prison. . . .

The Government are apparently anxious to get as many troops abroad as possible; accordingly at the request of the Brigadier the Colonel enquired of the officers whether in the event of his volunteering the Battalion for foreign service, he would be supported by officers and men. Every officer and about 90 per cent of the men agreed to go in the event of the offer of the Battalion being accepted. . . .

Further, the general feeling is that all unmarried officers should hold themselves in readiness to go abroad in the event of the necessity arising. As a preliminary I have refused to go as an individual, but I have said that if a definite request is made to me, I will consider the matter further.

I have also said that in the event of a composite Battalion being formed from the Fusilier Brigade, I should be prepared to give favourable consideration to the suggestion that I should go with them.

Naturally he also discussed the question of overseas service with his partner in Finsbury Square, whom he was given leave to go up to London and see. 'If the bulk of officers from the Battalion are going abroad,' he told Oppenheimer, 'I cannot stand out.' To this Oppenheimer agreed. In their deed of partnership Oppenheimer had guaranteed the payment of not less than £700 a year to his junior partner. He now agreed to continue to pay £500 and to allot the difference to the salary of a managing clerk so long as Nathan remained absent on military service. Out of the £500 Nathan proposed to hand over £400 to his father. 'I should be able to manage on the odd £100 together with my pay,' he told his father, 'as the expenses of actual service are not likely to be great.'

In recruiting the 'new armies', Lord Kitchener, the War Minister, discarded the county system on which the territorial army had been built up. His experience in the South African War had led him to distrust the influence of county magnates, and he had no first-hand knowledge of Haldane's reforms, so that he was disinclined to expand the existing territorials to reinforce the regular troops. He contented himself with appealing to the territorial army to volunteer for service overseas, particularly for the purpose of taking over garrison duties, in places like Egypt, Malta and Gibraltar, and so relieving the regulars for service in France. By December, 1914, nearly 2,500 officers and 67,000 other ranks of the territorial army had gone overseas. Shortly afterwards the first volunteer reserve battalion of the Royal Fusiliers, to be known as the 2nd Battalion, the 1st London Regiment, was ordered to Malta.

The battalion sailed from Southampton on February 1, 1915, in H.M. Transport *Galeka*, a vessel of 7,000 tons belonging to the Union Castle Line. Harry's first letter on board was posted to his parents when he reached Gibraltar.

> Each officer has a cabin to himself, and I have another for my luggage, so I have been far more comfortable than I antici-pated. The officers are, on the whole, very well treated: we are in the same position as first-class passengers, with the advant-ages that everything, except of course drinks, is provided by a generous Government: we have very good fare, and are getting fat and sleek.
>
> The men's quarters are not nearly so comfortable. There are a number of what are called troop-decks below the main deck, in each of which are tables and forms and eating utensils for 14 or 16 men to a mess, the number of messes on each troop-deck varying with the size of the troop-deck. Fear of the Censor prevents me from telling you how many men there are to a troop-deck, and also certain other details. The men sleep in the same troop-decks in hammocks slung over their mess-tables, and as the troop-decks are only about 9 feet high and the only ventilation—at all events, by night—is a single

36

Constance Nathan

Michael Henry Nathan

6 Bassett Road, Kensington, where
Lord Nathan was born

Harry Nathan as a child

Subaltern in First World War

hatch-way, you can easily understand that at night there is a fine stench, and how the men can stand it at all is a perpetual marvel to me . . .

As soon as we got into the Channel we found very choppy weather: the result was that most of the officers and about 90 per cent of the men were absolutely *hors de combat*. By Tuesday night [the third day out] it had blown into a gale and the boat was pitching and tossing and rolling far more than I thought that any boat could do without going under for ever. Fortunately I myself have got through comparatively well, though I had to miss dinner on Tuesday evening after having been violently sick as the result of inspecting the troop-decks, where the conditions were beyond description. The Captain of the boat says that the gale was a full gale, and the water seemed literally mountains high, time after time washing the deck. Yesterday our discomforts were added to by sleet and rain: so strong was the wind that the rain fell in almost horizontal lines. During the night the rolling was so great that it was impossible to keep still in one's berth, while the amount of crockery which has been smashed during the past few days would, I imagine, be sufficient to set up all the Belgian refugees for life!

Today, however, the conditions are very different: sun, blue sea, warm breeze. All the officers and most of the men are again full of vigour, and taking nourishment! . . .

There are other things which I might have told you, but we have been warned to be very discreet, and to make no mention of escorts, number of troops, etc.

At sea.
10 February, 1915

. . . We only stayed at Gibraltar about 1½ hours, and then really only for the purpose of sending to Hospital ashore one of our fellows who was down with pneumonia. While we were anchored, of course the usual pedlars came alongside in their boats, and I bought a box of 100 Manila cigars—for 7/-!—and quite good they are too.

I could not help thinking—like many others—when we left Southampton that it was rather a solemn moment in one's life, but I am not sure that I was not more impressed at Gibraltar to hear the citizen soldiers on shore cheer the 'citizen soldiers' on board. It is among the things that one will never forget. . . .

Since we entered the Mediterranean we have been allowed to show a few lights on deck, and I have our cabin port-holes open, but before we reached Gibraltar not a light appeared after dark.

The daily routine has been something like this (I take yesterday): Reveille 6.0; Orderlies draw men's rations 6.30; Men's breakfast 7.15; Officers' breakfast (and a very excellent one) 8.30; inspection parade 10 to 11; Men's dinners 12.0; Officers' lunch 1.0; Kit inspection 2.30; Officers' tea 4.0; Men's tea 5.0; Officers' dinner 7.0; Lights out 9.15; we go to bed 10 to 10.30.

Although the officers are living like fighting cocks, we have nothing to pay except for drinks, as everything is provided by the Admiralty. On the other hand, however, we get no allowances, but only our bare pay, out of which we have to give fairly substantial quantities to the Steward.

The men's food is, on the whole, distinctly bad. The dinners are fairly good, but the amount of food allowed for breakfast and tea (which with midday dinner are the only meals) is far too little; it bears very unfavourable comparison with the War Office scale, and still more unfavourably with what we have provided for our Brady Club boys in Camp. Speaking generally, I do not think that as far as provision for the men is concerned (both food and otherwise) matters can have improved much since the time of the Crimean War. In a word, it is scandalous.

Tonight we hope to get to Malta, and we shall probably disembark in the course of tomorrow.

2

The normal peace-time strength of the British garrison in Malta was 9,000 regular soldiers, and it was these that the Royal Fusiliers and other units of the territorial army were sent to relieve. The island was the Headquarters of the Commander-in-Chief of the Mediterranean Forces, a command recently relinquished by General Sir Ian Hamilton, who was now to assume command of the Anglo-French force being assembled at Mudros with the object of supporting the Royal Navy in a concerted allied plan to force the Dardanelles and establish contact with the Russians in the Black Sea, at the same time knocking Turkey out of the war.

St George's Barracks,
Malta.
20 February 1915

We steamed into the Grand Harbour at Valetta at about nine o'clock. All sorts of military officials—from the General down to a R.A.M.C. Lance-Corporal came aboard—and, as soon as the necessary preliminaries had been completed, we began the disembarkation. We went off in lighters, and landed on the quay without the least sign of excitement or even interest on the part of the bystanders. . . .

The first thing we did was to draw rifles. We then started on a very toilsome march to these Barracks, which are about five miles from Valetta. It was an extremely hot day; the roads were glaring white and rather hilly; and, as we were rather soft as the result of ten days or so on board, I must confess that we found the march rather trying.

These Barracks are supposed to be the finest on the Island; they are quite modern and fairly commodious.

The officers' quarters are first-rate: we have a spacious Mess —ante-room, dining-room and billiard room—and our bed-rooms are very airy. I have a bedroom with, in my opinion, about the finest view of all, looking across a bay over a strip of land reaching out into the sea on to Valetta. It is really a gorgeous view. I am within about 50 yards of the sea. The room is about 22 feet by 17 feet, and is about 15 feet high. It is provided with quite a comfortable bed, but no bed covering save a mattress and a pillow. It is very cold here at night (though quite hot during the day), and I am very grateful for my blanket and the rug, to say nothing of my great-coat. We have had to buy sheets and pillow-slips (the men get them issued by the Government), and I have slept quite well with a large double window looking on the sea open all night.

The men, too, are quite well situated: there are on an average twelve to a room large enough to accommodate six-teen with comfort; they get bed, mattress, bolster, sheets and blankets; a locker in which to keep their kit, and all necessaries for feeding. They seem to be reasonably happy. The first few days were rather hell; but, now, the organization is about complete, and we are fairly well settled down.

I have command of a double company of 240 men, which, you can understand, means a considerable amount of work and organization.

We are quite hard worked. At present we have Reveille at six and breakfast at 7.30; then we are at work (to take yesterday as an example) from about 8.30 in the morning till about 7 in the evening, with an hour's interval for lunch. Then, after changing into slacks and light boots and having had a wash, we are ready for dinner at eight. By the time dinner is over—about 9.15—we are quite worn out, and count the minutes to bed-time. As a matter of fact, we were most of us working after dinner till eleven o'clock. I think from what I have said that you will understand there is neither leisure nor inclination for sitting down to write letters during the week.

I ought to have said that, for the present, Thursday afternoon is a half-holiday, and on Sunday we are generally likely to be free after lunch. Last Sunday I went to Valetta, and also on Thursday afternoon. Most of us are joining the Union Club, where one can see the latest papers etc. as soon as they arrive. It is quite a fine building but rather cheerless. Valetta itself is not particularly interesting: it is like a fourth-rate provincial town in Italy. Italian is the language mostly spoken, and it is with French and English (of which one hears comparatively little) the 'official' language of the Island.

I don't think that I shall go to Valetta much, as it is rather a long way—one has to take a carriage (called a *carrozza*) and cannot get there and back for under 3/– or 4/–. There is an Opera House, and one or two officers went to see *La Tosca* on Thursday evening, but I have not yet been and have no present intention of doing so.

Even if I wished to do so, I am afraid there might be some little difficulty, as, owing to a slight outbreak of mumps, the whole Battalion was yesterday placed in quarantine for the time being—which is rather a bore.

The food is nothing to boast of. There is no grass: such soil as there is has been imported from Sicily, and little or nothing is cultivated here save potatoes. There is no cattle save a few goats, which appear to live mainly on one another's fleas and empty tins. Cow's milk is unobtainable, so all the milk we get is Nestle's. The beef etc. comes from Egypt and is rather tough.

A telegram from his parents anticipated the arrival of the official announcement of his promotion to the rank of Captain. 'It was, of course, rather gratifying, though so long delayed,' he replied. 'I showed it to the C.O., who told me it was the fact that he had sent in the recommendation, and that he had expected the notification to appear. I am unable, however, to get my uniform altered until the copy of the Gazette containing the announcement actually reaches [here], which should now be within a very few days.' In due course he was able to have the third star put on his jackets and felt 'proportionately dignified in consequence'.

Training continued in St George's Barracks for the next five weeks, slightly relieved for Nathan when he was deputed to sit on a District Court Martial on two prisoners at Government House— 'a most imposing function, I can assure you,' he told his parents, 'with power in the Court (two officers of another Battalion and myself) to inflict, if we thought fit, any penalty including death! There were about twenty officers present to learn how things should be done! We sat for just over six hours on the two cases.' On April 9 he wrote home: 'You will be interested to hear that I have a new subaltern in one Graham Carritt: he was at Rugby and New College, Oxford, and knows Philip Guedalla. He plays the piano very well, and is a very charming fellow, and, as far as I can judge as yet, likely to prove a competent officer.'

At the beginning of May, they had to move to a nearby camp at short notice, since Malta had become a base hospital area for the casualties in the Dardanelles campaign, and St George's Barracks were required to accommodate the wounded troops.

Pembroke Camp, Malta, 9 May 1915. . . . we were turned out at twenty-four hours' notice, and have pitched Camp on one of the most God forsaken and unsuitable sites that you can imagine. It is far from being as comfortable as in Barracks; indeed, if we were asked to stick it for any length of time, I scarcely know how we shall do it. I have fortunately, a tent to myself. . . .

Isn't it dreadful about the *Lusitania*? That incident, Hill 60 being lost and one or two other things which I have been able to observe make me more pessimistic about the length though not as to the result of the war.

The prearranged programme of training was now complete, and the battalion was ready for active service, at least in theory. 'I hope however that we shall have a little time longer, as I feel that there are a number of respects in which improvements might well be made,' wrote Nathan on May 12. 'The Battalion now is quite different from what it was when we left England, and I doubt whether anyone who knew it then would recognize it now as being the same.' It is clear from Nathan's letters that, as he put it, 'we are a small but very happy party here', and this situation continued when their numbers were increased. He was very pleased with the subalterns allotted to his company, particularly Graham Carritt and a socially well-connected youngster of twenty-two from the north of Ireland named William ('Willa') Chichester—he was a nephew of Lord O'Neill. ('I think that I have probably the best subalterns in the Battalion. Chichester, though young, is extraordinarily useful and level headed, and has a very nice way with the men who will do anything for him.') For Chichester, who was later to be killed fighting in France, Nathan developed a strong sentimental affection, akin to what he had felt at St Paul's for Arthur Bolter. Afterwards he wrote that in 'the days of our work together for a common cause', Chichester had often helped and never failed him. 'He has shown himself to be "the very perfect gentleman" which each of us in his heart of hearts would always wish to be. To have known him is a kind of religion.'

At the beginning of June, Pembroke Camp was needed to accommodate the ever-increasing stream of wounded from the Dardanelles, and the Battalion moved again, this time further along the coast to an isolated spot called Ghain Taffeiha. 'You have no idea what this is like,' Nathan wrote on June 6: 'there is no village of any kind, and the nearest town where anything can be bought or a newspaper seen is Valeta [14 or 15 miles distant]. The scenery by the sea is gorgeous, and is the only redeeming feature of the place though the bathing is not bad. We thought that the Pembroke camping ground was the "limit"; this is indescribably more depressing. We are all hoping that our next move will be out of the Island and that it will come soon.'

In fact the wished-for move did not come for another three months, and except for the final week or so, which they spent in some school buildings in Sliema immediately prior to embarkation, Ghain Taffeiha remained the battalion headquarters for the remainder of their stay in Malta. The working hours were considerably reduced, partly on account of the excessive heat and partly because some of the men were showing signs of strain. There were also plenty of bathing parades which were much appreciated. 'Since I have seen the men undressed in the water,' wrote Nathan at this time, 'I am struck by the very considerable improvement in the physique of most of them since we have been in Malta. . . . The errand-boy slouch has given place to something resembling a soldierly bearing—which, of course, is all to the good.'

There seems no doubt, on the other hand, that the men were as Nathan put it, systematically overworked and underfed during their long stay in Malta, a state of affairs for which Nathan blamed Field Marshal Lord Methuen, the septuagenarian veteran of the South Africa War who was the Governor and also commanded the forces in the island. 'Often and often did I protest and ask that my protests might be carried to higher authority,' he was to write after he had left, 'and sometimes I believe my remonstrances had a momentary effect. But on the whole the treatment of the men on the part of the Governor lends point to the remark of the Australians, who when they arrived wounded in Malta and found no food, no beds and no blankets for them, told him to his face that they would sooner be dead in Gallipoli than alive under him. The maladministration in Malta would in times of peace mean the impeachment of more than one highly placed official.'*

Since the officers were entitled to an allowance for keeping a horse, Nathan bought a nice-looking Arab mare for exercise. But he was not particularly lucky with her. Once she got frightened by the picketing and dashed off into some barbed wire. The second accident was more serious.

2/1st. Bn. The London Regt. Malta. 14 July 1915. . . . On Sunday I went off at 7 a.m. with Wiltshire, our transport officer and Deputy Town Clerk of Birmingham, to a place some 18 miles away at the other end of the Island where we breakfasted, bathed, lunched and, in fact, spent a very pleasant day, leaving for Camp at about 5.30 or 6.

It got darkish before we could get back. Just as we were coming into Camp, a silly ass flashed an electric torch two or three yards ahead of me, which rather startled my steed. The horse turned to one side towards a wall about 4 feet above the level of the road, and I tried to turn it again in the direction in which I wished to go, when the light flashed again. This was the last straw, and the horse took a flying leap over the wall—which is about 3 feet thick—and down into a field 4 feet below the level of the road, i.e. a drop of about 8 feet in all. The poor beast came down on its head and forelegs, and I on top of it, though I am glad to say that the saddle and my backside did not part company until after we had alighted. As far as I am concerned, I got off very lightly with a bruised elbow and a slightly strained wrist. The horse, however, got nasty scratches in several places, and cut her knee very badly, right across the bone. . . .

The horse is rather high spirited, but is very docile: it is about the fastest trotter in the Island—I did 12 miles in an hour and ten minutes the other day. I am very sorry about it, but must confess that my regret is to some extent tempered by thankfulness that I was not killed or more seriously damaged, which, as you can imagine, might easily have been the case. I

---

* This opinion contrasts strongly with the view expressed in the laudatory article on Methuen in the *Dictionary of National Biography 1931–1940* that 'it was thanks largely to his foresight that Malta found itself so well equipped with hospitals and staff for the Dardanelles expedition'.

have been most unfortunate with this horse and with the last: it is very disheartening, but it has not on any occasion been due to any fault of mine.

Nathan felt very strongly about young men not joining the forces when in his view they should do so, particularly when they were family friends. An advertisement of a book by Philip Guedalla, *The Partition of Europe*, which dealt mainly with the wars of the eighteenth century, prompted an angry outburst in the same letter as that quoted above, since Guedalla was carrying on his barrister's practice. 'It makes me absolutely vomiting sick to think of him, perfectly hale and hearty, staying at home . . . and . . . writing books on war,' he wrote. 'There can be no possible excuse for him, for I have not the least doubt in the world that he would earn far more even as a junior subaltern than as a barrister at present. . . . It is quite the worst case of which I have heard, and makes me so angry that I really can't think about it. He seems to me to stand in a very different category from those who are prevented by ill-health or domestic responsibilities from joining.' No doubt he was even more furious when he heard that Guedalla had secured a comfortable billet for himself in the War Office as a legal adviser to the Contracts Department.

Before they left Malta, the Battalion received a piece of disquieting news from Whitehall that, in spite of a pledge previously given that its entity was to be preserved, it was now proposed that it should in effect be broken up by being used to supply drafts to reinforce the First Battalion already in Gallipoli. One draft was in fact got together, and then much to everyone's relief the order was cancelled when the authorities decided that the Second Battalion should keep its integrity as a part of the Mediterranean Expeditionary Force.

Prior to embarkation, a number of personnel changes took place which affected Nathan. First, their Commanding Officer, Colonel Ekin, was taken to hospital with a severe attack of gastritis, and he had to be left behind. Then, the officer second in command was appointed commandant of the prisoners-of-war camp in Malta. As a result, another field officer, Major Christopher Tatham, took over the battalion command, while Nathan became acting second in command in addition to being a Company Commander.

> Never did I anticipate that I should go out to fight as second in command of a Battalion—for I shall have to act as such till the Colonel returns (if he ever does, which is more than doubtful). With command of a double company also I expect to have a busy and anxious time. It is a heavy responsibility. . . .
> I think the Battalion will put up a good show in whatever work is allotted to us; the officers are keen and, on the whole, efficient and have the great advantage of all working happily together. I don't suppose that any body of men have lived in intimate association day by day as he have, among whom there has been less friction. The men have been splendid throughout the period of our long and severe training, and under circumstances which have seldom been propitious.
> I shall try to give a good account of myself, and, whatever may happen, it will be an honour to have fought in such a cause with our officers and our men.

Unfortunately Nathan was to lose his two best subalterns, Graham Carritt and shortly afterwards Willa Chichester, who went down with jaundice; both were subsequently invalided home. 'It is awfully bad luck on him,' Nathan wrote of Carritt at this time. 'However, I have taken the best medical advice that can be got, and, as the advice is that he must get away at once, I am afraid that there is no help for it, as I cannot sit quietly down and watch him fade absolutely away under my eyes. He has done very good work out here, and his men would have gone anywhere with him. I fear that he will not be able to rejoin us even after a rest, as this kind of climate is quite unsuitable for him. . . . We shall miss him very much.' Unlike Chichester, Carritt was to survive the struggle and lived to work with Nathan again, this time in the Second World War.

The Governor's inability to bid good-bye to the two Battalions of the City of London Regiment on the ground that they 'would have made too small a muster for an Inspection owing to the detachments funeral parties and fatigues' did not go down at all well, particularly with the officers. However, Lord Methuen tried to make some amends by issuing a Special Fortress Order in which he commended the behaviour of the Battalions during the period they had been under his command. 'Their conduct has been excellent, under trying conditions lately, on account of the heavy and increasing fatigue work they have had to perform. Their appearance in Valetta, the smart way in which the men salute, the alacrity of the Main Guard in turning out, all show the efficiency of the Battalions.'

After ten days in the sweltering heat of a transit camp in the desert outside Cairo, the Battalion left Alexandria in the troop transport *Manitou* bound for the Dardanelles. (This was the vessel at which, when recently lying in Mudros harbour, a Turkish torpedo-boat had fired three torpedoes at point-blank range, all of which had missed.)

Captain Nathan marched out of the camp at the head of his half of the contingent—over 500 strong. 'Never did I imagine that it would fall to me to command such a body of men marching almost directly to the field of battle. It is an experience never to be forgotten.'

3

After touching briefly at Lemnos, the Battalion landed at Suvla Bay in the Gallipoli Peninsula on a late September afternoon in 1915. As they approached the open beaches, they were met by a patter of enemy shrapnel and intermittent shell fire. Everything was most primitive—improvised rickety piers, long lines of mules, dirt and dust, scruffy dug-outs, miscellaneous dumps of stores and the hazards of landing everything by hand in a glaring sun. Nathan was the first person in the Battalion to set foot on Turkish soil. After keeping his half of the Battalion in the shelter of a nullah for the night and much of the next day they marched about two miles to the positions of the Reserve Brigade of the 29th Division, 'the incomparable 29th', of which they were now to form a part.

The campaign had now lasted for five months, and the little progress that had been made had been at immense cost of life and limb and material. A month before the Second Battalion reached the scene, the greatest battle of the campaign in terms of numbers had been fought, when General Sir Ian Hamilton launched a massive attack on the Turkish-held heights above Suvla. Although the Turks were forced to bring up their last reserves, the British suffered 5,000 casualties, mostly from the 29th Division, which included the First Battalion of Nathan's regiment, losses which Winston Churchill later described as 'heavy and fruitless'. Morale sharply declined as a result of what the campaign's official historian called 'the miasma of defeat rising from Suvla Plain'. Major Hore-Ruthven, V.C., a staff officer from G.H.Q., reported at this time: 'Every visit to Suvla discloses confusion, inertia and magnification of difficulties, due to the pessimistic attitude of higher commanders and staffs, which filters down to the troops.' At Suvla, as elsewhere in Gallipoli, the situation developed into a stalemate, while the opposing forces faced each other and dug themselves in for the winter in trenches two to three miles from the beaches.

27 September, 1915. I am writing this in a dug-out some six feet underground with shrapnel and high explosive shells passing overhead at frequent intervals—indeed, as I write. We are at the moment in Brigade Reserve, and stray rifle shots pass over us more than is pleasant, but I don't think that we have any casualties as far as rifle shooting is concerned, though we have had a few—remarkably few from shrapnel. My Company has got off pretty lightly—one fellow wounded yesterday and one today.

The sensation is novel and harassing—but the men have borne the unexampled experience with a nerve and stamina which are beyond all praise.

Generally speaking, we are working as navvies all night and most of the day and are more or less beasts of burden in between times. We—i.e. my Company—have not yet been into the firing line, but I rather anticipate that we shall be going up tomorrow. I hope that we shall give a good account of ourselves.

4 October. Since last writing I have had my Company in the firing line, and got off with only two casualties. It was an interesting experience, but rather trying. We were placed within 40 yards of the Turkish trenches and through a peephole I could quite distinctly see the enemy in their trenches. Yesterday we had some shrapnel over us, and I am sorry to say that my orderly was hit while I was speaking to him—rather disturbing. He is not badly hit—a bullet in the back. I was able to put on a temporary bandage and hope that he will get on alright. He has, of course, gone off on a Hospital ship and I have had to find a fresh servant.*

I have, since I have been in the Peninsula, seen sights which, in normal times, would have turned me up altogether—but I make a point of thinking about these things as little as possible, and seem gradually to be becoming almost callous to them. Anyhow, casualties are inevitable and it is no good worrying unduly as long as one has taken all reasonable precautions to avoid them. I had five in my Company yesterday at one fell swoop.

For this visit to the firing line, Nathan's Company was attached to another unit to give them experience. After this brief 'baptism of fire', they went back to reserve.

6 October. . . . I am continuing this at 8 at night, crouched in a most uncomfortable position in my dug-out lighted by a solitary candle. My dug-out is in the side of a hill and, while in it, I am safe from stray bullets and practically safe from shrapnel. I think that you would be rather amused if you could see me, and certainly neither you nor I ever imagined that I should be able to get on at all in circumstances like these, down in the bowels of the earth with bullets whizzing all round. One of the great differences between the campaign in France and here is that in France when in reserve one is, I understand, practically safe, while here one has perforce to be kept so near the firing line as continually to be liable to get damaged. . . .

I would give much for a hot bath. I have only had one hot bath since the beginning of May, though I had a cold one every

---

* He was Private Thomas Snooks and was to make a dramatic reappearance during the Second World War: see below, p. 148.

day until we left Egypt. Since our arrival here, it has not of course been possible to get a bath at all, but I have managed twice to get a wash all over. Each day so far I have been lucky enough to get a shave and a face and hands wash in something over a pint of water! Some of the men have not been able to wash or shave for days. Except that I have changed my under-clothing twice, I have not had my clothes off day or night since we arrived in Gallipoli. My dirty clothes are washed as well as may be in my dirty water after I have finished washing and shaving and my servant also washed in it! So you can see that we are living the simple life.

Since my servant has been wounded, I have been looked after by Chichester's servant; he does me very well. We have the same food as the men, and eat in our dug-outs with our food on our knees. My new dug-out is about 2 feet 6 inches wide and about 6 feet long and $4\frac{1}{2}$ feet deep. I am very lucky to have such a large one all to myself. My servant has fitted three boxes in the wall and tied two blankets over the top to keep the sun from me. So I am really quite comfortable and cosy.

9 October. Since last writing to you I have had my Company for a short spell in the advanced firing line—only one casualty, man killed instantaneously by a shot through the temple. It was, as you may imagine, an unpleasant spectacle, especially to see the flies swarming round. . . . It is the first outright 'kill' that I have had in my Company.

It was last night that I was relieved. The sky suddenly be-came pitch black—you literally could not see 6 inches or even 3 inches in front of you — and as the trenches are narrow and winding the difficulties of carrying out the relief were immense. However, by dint of careful going and each man hanging on to the jacket of the man in front of him, we managed to get the new Company in and my Company out. At the same time we had some very heavy rain—the first we have had since, I think, the first week in June—so that altogether the con-ditions left much to be desired. The discomforts were added to by the fact that the Turks took advantage of the change in weather and wind to send along some asphyxiating bombs, so that we had to be ready with our respirators. However, none came near us.

The march home—about 1,000 yards in all—along slippery, narrow winding trenches in the inky darkness was a nightmare, and I was very much relieved to get back without casualties, or losing the way. Of course, we were sniped at all the time. At the time I hated it, but it is an interesting experience to look back upon. When we arrived at our dug-outs, it was still raining, and I could not help chuckling when I thought of what you would have said if you had seen me drop into my little brown hole in the earth and lie down to sleep with my Burberry round me and the rain pouring upon me. However, I soon fell asleep, as I was absolutely tired out, and this morning the sky was blue again. Unless one sees the humorous side of some of the incidents out here, I don't know how we should get on at all.

We anticipate that, each Company having been in the trenches attached to a Regular Battalion and so having gained experience under favourable circumstances, we shall shortly go up as a Battalion.

It is rather eerie work, especially at night, looking over the parapet for advancing Turks, with snipers' shots whizzing over your head and all round you. The only wonder is that there are comparatively few casualties.

The trenches are very wonderful—mile after mile over the the whole country side winding over hills and through valleys —fine trenches and supports—with the Turkish trenches anything between 40 and 400 yards distant the whole way. The feeding in the trenches is just as good as in reserve, and on the whole the organization is very complete, especially considering the primitive conditions which have to be met—for instance, there is not a habitation anywhere to be seen.

It is rather pathetic to see here and there small patches of ground wired in containing the graves of some of the fallen. They all seem to be well tended. . . .

By the way, one often hears talk of what one's sensations have been when one has first come under fire. I was rather apprehensive in anticipation, but when the time came I think that all I felt was a sort of mild surprise. Perhaps the best description I have seen is in a letter written by one of my men which has today passed through my hands for censoring—he says that when he heard the first shell whizz past him and explode, he was so astonished that he accidentally fell into the nearest dug-out. Astonishment is, I think, the keynote of one's first sensation. As it happened, I had a man wounded by the first shell and had to look after him. I daresay that if there had not been something which had to be done at once, I should have been in the deuce of a funk.

A few days later, they returned to the firing line, this time as a complete Battalion.

13 October. We came up as a Battalion yesterday and are here indefinitely. Of course it is a little wearing—chiefly owing to lack of sleep on account of the fact that the dangerous time is the night and that during the day one is busy with administrative work. Last night I was out just in front of our lines and tonight propose to reconnoitre to find out what Mr Turk is doing about a couple of hundred yards in front of us. Apart from the fact that one may knock up against an enemy patrol or stop a stray bullet, the job is more nervy than risky.

I have got a dug-out about 40 yards back from the firing line, and while there am quite reasonably safe. I am afraid that when the really wet weather comes, things will be devilish messy.

15 October. I wrote you in my last letter that I was going to do a little reconnoitring. In fact I took out a couple of N.C.O's and got out about a couple of hundred yards to within 80 yards of the Turkish trenches, and was able to get a little information about their wire entanglements, but as the devils began firing at a range rather closer than was pleasant, I beat a retreat, as I had no desire to make a present of myself to Mr Turk. I was also out helping to lay down wire in front of our lines. It is a little nervy, but on a reasonably dark night not nearly so dangerous as you would think. Last night the moon made it too bright to go out.

A night or two later, he had what he modestly called 'an interesting experience out in front'. But it was also an extremely risky one, and a brother officer who witnessed it—John Burnaby, later Regius Professor of Divinity at Cambridge—felt at the time that Nathan was bound to be hit by the Turkish bullets. But fortunately he came through without a scratch.

Allied troops in Anzac Bay, 1915

The Battalion Commander in his dug-out, Gallipoli, 1915

Liberal M.P., 1929

Chairman for
Lloyd George, 1932

The Engineers wanted to put up barbed wire in front of our trenches and my Company was ordered to find a covering party, i.e. a party to get in between the Engineers and the Turks so that, in the event of the latter attacking, the covering party would be able to give warning and hold up the attack momentarily while the Engineers got back into the trenches. As soon as it was dark I took out the N.C.O.s to show them where the covering party was to go. I ought to have said that at this point the trenches are only 80 to 100 yards apart.

When the time came for the covering party to go out (it was a fairly moonlight night), I stopped with the flank of the party nearest the Turks' trenches and sent the Sergeant to the place which I had taken them to earlier and pointed out as the spot for the other flank of the party to rest on. Unfortunately he mistook the way—a mistake of 30 yards makes all the difference at that point—and ran slick into the Turks. The first I knew of anything wrong was on hearing shouts of 'Allah! Allah!' followed by firing. It was only 100 yards from me, but I could not, even in the moonlight which was gradually waning, see exactly where they were. (In fact they were hidden from view in a nullah.)

I got my part of the party down and began rapid fire, but as there were only about 8 of them and the Turks seemed to be about 40, I gradually got them back to the trenches and then went to find the other part of the party. When I found them (there were only 12 of them), they were doing quite well, but as I knew that the Turks outnumbered them several times over, I gradually withdrew them (under fire, of course) to our trenches, but when the roll was taken found that we were three short. So I had to go to find them.

I found one and managed to carry him in—I never knew that I could carry a man on my back before, but it is wonderful what one can do in an emergency—and then went back to look for the others, of whom one was the Sergeant who had led the men astray. He had managed to crawl a short distance towards our trenches, and with my assistance was able to walk back. The third man ought, I knew, to be at the other end of the line, so I had to go to look for him. I found him lying down where he had been put originally, and he had not heard the order to retire back to the trenches; he was unhurt. Then I really got angry, as it is not a pleasant job walking about to look for missing men in the open with people firing at you and trying their best to knock you out.

The place to which the Sergeant had led the party was the same place as I had been to to reconnoitre on the previous occasion; there were no Turks there then, though their trenches were within a very few yards. It appears that he ran right into them before he saw them or they him—and the firing was at a range in places of 7 yards. The party of Turks was apparently a strong patrol. Of course, I couldn't stand that kind of thing, so when I had got all my men back, I sent up a couple of flares to light the place up and to give the devils a few rounds of rapid fire to take back to their trenches with them.

Well, the work was important and I thought ought to be done, so I took out the covering party again and this time placed every man out myself. We got the Engineers to work, and they finished by daybreak. The Turks had apparently re-tired from the position where we found them (they had not returned there the following night, so I think we have fright-ened them away for the time), and though we were under a fast and furious fusillade the whole time—mostly over our heads—we managed to get the work completed without further casualties to ourselves or the Engineers. Everybody is rather pleased with the way things were done from the General down-wards, so it is an interesting experience to look back upon, though rather damnable at the time.

The following night we had the covering party out again in the same place, but without incident.

Of course, these small scraps etc. are going on all the time. The men were absolutely splendid, and are very proud of being some of the very few who have actually seen a Turk. Total damage: three wounded.

24 October. The discomforts have, of course, been consider-able—inevitably so—but I have heard no 'grousing' except an occasional murmur as to lack of sleep. Especially in the trenches, when constant and continuous alertness is the only safeguard against disaster, sleep is a minus quantity. Person-ally, I didn't see my bed (so-called) for upwards of 55 hours on end—from the Sunday morning when I got up until the Tuesday afternoon when we returned to our dug-out from the firing line. The only ill effect was that I was so overcome with sleep at the end that I was unable to write or dictate reports, and had to give up the attempt till I had had a good sleep. . . . Our 'family party' out here continues to be happy and without friction, but it is diminished in number sadly—so sadly. We don't see a great deal of one another nowadays and of course have no Mess. Most of the officers I have not seen for over a week—some are a couple of miles away, and we don't pay visits while shot and shell are flying about.

By the beginning of November the number of officers had dwindled to nine, and of these all except Nathan were 'under the Doctor' for some ailment. 'At present we here live in the past and for the day only,' he wrote at this time. 'Perhaps it is as well: for, as far as I can see, we are a great deal nearer Eternity than Constantinople.'

Colonel Ekin now rejoined them, but after a fortnight left again this time for good ('He could not stick it at all'), and Major Tatham once more took command of the Battalion. ('I must say that during the week in the trenches he gave me every assistance which a Commanding Officer could give. The remaining officers were either sick or in support.') Shortly afterwards, Tatham went down with jaundice, so that Nathan became 'to all intents and purposes', as he put it, 'responsible for the whole show'. A fortnight later Tatham was evacuated in a hospital ship, and Nathan officially took over the command.

'I certainly never contemplated in my wildest dreams that I should ever actually command a Battalion in the field in war,' he wrote on November 25, 'nor indeed, was it ever one of my particular ambitions to do so. As I look back upon the last ten years, I cannot help thinking how responsibility after responsibility has fallen upon my shoulders—from the day when I first became Honorary Secretary of the Union at St Paul's until now when I am responsible immediately, I suppose, for the safety and the lives of several hundred men, and, indirectly, for the creditable carrying out of some part of the operations out here. I don't suppose that there are many—if, indeed, there are any Commanding Officers—of my age; but pleasant though it sometimes feels to think that one is taking a responsible and important part in the work on hand—whatever it may be, from collecting the pennies in an East End Club to commanding a Battalion on active service—I fear that with each additional burden, the shoulders become less able to bear fresh weight.'

4

During the two months that Nathan had been in Gallipoli, important changes had been taking place in the military theatre. Bulgaria had entered the war against the Allies and this meant that greatly improved guns and ammunition would soon be pouring into Turkey from the Central Powers; indeed, had the Turks had adequate artillery support after the original allied landings, they would soon have driven the allied troops into the sea. As things were, the Allies had failed to make any appreciable headway, and for this General Sir Ian Hamilton was blamed at home, with the result that he was recalled in the middle of October. 'Sir Ian was of the old chivalrous school,' wrote one of his staff officers afterwards; 'his war was to be "run on gallantry"—the Englishman never knows when he is beaten, and all that. And so he blinded himself to the truth.' Evacuation was strongly recommended by Hamilton's successor General Sir Charles Monro, who arrived towards the end of the month from France where he had been in command of the Third Army. The decision was not finally taken by the Cabinet until Kitchener himself had paid a quick visit to the Dardanelles and appraised the situation. On November 22, the War Minister advised the Cabinet that Suvla and Anzac should be evacuated forthwith, but that Helles should be retained as a foothold in the Peninsula, 'at all events for the present'. More troops had also to be sent to Salonika to fight against the Bulgarians.

In October there had been some heavy rain and high seas, which had smashed the piers and there was some further rough weather in the middle of November. But this was nothing to the violent storms and blizzards, which began on November 27 and raged over the whole Peninsula for nearly a week. 'It has been the most awful few days that I have ever experienced or imagined,' Nathan wrote on December 2. 'Last Friday we had the most *terrific* storm—hail, lightning, thunder and rain by the bucketful. On the top of this we have had a very keen frost. We have, of course, been flooded out and for abject misery and hopelessness the situation could not for a few days be surpassed. . . . The authorities have issued officers with port wine and everybody with any amount of rum: everything possible under the distressing circumstances has been done to alleviate the conditions, but they would never have been so bad if ordinary foresight had been exercised.'

The torrent came rushing down from the hills above Suvla, carrying with it the bodies of drowned men and mules and a huge mass of debris. All thoughts of fighting were set aside in the struggle for survival on both sides. One British soldier wrote of 'the dead lying about in hundreds all swollen and black and in every conceivable place and attitude, trenches broken down and filled with water, and equipment of all sorts everywhere'. In all 280 men died as the direct result of the storm and blizzard, and at Suvla alone there were over 12,000 cases of frostbite and exposure. In the words of the Special Army Order from Monro thanking all ranks for their strenuous and self-sacrificing devotion to duty, 'the conditions prevailing were probably more severe than any to which our troops in France were subjected during last winter and the hardships which our men have suffered have consequently been intense'.

5 December. You say in one of your letters that you cannot think that we can go on indefinitely without undressing. Well, we have managed so far: I have never had any of my clothes off (except to change underclothing) since we left Lemnos, except that I have taken off my leggings and boots most nights when we have been in reserve. . . .
The wastage is far greater than appears from the casualty returns, for there is inevitably a large amount of sickness—apart from that resulting from such untoward incidents as the

storm. The problem is not only how to get the armies but how to keep up the numbers.

13 December. The storm, of which I wrote you previously, is still a dreadful nightmare to look back on, and we are still suffering from its effects. As far as I am concerned, I was at the time not quite so much affected as some of the others, though for about 10 days I was unable to get into my dug-out which was 3 feet deep in water, and my baggage was all awash! —and I had to get what rest I could sitting up on a ledge of earth in the only dug-out which was not swamped: that was the Headquarters dug-out over which I had got a little corrugated iron, and where I gave refuge to the only 6 other officers who remain from those who landed in September. That was in itself very trying, especially as after the actual storm we continued to have rain and snow and ultimately about 15 degrees of frost for some days.

The sole of one of my boots was partly broken away by the suction of the deep mud—which was often knee, and in places waist deep—and my other pair had got wet through in my dug-out. However, I had to manage as best I could. The result, however, was that I got a slight touch of frostbite and very severe rheumatism in my feet. I massaged my feet regularly with warm oil, but was not allowed to take off my boots for more than a few minutes at a time lest my feet should swell, and the boots not go on again. The pain for days was excruciating, and resisting it sapped most of my remaining strength: until the past few days I have been as weak as a child, unable to walk more than a few yards without wanting brandy to pull me together again. The severe pain in the feet left me, and the rheumatism distributed itself pretty evenly over all my limbs. However, save for a slight stiffness in the legs after I have been sitting for any length of time, I have been able to throw it almost entirely off, and also a slight attack of jaundice which so far has not mattered, and doesn't seem likely to. I have really been absolutely beaten, whacked and dead to the world, but am now more or less myself again, and hope to carry on to the bitter end.

From what I have said of myself, you may be able to form some opinion of what the men—under less favourable conditions—have suffered. It has been a gigantic tragedy.

After the severest weather was over, Chichester arrived and brought with him a number of new officers, and, within a few days, a couple of our other old officers also rejoined, so now we are quite a large party again. . . .

I wonder if you realize that those of us who remain are quite veterans after our three months here. There are very few officers now in the other Battalions who were here when we arrived: one could count them on the fingers of one's hand.

The plan was for a gradual and secret withdrawal, while at the same time pretending to the Turks that a large army remained. The troops by and large entered into the spirit of this deception, and by the middle of December the evacuation was well advanced, thanks partly to a spell of good weather. But General Birdwood, the future Field Marshal, who commanded the Australian and New Zealand (the Anzac) Corps, and quite a number of his men, said they would rather die than leave; in fact Birdwood was put in charge of the evacuation and he afterwards related how one Australian said to him nodding in the direction of the ragged cemeteries, 'I hope *they* won't hear us going down to the beaches!' Every night flotillas of small ships would slip into Suvla Bay and Anzac Cove and take on their human cargoes, leaving the sea empty again before morning. By December 18 only 40,000 men were left, and these were all taken off during the two following nights.

Mudros. 23 December. You will have read in the papers ere now of the evacuation over the week-end of Suvla and Anzac. The whole operation went off very successfully, and as far as I have been able to ascertain the casualties were not more than on an ordinary night when nothing special is in the air. Our Brigade covered the retirement of the 29th Division.

The evacuation had been begun, as far as stores etc. are concerned, before the storm, but that, of course, upset all calculations and entailed a considerable postponement. The final stage of the operation covered Saturday and Sunday [18–19 December]. I left with my Battalion on Saturday night and brought with me about 850 others of the Brigade, so I had a pretty good command on that eventful occasion. My Battalion was in reserve, and for some days prior to the final stage, we had been sending away stores etc. including all our own personal baggage and belongings. I retained my mackintosh* (and lining) and my shaving tackle in addition to a mackintosh sheet and one blanket. Otherwise neither I nor anyone else had for the last two days anything but what we stood up in. At the end I buried all stores that were left, so that the Turks will not have found any booty where we have been.

It was a little eerie forming up in the darkness prior to the flit and marching back to a splendidly constructed line of defence near the shore (which my Battalion had done much to build), fearing that at the last the Turks might have discovered what we were up to and come swarming after us, and so necessitate the holding of the line of defence. However, the Turks never seemed to realize the true position, and for some days were feverishly engaged in wiring themselves in behind a regular birdcage of wire. They must have thought that we were about to make an attack and were landing reinforcements, especially as we gave them one or two terrific bombardments both from sea and land. We got down to the line of defence alright, and as the Turks had made no move proceeded to the beach, where we embarked on the same boat as had taken us to Suvla in September.

We were brought to Mudros and there transhipped temporarily on to a transport, where we were provided with breakfast and lunch. You can imagine how we enjoyed the decent food after what we have been through. In the afternoon we disembarked, and marched to the Camp where we now are at Mudros West. The march was very trying, and I never realized before how worn out and 'whacked' we all are: it was only about 2 miles, but it took me all I knew to manage it. Of course, the conditions here are not ideal: you would imagine that the army had had possession of the island for 36 hours instead of 6 months, but I suppose we ought to feel lucky at being safe and sound away from the incessant shot and shell. . . .

I am in a bell tent, which I share with the Doctor: my bed is a stretcher, and as we had rather a heavy storm two or three days ago which turned everything into liquid mud, I am thankful even for an uncomfortable stretcher—sprawling on which I am writing this letter.

---

* The mackintosh now belongs to the present Lord Nathan.

Mudros is a loathly place; the prevailing view is mud; the prevailing smell, burning refuse.

Yesterday I went on board the *Aragon*, the ship on which the General Headquarters of the M.E.F. are stationed, as I wanted to see some officials there. I had a tip-top lunch, which will live in my memory; to drink out of a glass again, and to see a clean tablecloth and use a table napkin to say nothing of cleaned cutlery and crockery seemed a luxury almost undreamt of.

We are staying here—for how long or how short a time we do not know—'prior to transference to a fresh sphere of activity'. The 'fresh sphere of activity' which I should like best is England, but I fear that there is no hope of that.

The evacuation of Suvla is, of course, an event which will live in history; I am not sure that what I felt most about it was not leaving behind the bodies of so many men who had come out with us and were killed. We left the graves marked and I hope that the Turk will not disturb them. . . .

Snowdon [one of Nathan's subalterns] went to Hospital yesterday—absolutely done in; he never got over the storm. So now there are only five of us who have been through the whole show with the Battalion. The losses from the storm were tremendous, but so far the only serious results among our men, as far as I have heard, has been one death and one man who had his feet taken off: I dare say I shall hear later about the balance of the 280 men who were 'drowned' by the storm. It is impossible to visualize what it was like, and it makes me ill to think of it. It stands out in relief from all the other sights and sounds that I have experienced out here.

I think that, if we could get to Egypt and civilization again, it would do much to brighten us up and would make new men of us. I don't see how we can carry on for long as we are. The men have been throughout quite admirable, and especially during the evacuation, when the exercise of the most rigid discipline was necessary, compared very favourably with the Regulars.

Looking back on the Suvla evacuation some weeks later, Nathan described it as a marvellous piece of organization, and rather thrilling. 'Though not actually the rearguard, we took part in the final stage of the evacuation,' he wrote, 'and I had under my command when we left about half our Brigade. We had no particularly large part in the operations—no individuals had: but I was present at all the preliminary conferences etc. of C.O.s with the General. The only praise that is due to us is for carrying out what we had to do intelligently and quietly. The night we left was the quietest and brightest that we had while in the Peninsula: the Turkish communiqué, "No prisoners on account of fog," much froth, "English driven into the sea," etc. etc. is a tissue of lies from beginning to end.'

5

Since the French had insisted in withdrawing their troops from Helles, General Birdwood had to call on the 'incomparable' 29th Division to fill the gap there. While he was having his Christmas dinner with his Battalion, Nathan received orders to embark first thing the following morning. So he and his men had to endure another weary march, though for him there was the compensating news which reached him before they left that he had been promoted to Major so long as he commanded the Battalion.

That same night we arrived at Helles, and remained standing by until 6 next morning: there was a good deal of rain, and it was too rough to take us off, so we steamed to Imbros, where we remained for the day, returning in the evening to Helles, where we disembarked at about 9 o'clock. Disembarkation may sound a very easy thing, but it is by no means so simple as it sounds. First, we had to tranship into a small tug, and, as there was still a heavy swell, this was quite a dangerous operation, and each man had to be helped on board independently—no gangways or anything like that. However, we managed to tranship without accident, and then were taken to the *River Clyde*, which, you may recollect, was a transport which was run ashore at the original landing. It is now used as a sort of pier.

On the Asiatic side of the Straits there is a large [long range Turkish] gun known as 'Asiatic Annie': she sends heavy high explosive over to the landing beaches every few minutes: the flash can be seen from the *Clyde,* and a horn is blown as a warning that the shell is coming, and, in about 15 seconds, it comes over, making a noise like an express train, as it rushes through the air. The bugle sounded and a shell came while we were forming up on the beach: not a very comfortable sensation, when you know that you can do nothing to save yourself, except lift up your hands and pray! Of course, it is merely blind firing by the gun, they can't see a target, and don't know what they actually hit: but now and then they are bound to —and do—get a bag.

The night was pitch dark, the roads ankle deep in mud, and the guides twice lost their way; so you can imagine that we had a jolly march. At last however, at about 3 o'clock on the Tuesday morning (28th) we got to our dug-outs, and by 4 o'clock had settled down, dead tired, for a couple of hours sleep in six inches of mud.

The first thing that I knew on waking up on the Tuesday morning after two or three hours fitful slumber was that there was an aeroplane up above making a thorough nuisance of itself and dropping bombs: one came down, with a sizzling noise, about 15 yards from my dug-out: it only damaged two picks. However, it wasn't a very cordial welcome to Helles. . . . The firing line was certainly not so comfortable as at Suvla; but Helles had many compensating advantages in spite of the fact that in places 'no man's land' between the Turkish lines and our own was only 7 yards wide. We never went up to the firing line there as a Battalion, though I had (and left) detachments there until almost the last moment.

During the time that we were there, the shelling grew extraordinarily heavy: the Turks seemed to have brought up many new guns (probably from Suvla and Anzac) and to have received unlimited supplies of first class ammunition. During the day there was scarcely a square yard from the front right away back to the beaches which was not searched by high explosive and shrapnel. We all of us, of course, had many narrow shaves and many miraculous escapes: on one morning a high explosive burst in one of our dug-outs about 10 yards from my own— and badly damaged the occupants, and elsewhere one of my fellows had his leg blown off and died. On the whole, however, both of my own Battalion's casualties and the casualties generally were small out of all proportion to the enemy's expenditure of ammunition. One great advantage of Suvla was that, unless one was in the firing line, one was immune from stray rifle shots: our dug-outs were about a mile behind the firing line, whereas at Helles we were only 600 or 800 yards behind. There was a certain amount of shelling of the beaches at night (apart from 'Asiatic Annie', who was rather a terror), but, on the whole, after sundown the guns were pretty quiet.

General Birdwood was convinced that the only chance of success at Helles lay in a policy of aggressiveness, and he issued orders in this sense. These orders met with a spirited response from his troops, and, as Robert Rhodes James points out in his excellent account of the Dardanelles expedition, within a week of the Suvla and Anzac evacuation the British at Helles had obtained a tactical superiority over the enemy which remains one of the least publicized but crucial triumphs of the entire campaign.* But the Cabinet had already agreed that the troops should also be withdrawn from Helles after this course had been strongly advocated to Kitchener by Sir Charles Monro, who knew that the Turkish commander, General Liman von Sanders, angry that the British had slipped through his fingers at Suvla and Anzac, was preparing for a massive assault upon their positions at the southern tip of the Peninsula. Monro accordingly urged upon Birdwood the vital necessity of speed, and the reluctant Birdwood intimated that, weather permitting, the evacuation should be completed on the night of the 8/9 January 1915.

Nathan described how it happened through his eyes when he had reached Egypt:

> When we arrived [in Helles], nobody thought of evacuation, but it soon became pretty evident that something was in the air. My own Battalion had a good deal of work to do in the way of building barricades, etc., and a few days after our arrival we were ordered to send away our valises and packs, which we had recovered on our arrival at Helles: so once again we were left with nothing save what we stood up in!
>
> The final evacuation took place on Saturday 8th January.

---

* James. *Gallipoli* (1965), at p. 344.

We left on the night of Thursday 6th, at ten minutes' notice. We were in the middle of tea when, at 5.30, the order came to rendezvous at 6 o'clock at a place some ¾ mile away. So we left the remnants of our meal on the table, packed up and paraded: then came a very trying march to the beach, passing ghost-like bodies of troops marching down silently also to the beaches, each one of us catching his breath, however little, as the shells hissed overhead. Fortune, however, was again with us, and 9 o'clock found us—without a single casualty—on the *River Clyde* once more. As we were getting ready to embark, 'Asiatic Annie' spoke more than once: some French troops near us rushed for shelter behind the walls of Sedd-el-Bahr Fort, but my fellows stood firm as a rock, though the shells plunged down only 30 or 40 yards from us. Similarly at Suvla, my men by their self-restraint and discipline put to shame the discipline of the so-called Regulars, most of who are of course much junior soldiers to us. In fact, whenever we have failed to beat the Regulars at their own game, it has been by reason merely of our inferior physique: our strongest men all went down with dysentery within 3 weeks of our landing.

From the *River Clyde* we embarked on a lighter, and thence transhipped to the *Minneapolis*, which after waiting at Mudros till the 12th sailed for Alexandria which we reached on the 14th and from where I cabled you that I was safe and sound.

The voyage was very restful and the food first rate.

It was with feelings of profound relief and thankfulness to be still alive that Nathan recorded that the Battalion's period of service in the field was for the time being at an end. 'As I look back upon the momentous incidents of the past few months,' he wrote to his parents at this time, 'I don't think that I have a great deal to regret, except the loss of so many excellent fellows from wounds and disease: on the other hand, I have had the honour of commanding a Battalion in the two evacuations, each of which is in itself a memorable event. I believe this is the only Territorial Battalion— it is certainly the only 2nd Line Territorial Battalion—which has been through both evacuations; and to have had this experience as a unit of "the incomparable 29th Division" makes it a very signal privilege!'

6

The Battalion was accommodated in a camp about thirty miles from Cairo, which was to be their home for the next three months. Since his luggage had not arrived after several days, Nathan went to Cairo for forty-eight hours to fit himself out with some necessaries. He stayed at Shepherd's Hotel, which he did not find as pleasant as during the previous September. Everything was much more expensive. 'If you wear two stars you are fleeced: if you wear a crown, as I have been doing, you are simply asking, so to speak, for robbery with violence.'

On January 19, 1916, whilst he was in Cairo, Nathan received a telegram from Camp, much to his surprise and chagrin, to the effect that Lieutenant-Colonel A. C. H. Kennard had joined for duty.

I had never heard of the man, nor of any suggestion (beyond a vague rumour from a N.C.O.) that any new senior officer was coming out. However, I returned on the 20th and there met the fellow. He seems pleasant enough, and, no doubt, capable; but that is a very poor satisfaction to me. It appears that he was formerly in the Rifle Brigade, and went through the South African War, retired and joined the 19th County of London Regiment, returning in May sick. In November, being tired of slacking—this is his own story—he went to Sir Francis Lloyd, G.O.C. London District, and asked for a job. Ekin had just gone home, so the command was vacant and Lloyd offered it to Kennard, who, of course, jumped at it. That this should have been done without any reference to the abilities of the people on the spot seems to me to speak for itself, and to make the whole thing nothing less than a scandal, which is added to by what Kennard himself tells me, namely that he is having sent out a new second in command, new adjutant and new quartermaster.

How a man can have the mere cheek to do this without seeing his new Battalion and without meeting any of his officers is to me quite incomprehensible. It only goes to prove what I have all along felt—that the people on the spot in London can pull the strings, while we poor devils who have been away for months and done all the work are simply shoved from pillar to post—because the Censorship regulations gag us, and we can't speak what we know neither for our own benefit nor the public's. The authorities, therefore, to appease those who are nearest and loudest become mere time-servers and, to stop the annoyance and noise at home, have no hesitation in acting in however dastardly a fashion towards those who are away.

It is indeed disappointing. . . . What I feel so bitter about is that I have been passed over without any reference to what I have done because Kennard has made sufficient noise to become a nuisance. He is a member of the L.C.C. and sits for West St Pancras.

Nathan thought that with the arrival of a new second in command his acting majority would go as a matter of routine and that he would revert to being a company commander. However, it appeared that before leaving Gallipoli one of the Brigadiers of the 29th Division had recommended his promotion to temporary rank. Fortunately this came through before Kennard's choice could reach Egypt, with the result that Nathan being the only officer of field rank in the Battalion automatically became second in command. He was further promoted retrospectively Lieutenant-Colonel, for the period when he commanded the Battalion in Gallipoli, but the notification was not published until after Colonel Kennard had joined up; otherwise, as Nathan put it, 'I should have been able to keep him out—rather annoying, as it also prevented me from wearing the star as well as the crown.'

In March, the unwelcome Kennard was ordered to take over the command of a Brigade in another part of Egypt, as a temporary job, with the result that Nathan again became acting Battalion commander. He had already applied for home leave, and the news that he had been granted a month's leave reached him the day after Kennard's departure. In the circumstances he felt that he should withdraw his leave application, which he did. He might just as well have taken the leave, since about ten days later he heard the news that the Battalion was being sent to 'somewhere in France'. This

meant that all officers on detached duty such as Kennard were recalled, and Nathan once more became second in command.

Alexandria. 12 April 1916. I am not overjoyed at going to
the Front again, especially under Kennard, who has failed sig-
nally to obtain anyone's confidence or respect either as a soldier
or a man. I am about the only one who is on even superficially
good terms with him, though courtesy always prevails with
everyone. However, no doubt, Snowdon [who had gone home
on leave] will tell you all about him!

I am quite fit and well, though perhaps not quite so vigorous
in mind or limb as six months ago. I don't think my nerves are
as good as they were, but I hope to put up a tolerably creditable
show. The officers (with the conspicuous exception already
mentioned) are a pretty good lot, though not so good as those
who left Egypt in September. Of the latter, 11 are now with us.
We have been a singularly happy mess throughout the existence of the Battalion. Besides myself, there is, as I think I have
previously told you, only one officer—a Captain, John
Burnaby—who has been with the Battalion right through
from the old Handel Street days to the present time. He,
Snowdon and myself—and, of course, Chichester—have been
very good friends all through. Snowdon, as you will doubtless
gather when you see him, is a broken man, physically and
mentally, and I doubt whether he will return. The strain was
too much for him, though he always managed to get things
done. I do not think he will ever recover fully. Burnaby has
been remarkably fit all through, and Chichester has been quite
strong since he rejoined in the early days of December. Several
of the others are not the men they were, but of course the
youngsters who have recently joined us are able to infuse a
considerable amount of vim and vigour into the show. As for
the men—those that remain and form the 'Battalion' as it now
is—their recovery has been wonderful. They are, as they have
always been, a first-rate set of men. They can be relied on: and
in war that is everything.

Five days later the Battalion, under the command of Colonel
Kennard, sailed for Marseilles in the troop transport *Transylvania.*

This is quite a comfortable old tub, but rather crowded.
For the first time, I don't get a cabin to myself, but share with

two others—Chichester and Burnaby. It is a decent sized 'state room', so we don't suffer overmuch inconvenience. We've got a proper dressing-table with drawers etc., a wardrobe and a real lavatory basin with running water. Though the feeding leaves something to be desired, it is the best we have had since we disembarked from the poor old *Minneapolis*. We wear life belts all day, and I am writing this sitting on deck with a body belt on, but I am afraid that there is a precious poor chance of many of us surviving if a submarine should come up with us.

Where we shall be or what we shall do when we get to France I do not in the least know, but I hope to get early leave, and Kennard has promised to put in a strong application for me and all of the others who have been away for the past 15 months. . . .

By the way, I couldn't help remarking that we left Egypt for the Peninsula on 17 September—the Day of Atonement—and for France on 17 April—the first day of the Passover—rather a curious coincidence. I wonder what the superstitious would make of it? . . .

There is much to be said for us on embarking on this latest stage of the great adventure—that we now have a fair amount of experience to guide us, unless indeed things are radically different in France from what they were at Gallipoli, and that should give us a certain amount of confidence in ourselves. Whatever the future may hold for us, we go to meet it with an enthusiasm that is tempered, at all events, with a certain confidence and determination, ready for whatever may come.

At this point there is a gap in Nathan's correspondence, due no doubt to his being granted a month's leave shortly after the Battalion reached Marseilles. When he returned to France in June, 1916, it was to find the 8th Army Corps, of which the 29th Division, with the London Territorials, formed a part, had become a reserve corps under the command of General Hubert Gough on the extreme left of the Somme Front. When the heavy artillery bombardment of the German lines began on June 24, in preparation for the all-out attack intended for June 29 but subsequently postponed until July 1, the 29th Division was moved into the battle area between the village of Beaumont-Hamel and the river Ancre. The whole British attack was on a front of approximately one and a half miles and in the event engaged fourteen British divisions. The 8th Corps attacked the enemy positions north of Beaumont-Hamel, and though its central division penetrated the German front line it was eventually driven back to its own trenches. Most of the other divisions on the front fared equally badly, with the result that this was the greatest loss and slaughter sustained in twelve hours in the whole history of the British Army, 60,000 being killed, wounded or missing on that terrible day. The extent of the catastrophe was concealed by the Censorship, and with the continuance of the fighting on a smaller front, reduced to about 7,000 yards, the full significance of the initial confrontation was not generally appreciated. Nevertheless, the total British losses amounted to 171,000.

8 July 1916. You will, of course, have been interested in the news of the ? Big Push. As far as I am concerned, you need have no particular anxiety, for, at present, things are more or less normal with us. How long they will remain so I cannot of course imagine or prophesy. I am glad to observe in such newspapers as I have seen a restrained enthusiasm. I think it very necessary, and that one must not allow one's hopes to be raised too high. The cost will be necessarily great: the profit—who knows?

I have never known such a summer as this. Nothing but rain, rain, rain. It may be as calamitous here as it was on the Peninsula in November. I wonder if the constant firing of big guns has anything to do with it.

The Censorship regulations are now so strict that it would be almost impossible for me to give you any information, even if I had any to give. I do not think I can say more than that my Battalion is now back from the Line, and that while in the Line, I had one interesting night not without an element of excitement in connection (not immediate) with one of the raids which has been casually mentioned in the papers.

I think I have previously told you that in this Battalion there is a system of small Messes. Last night I dined with Headquarters as the guest of the C.O. They are all quite pleasant. . . .

Though the feeding out here is good, it is apt to become a little monotonous. If you think it practicable, you might *occasionally* send me a dozen kippers or bloaters, or a cooked chicken.

On July 15, he wrote a brief note to say he was 'still alive and well' and to ask his parents to send him some tobacco and a book on Patience with two packs of cards which 'would help to pass some weary hours'. But before there was time for this letter to reach Bassett Road, a telegram arrived from the War Office to say that he had been seriously wounded in the head and was on the danger list. He was taken to a casualty clearing station behind the lines, where he was visited next day by the Jewish Chaplain to the Forces, the Reverend Vivian Simmons, who stayed with him just long enough to take down a few lines at his dictation. 'I got a sniper into me yesterday and am likely to be out of action for a short time,' he wrote. 'Happily the steel helmet saved me. I don't know how long I shall be here, but I dare say I shall be finding my way home in a reasonable time.'

Apparently the bullet went clean through the base of his head. At first the doctors thought that his skull had been fractured and his brain damaged. But careful examination revealed that fortunately this was not the case, and a further communication from the military authorities informed his parents that the 'prognosis for complete recovery is probably good'. On July 24, he was able to dictate another short letter to his parents. 'There is the chance that I may not be fully recovered for a long time,' he told them. 'I have had very considerable pain, but I am glad to say that now it is decreasing. I cannot yet read or write, or rather I couldn't yesterday, but today with a great effort I have managed to read Mother's letter. I shall probably be sent to the Base in a day or two and presumably thence to England. I hope that I shall be sent to a hospital near home, and I understand that when I am convalescent I shall be allowed to go home. I have been treated very kindly at the hospital here and couldn't have had more attention. So you need not have any anxiety as to my not being properly looked after.'

Nathan did make a remarkable recovery, but the process was long and painful. On being evacuated from France he was sent first of all to the Palace Green Hospital for Officers in Kensington. While he was there he heard the tragic news that his dear friend Willa Chichester had been killed in action in France on September 15, 1916. It was a terrible blow, since Nathan had been closer to Chichester than any other officer in the Battalion, and the realization that he would never see him again added to the melancholia which he experienced at this time. He could never forget Chichester, and for the rest of his life on the anniversary of his friend's death he inserted an 'In Memoriam' notice in the newspapers recalling the event.

He could well ask with the author of the poem 'To Any Dead Officer':

> Well, how are things in Heaven? I wish you'd say,
> Because I'd like to know that you're all right.
> Tell me, have you found everlasting day
> Or been sucked in by everlasting night?

After spending several months in the Palace Green Hospital, he showed no signs of recovery, and in the hope that a change of air would make a difference the doctors sent Nathan off to a hospital in Bournemouth, where he spent most of the ensuing winter. Again there was no appreciable sign of improvement. His eyes had been affected, he suffered from acute headaches as well as melancholia and 'nerves'. It was eventually decided to try psychiatric treatment and with this end in view he was despatched to Craiglockhart War Hospital, a requisitioned hydro on the outskirts of Edinburgh, where he was put under the charge of Dr William Rivers, a brilliant medical officer, who had recently been awarded the Royal Society's Royal Medal for his work in the field of physiology and experimental psychology. Here he was kept in a darkened room for many weeks with other seriously wounded and shell-shocked officers.

Only one letter which he wrote to his parents at this time has survived.

Craiglockhart Hospital, Edinburgh. 14 June 1917. Life continues to be carried on here along normal lines, or rather along as normal lines as can be expected in a place where no one is absolutely normal.

72

I've not very much to tell you. I have not been out of the grounds since I wrote last, and have had a fairly restful time. As I am not taking any exercise, and as reading and writing are more of an exertion than they used to be or should be, I really haven't anything much to write about. The other officers here are of all sorts and classes, and come from practically every regiment in the Kingdom. Some of them are quite pleasant, others absolute outsiders. I manage to get on pretty well with all of them, though as there are over 150 here, I need scarcely say that I do not know all of them—the more so, as a few are continually coming and going.

I had a talk with Rivers yesterday, and though, as I wrote you in my last letter, he is of opinion that I shall be fit for general service again within a measurable period of time, he told me that he did not think that I should be fit for any kind of duty for another three months. Of course, as time passes, he may modify this view, and in any case, I'm not clear as to whether it means that I am likely to be here for that time. I hope not, as I am sure I shall get bored to tears within a comparatively short time. After a time, I may be sent to a place called Bowhill, which the Duke of Buccleuch has lent us as a sort of convalescent home to this place. . . .

I am writing this in the garden which is quite picturesque and, being fairly high, gives one a good view over Edinburgh and towards Stirling. The Pentlands are about three miles away. Everything is backward here compared with England— lilac, laburnum, wallflowers, lilies of the valley, etc., are flourishing now, though in the South they were over long since. The rhododendron is only now in bloom, though in January it was flourishing in Bournemouth.

The other patients at Craiglockhart included three outstanding poets and writers, Siegfried Sassoon, Robert Graves and Wilfred Owen. But the only one of the trio whom Nathan seems to have remembered afterwards was Siegfried Sassoon, partly because they shared a love of horses and hunting and partly perhaps because Sassoon had recently been in the news because of his anti-war protest, which led to questions being asked about him in the House of Commons and a ministerial statement that he was suffering from a nervous breakdown. ('I believe that this war, upon which

I entered as a war of defence and liberation, has now become a war of aggression and conquest.') Did Nathan inwardly share some of Sassoon's misgivings? Quite possibly. At least he had some sympathy with Sassoon, who wrote 'To Any Dead Officer' quoted above and was afterwards to write in *Siegfried's Journey*:

> I could no longer indulge in fine feelings about being a hero, for although my period of active service had given me confidence in myself as a front-line officer I was ceasing to believe in the War itself. Like most of the infantry, I had expected too much of the Battle of the Somme. We had been told that it would be 'the Great Advance'. It was now obvious that it had been nothing of the kind, and disillusionment was inevitable. The feeling was intensified by the fact of the battalion I had served with having been rendered almost unrecognizable by heavy casualties, which naturally took a good deal of the heart out of me. The prospect of rejoining my former companions could have kept my fortitude up to the mark. But of those I'd liked best, very few remained, and those few must by now be much dispirited. My old friend the Quartermaster had written advising me to stay away as long as I could, until the worst of the winter was over. He said that after being up to their necks in mud in front of Beaumont-Hamel they had now got half the battalion being treated for frost-bitten feet.

When it became clear, at the end of eighteen months, that he was still unfit for any kind of further military duty, Nathan was 'invalided out of the Service on account of wounds received in action' with the honorary rank of Major. On the other hand, the treatment he received from Dr Rivers, which in effect amounted to psychoanalysis, had one remarkable result. He came out of Craiglockhart with new self-confidence, his former characteristic diffidence having largely disappeared. But for a long while afterwards he was to suffer the latent effects of his head wound in the form of eye strain and severe headaches, which made his ultimate convalescence painfully slow.

CHAPTER THREE
Liberal M.P.

In spite of the marked falling off in solicitors' business at the beginning of the war, the firm of Herbert Oppenheimer, Nathan and Vandyk had prospered during the junior partner's absence, so that Nathan had quite a comfortable practice to come back to, though it was still relatively small. Shortly after Nathan's return several important new clients began to call at the offices in Finsbury Square. These included Sir Alfred Mond, M.P., later first Lord Melchett, who was managing director of Brunner, Mond & Co., the great chemical concern, shortly to be amalgamated by Mond with other similar concerns to form the giant Imperial Chemical Industries, Ltd. An influential Jew of German parentage, Mond sat in the House of Commons as a Liberal; he had been a member of the war-time coalition government and was on close terms with the Liberal leaders, particularly Lloyd George and Herbert Samuel, as well as with the Lord Chief Justice and former Liberal Attorney-General, Lord Reading, whose only son and heir Lord Erleigh had married Mond's daughter, and who in fact introduced Nathan to Mond. Mond became a personal friend as well as being the professional client of both Oppenheimer and Nathan. He stimulated the younger partner's interest in Liberal politics, and when Nathan came to seek adoption as a parliamentary candidate Mond's backing as chairman of the Liberal election campaign organization was to prove of considerable help.

Nathan formed a tremendous admiration for Alfred Mond both as a business man and a statesman and also as an outstanding benefactor of Palestine Jewry. As his lawyer, Nathan had to carry out the formidable task of drawing up Mond's will for the disposition of an estate which in size and complexity was probably comparable with only one other with which Nathan was to be professionally concerned—that of the coal owner and former Air Minister, the seventh Marquess of Londonderry. In a notice which he wrote of Hector Bolitho's biography, Nathan had this to say of its subject:

> Lord Melchett possessed perhaps more than anyone in public life except Mr Lloyd George the power of being able to think ahead and search for plans for dealing with emergencies long before their arrival was visible to the ordinary politician and man of business. As long ago as 1910 he was working out the idea of a planned industry. The need became far more urgent with the war. He grasped at once the dangers that were arising from the enormous expansion of industry which the need for shells was creating. He adopted the gospel of high wages and short hours long before it had been popularized among the industrialists. He was one of the first to realize the inefficiency of production created by small firms engaged in ruinous competition. He became the leading apostle of rationalization and the Chemical Merger of 1927 probably represents the most important amalgamation in English industrial industry.*

It was Lloyd George who brought Mond into the Coalition Government as First Commissioner of Works and later as Minister of Health. In both departments Mond brought business methods to Whitehall. Nathan particularly liked the story of the civil servant in the Works Ministry who brought a voluminous file to the Minister, who looked through it quickly, grunted and said: 'The whole Book of Revelations occupies ten pages. I don't see why new wash basins in the Revenue Office at Leeds should take a hundred pages. Take it away and bring me a short one without details. It is for you to worry about them.' Nathan also admired the way Mond cut the cost

* *New Statesman*, April 8, 1933.

of local government housing when he was Minister of Health by eliminating waste. In September, 1920, the houses were costing £1,000 each; in six months the same houses were costing £600.

Not only did Mond succeed in making the Zionist movement 'fashionable' in England—in itself a difficult and considerable achievement—but he also wholeheartedly devoted all his experience and reputation as a statesman and industrialist to giving practical form to Zionist ideals and translating them into effect in Palestine. It was largely through Mond that Nathan now began to act professionally for various organizations and undertakings concerned with the development of what was to become the state of Israel. Following the Balfour Declaration in 1917, pledging official British support for a Jewish national home in Palestine and the placing of Palestine under British mandate with Sir Herbert Samuel as High Commissioner in Jerusalem, there was naturally much interest shown on the part of British Jewry in the new political experiment. In this connection Nathan became legal adviser to the Zionist Organization and the newly formed Economic Board of Palestine. Two of the economic projects with which he consequently came to concern himself professionally were to prove of immense value to the newly emerging country. They both owed their success to the initiative and enterprise of two Jews of Russian origin, Pinhas Rutenberg and Moses Novomeysky. Rutenberg's scheme was designed to provide the country with cheap electricity, while Novomeysky's aim was to extract potash from the shores of the Dead Sea by the natural agency of the sun and without recourse to artificial fuel. In particular, the long-drawn-out negotiations with which Nathan was closely involved as Novomeysky's lawyer, and which eventually led to the grant of the concession to Novomeysky and the formation of the Palestine Potash Company in 1930, form an interesting story and are referred to in more detail later in this chapter.

Also a client was Alfred Mond's brother, Sir Robert Mond, distinguished as a research chemist, archaeologist and philanthropist, whose Egyptian finds now enrich many museums and institutions. He founded, in memory of his first wife, the Infants' Hospital in

Vincent Square, Westminster (known as the Westminster Children's Hospital after it amalgamated with the Westminster Hospital in 1946), of which Nathan was to become chairman after Mond's death in 1938. His great Egyptian collection was kept in his London house, but he himself lived mostly in France with his second wife, a Frenchwoman who owned extensive property in Brittany besides a flat in Paris. Nathan's firm looked after her affairs as well.

Meanwhile an important event had been foreshadowed in Nathan's private life at the end of the war. During his lengthy convalescence he had got to know Miss Eleanor (Nellie) Stettauer, and a fortnight after the Armistice they announced their engagement. They had first met and become attracted to each other at a war-time gathering. Nellie Stettauer, who was four years younger than her fiancé, was an extremely intelligent young woman, who had been educated at Girton College, Cambridge, where she had graduated with honours in economics and mathematics. The young couple had a common interest in welfare work in the East End of London, where her father the late Carl Stettauer had been a member of the Stepney Borough Council and later represented Mile End on the London County Council. Carl Stettauer was a remarkable man, who had died in 1913 at the comparatively early age of 54, and his daughter undoubtedly inherited his talents. A native of Bavaria, he had as a young man come to London, where he founded the successful leather business of Stettauer and Wolff in Bermondsey. By the time of his premature death he had acquired a considerable fortune and was regarded as a leading authority on the leather trade in this country. Besides his public work in the East End, he had rendered conspicuous service to world Jewry, when at some personal risk to his life he went out to Russia in 1905 as a member of a small mission to render relief to the victims of the terrible pogroms which had taken place there, notably in the Ukrainian town of Kishinev. As Stettauer and his companions were leaving the railway station at Kiev, fighting was going on between the Jews and their anti-Semitic persecutors and it was only the personal intervention of the British Consul who had come to the station that saved the visitors from serious physical injury.* Carl Stettauer's wife, Nellie's mother, née Cohen, was a first cousin of the first Lady Reading, the wife of the Lord Chief Justice. It was through this family connection that Nathan first met Lord Reading, who was to give him much friendly advice and encouragment, particularly in the field of politics.

Harry Nathan and Nellie Stettauer were married on March 27, 1919, in the West London Synagogue by Rabbi Morris Joseph 'according to the rites and ceremonies of the Jewish Religion'. For the first ten years of their married life they lived in a house at 15 Lansdowne Road, Holland Park; in 1925 they bought a small place at Churt in Surrey as a retreat for week-ends and holidays. They had two children, a daughter Joyce, now Lady Waley-Cohen, who was born in 1920, and a son, Roger, the present Lord Nathan, born in 1922.

As Liberals, Nathan and his wife were both drawn towards politics. Because of their common interest in Jewish welfare work in the East End of London, it was natural that their first essays in public life should be in that area. In January, 1924, he was adopted as Liberal candidate for the Whitechapel and St George's Division. The seat was held by Labour with a majority of 2,200, the sitting Member being Mr Harry Gosling, sixty-three-year-old Minister of Transport in the minority Labour Government, which had taken office under Ramsay MacDonald's leadership following the General Election in December, 1923. Gosling, who had begun his working career as a Thames waterman and lighterman, was also President of the powerful Transport and General Workers' Union and had been the Labour Party Leader on the London County Council. He was generally popular in the division, so that Nathan faced a strong and experienced opponent. On the other hand, Nathan was himself no stranger to the Whitechapel constituency by reason of his close association with the Brady Street Boys' Club which lay within its

* A tablet recording Carl Stettauer's work on behalf of the victims of the pogroms was later erected in the hospital in Odessa, and he received the grateful acknowledgements of all the leading Jews in Russia. The report which he subsequently made and the photographs he collected were later presented by his daughter to the Mocatta Library.

boundaries. He had also helped his late father-in-law, Carl Stettauer, in his L.C.C. election campaign in Mile End before the war, before indeed he had ever met Stettauer's daughter Nellie. He immediately took steps to make himself known throughout the constituency by continuing his former welfare work as well as holding meetings; in this connection he opened two legal bureaux for free advice to the poorer electors, thus anticipating the present official Citizens' Advice Bureau.

The Labour Government was only in office on sufferance, since the balance of party strength in the House of Commons was held by the Liberals who could turn the Government out whenever they pleased. Nathan consequently realized that he had to be ready to fight an election any time, and he spent every possible moment in nursing the constituency. In July, 1924, he organized a great Liberal rally in the Pavilion Theatre, at which he took the chair and at which the principal speaker was Sir Alfred Mond. In his introductory remarks, Nathan reminded his audience that he had made his political début on the same platform ten years before when he had said a few words in support of Sir Herbert Samuel. He went on briefly to extol the achievements of the Liberal Party. 'It was,' he said, 'a Liberal Government that brought the House of Lords to its knees at the point of the People's Budget. It was a Liberal Government that gave independence and self-government to South Africa. It was a Liberal Government that put the Home Rule Act for Ireland on the Statute Book; and it yet remained for the Liberal Party to see that Ireland was put under a single government which would form one united Ireland, so that she might occupy her place among the nations of the world.'

The downfall of the Labour Government, which precipitated the next General Election, was occasioned by what T. P. O'Connor, the 'Father' of the House of Commons, described as a 'miserable tempest in the tiniest little tea-pot ever introduced into political life', namely, the action of the Attorney-General Sir Patrick Hastings in first authorizing and then withdrawing the prosecution of John Campbell, the acting editor of the Communist *Workers'*

Weekly, on a charge of sedition. The Conservatives, who put down a motion of censure on the Government, discovered in the course of the debate that they could not count upon Liberal support, since Sir John Simon for the Liberals moved an amendment calling for a Select Committee to investigate the circumstances in which the prosecution had been withdrawn. The Conservatives thereupon went into the division lobby in support of the Liberal amendment which the Government had previously refused to accept. In the result the Government was defeated by 166 votes, and the Prime Minister thereupon advised the King to dissolve Parliament. This was done and the Election took place during the second part of October.

2

Whitechapel had been represented in the past by two Liberals of the Jewish faith, Sir Samuel Montagu, later Lord Swaythling, and his nephew, Sir Stuart Samuel, Bart. There was a strong Jewish element in the constituency, for whose support Nathan felt justified in appealing. Accordingly, at the outset of his election campaign, he issued the following statement through the Jewish Telegraph Agency.

Whitechapel is, historically, a Jewish constituency, and the many thousands of Jewish voters in this district are therefore entitled to look to their representative in the House of Commons to safeguard and advance their legitimate interests. By no one can these interests be advanced more effectively or sympathetically than by a Jew who himself knows the anxieties, troubles and desires of his fellow Jews, and who has himself since boyhood taken an active part in the public service at large and of the Jewish community in particular.

There have been many Jewish Members in the House of Commons, but for many years past there has been no Jewish Member in Parliament qualified to do so by his knowledge of Jewish problems, particularly now that the political and economic position of Palestine is a matter not of Jewish politics alone, but also of British.

I am strongly in favour of the faithful carrying out of the Balfour Declaration and the establishment of a Jewish National Home in Palestine. I am no stranger to the whole problem, being the legal adviser of the Zionist Organization, the *Keren Hayesod* [the Palestine Foundation Fund,] the Palestine Electric Company, the Palestine Jewish Colonization Association, the Economic Board for Palestine, and many other political, cultural and economic enterprises established by the development of Palestine. It is hardly necessary to say that it will be my object to protect in the House of Commons the interests of all my constituents, irrespective of class, creed, race or party. Further, I shall feel it my duty to be in the constituency at regular and frequent intervals, ready and accessible on the spot for personal consultation with each one of my constituents— whether Jew or Gentile.

It should not be forgotten that a Liberal, Mr Lloyd George, as Prime Minister, was responsible for the idea and for the carrying into effect of the Mandate for Palestine, and that another Liberal, Sir Alfred Mond, has taken a distinguished and active part in the up-building of Palestine, and that a Liberal, Sir Herbert Samuel, is the first High Commissioner of Palestine; not only so, but when the British policy in Palestine was questioned in the House of Commons, it was due to the Liberal Party that the Mandate was accepted and continued as a solemn obligation on the part of this country.

It was the Liberal Party which was responsible for the emancipation of the Roman Catholics and Jews in this country, both political and religious, and which held the doors of this country open for political and religious refugees fleeing from persecution in Russia and elsewhere, at a time when they were the only political party that would stand for the equal rights of free men.

At first it looked as if there would be a three-cornered contest in Whitechapel, but at an early stage the Conservative withdrew, leaving a straight fight between Gosling and Nathan. It also proved to be an extremely rough fight. This was mainly because the Liberal candidates incurred the unwelcome attentions of the Communists, most of whom were of Russian origin, and who created rows at all his meetings, although Mr Gosling's meetings were left undisturbed. Nathan's largest meeting was held in Premierland, the great East End boxing hall, when both he and Sir John Simon, who was the star attraction among the supporting speakers, were howled down and were quite unable to make themselves heard above the din of shouting like the boxing referee ('one, two, three. .... nine, ten, OUT') and the singing of 'The Red Flag' by the Communist interrupters. The police had to be called in, and the meeting broke up in confusion, Nathan's chauffeur losing his dentures in the fray. The platform party was eventually hurried off by a back door under police guard.

During this hectic election campaign Nathan concentrated on the two local issues of housing and unemployment. Housing conditions in particular were a disgrace in Whitechapel. Not a single house had been built in the constituency since Labour had taken office, and local schemes which could have housed hundreds of homeless persons had been turned down by the Ministry of Health. This state of affairs gained Nathan votes, and he was also probably helped to some extent by an incident which occurred a few days before the electors went to the polls on October 29. This was the publication of the so-called 'Red Letter', which was alleged to have been addressed by Grigori Zinoviev, a prominent Moscow Communist, to the British Communist Party and designed to provoke disaffection in the armed forces of Britain and to organize risings in Ireland and the British colonies. Although denounced by Labour at the time as a forgery (which many years later it was conclusively proved to be), the Zinoviev letter was accepted as genuine by the large body of electors in the country and caused a stampede to the Conservatives on the part of those fearful of the 'Socialist menace'.

The result in Whitechapel was as follows:

Harry Gosling (Lab.)		10,147
Major H. L. Nathan (L.) ...		7,193
Labour majority... ...		2,954

These figures meant that the sitting Labour Member's majority had risen by little more than 750 as compared with the previous

General Election when there had been a three-cornered contest. But however satisfactory this result might be for the Whitechapel Liberals, for the Liberals generally throughout the country the results were catastrophic. In all they lost 118 seats and were never to recover from this staggering electoral blow. Thus the Conservatives were returned to power with a majority of more than two hundred over the combined strengths of the other two parties, the Liberals being reduced to a mere forty seats.

The Conservative victory made it clear that it was highly unlikely that the next General Election would take place before 1929. However, in Whitechapel Nathan agreed to carry on as the Liberal candidate. The officers and members of the Whitechapel Liberal Association presented the defeated candidate with an illuminated album containing an address of thanks for his efforts. 'We avail ourselves of this opportunity of expressing not only our gratitude for your services but the affectionate esteem with which we regard you,' so read this flattering document, 'and trust your association with this constituency will be long continued.'

In fact, Nathan remained the prospective Liberal candidate in Whitechapel for barely twelve months after the Election. Local government elections were due to be held in November, 1925, and as the time drew near the Liberal Association Executive announced that it would support a list of ratepayers' candidates, comprising both Liberals and Conservatives, which had been approved by the local Union of Ratepayers. Nathan strongly objected to anything in the nature of a political pact between normally opposing parties, even in municipal affairs. Indeed he felt the position, as far as he was personally concerned, to be intolerable, since he had refused an alliance with the Conservatives during his own parliamentary contest, and he lost no time in telling the Executive Committee so. 'I have throughout adopted the position that I stand on a clean Liberal ticket, without commitments towards any other party,' he wrote to the Association's Chairman. 'The resolution passed by the Committee with regard to the Borough Council election obviously cuts the very ground from under my feet. I am not prepared in the present state of politics to accept the position that it is necessary either to combine with the Tories to keep out Labour, or with Labour to keep the Tories out.'

In the circumstances Nathan felt that his only course was to withdraw from the position of prospective Liberal candidate for Whitechapel and St George's. His decision was accepted by the Executive Committee 'with much regret'.

3

While he was nursing the Whitechapel division, Nathan had been active in forming the London Liberal Candidates' Association, and he became its first Honorary Secretary. This body was to serve as the model for the larger Liberal and Radical Candidates Association, which came into being after the General Election in October, 1924.

On the eve of the opening of the new Parliament, Lord Beauchamp, the leader of the Liberals in the House of Lords, gave his customary party reception in his London house, to which the defeated candidates at the General Election as well as the new Liberal M.P.s were invited. The fact that only 40 Liberals had been returned to the House of Commons was a cause of concern to one of the defeated candidates, Mr W. H. Pringle, an able and energetic individual, who had served in the previous Parliament. What worried him particularly was the greatly reduced Liberal membership of the House in relation to the electoral strength of the party in the country, approximately three millions. Accordingly he buttonholed all the defeated candidates present, including Nathan, and invited them to an informal meeting at the National Liberal Club next day. Everyone approached agreed to come, and at the meeting Mr Pringle urged the necessity of their forming themselves into some sort of organization which should watch the actions of the 40 elected M.P.s and, by exerting their influence, preserve the Liberal cause from any hasty and ill-considered action the M.P.s might take and which the candidates would otherwise be obliged to defend in their constituencies. Pringle, who stood alone on the platform, made an eloquent appeal, which closed with Blake's famous lines:

> Nor shall my sword sleep in my hand
> Till we have built Jerusalem
> In England's green and pleasant land.

Before the gathering broke up, a Liberal Candidates' Association was formed by those present. Officers were appointed and it was agreed that the Association should meet regularly.

Both Liberal Candidates' Associations brought Nathan into touch not only with able young candidates like Robert Bernays and Leslie Hore-Belisha, but also with the party leaders whose help he could count upon in his search for another constituency. Fortunately for Nathan the search did not take long, and as things turned out he found a new constituency next door to Whitechapel. This was North East Bethnal Green, where the Liberals adopted him in June, 1926, following the resignation of the previous candidate, a local Councillor named Garnham Edmonds. As in Whitechapel, the sitting member for North East Bethnal Green, Mr Walter Windsor, represented Labour, but he had held the seat at the 1924 Election by only 95 votes in a straight fight with a Liberal, and since the present Parliament had in the nature of things three more years to run there was a good chance of a hard working candidate such as Nathan being able to win the seat. 'We are going to have no fewer than 500 candidates,' Nathan spoke optimistically at one of his first meetings. 'We shall fight as one party, and we shall present within the House of Commons an amount of experience and brains which no other party can possibly compete with. We are the party which is doing the thinking for the nation, and we are looking to the next General Election to give us the opportunity, not only of doing the thinking for other parties, but doing the thinking for our own party, and carrying our policy into practical effect.'

Nathan's energy and enterprise drew praise from two of the Liberal leaders in particular, Lloyd George and Sir Herbert Samuel. Lloyd George sent his young daughter Megan to North East

Bethnal Green, where she made her London political début, address-
ing a women's demonstration which the Liberal candidate had
organized. 'If the harassed housewife seeks the aid of Liberalism,'
said Miss Lloyd George on this occasion, 'she will discover that all
her problems have been answered.' So far, she added, men had had
things all their own way, at least so far as the government of the
country was concerned. 'Women are to have their revenge,' she
went on. 'Men have admitted that women have outwitted them.
They will soon have to admit that women have outvoted them.' In
the same month—May, 1927—as Megan Lloyd George spoke in
this sense, her prophecy was in some measure realized both in
Nathan's constituency and his own home, when his wife was
adopted as prospective Liberal candidate for the L.C.C. Eleanor
Nathan was already known not only as the parliamentary candidate's wife, but also in her own right for the welfare work she had
done in the East End and also by reason of her father's interest in
London local government and service at County Hall. It was a
striking political partnership between husband and wife in the same
constituency.

Meanwhile Nathan was actively helping the party leaders,
particularly Lloyd George, in hammering out Liberal policy. He was
on the Committee of the Liberal Industrial Inquiry, he assisted in
the organization of the regular Liberal summer schools, and he
helped to edit two volumes of addresses given at these schools
and Liberal candidates' meetings—*Liberal Points of View* (1927)
and *Liberalism and some Problems of Today* (1929)—which formed
useful campaign handbooks for candidates, as did his *Free Trade
Today*, which he produced at the same time. In the industrial and
economic field, Nathan also put forward the germ of a brilliant idea
which he hoped might commend itself to all parties and in which
he anticipated by some thirty years the rise of the unit trust movement. In 1927 he suggested the formation, on the lines of the
building societies, of some organization that would help to invest
the savings of the small man. 'It could secure very much better
terms than he himself can obtain,' he said, 'and, by giving him a

direct financial interest, outside his daily work, in the industry of the country, it would promote an interest in the economics and stability of industry which would be of immense social value.'

At the same time, Nathan continued to do much voluntary work for Anglo-Jewry. Besides the concerns already mentioned for which he acted professionally in Palestine, he was Honorary Legal Adviser to the Union of Jewish Women, Honorary Treasurer of the Friends of the Hebrew University of Jerusalem, and Chairman of the Balfour Forest Committee. The object of the latter committee was to raise funds for the planting of 5,000 trees in the Valley of Jezreel in Palestine as a lasting memorial to Lord Balfour, the author of the famous Declaration in 1917 of British Government policy towards Palestine. In this connection Nathan organized a banquet in the Guildhall in London, on July 3, 1928, at which he took the chair, the gathering of some 700 guests being addressed by Lords Reading, Melchett and Birkenhead. In his own speech, Nathan was able to announce that nearly £16,000 had been collected as a result of this function, the first of its kind ever to be held in the historic Guildhall. Lord Balfour himself was unable to be present, but he sent a message which the Chairman read out.

I am profoundly touched by the action of the Anglo-Jewish community in bringing into existence a living and enduring symbol of their participation in the regeneration and development of Palestine. I like to think of the Balfour Forest not merely as evidence of goodwill to myself personally, but as a token of the loyal co-operation between Anglo-Jewry and the British people in the fulfilment of a great enterprise.

Both the Municipal Elections, which took place in November, 1928, and the L.C.C. elections in the following March, augured well for Nathan's political prospects. In every ward in Bethnal Green the Socialists were defeated by Progressives (Liberals), including that won by Mrs Nathan in the North East Division. 'The result clearly shows that every seat can be won by hard, continuous and intelligent work,' Lloyd George remarked in his message of congratulation to Mrs Nathan and her colleagues. 'An electoral victory is not won by rush tactics, but by cheerful preparation and persistent work. That is the real lesson of your notable achievement.'

In the national and parliamentary field, Lloyd George's aim was to make the Liberal party the party of ideas. Hence the summer schools and the inquiries by economists into a wide range of subjects from coal and agriculture to town planning and industry which were promoted and financed from Lloyd George's private political fund. Early in 1929 the fruits of these investigations were distilled into popular form, being expressed in a handbook with the ringing title, *We Can Conquer Unemployment*. On March 1 'L.G.' affirmed the pledge at a meeting of Liberal candidates. The traditional Gladstonian principles of balanced budgets and classical economics were to be discarded, and instead there was to be a great programme of public works, such as roads, houses and electricity undertakings to be completed on a deficit. The unemployed would be set to work on these projects, which would generate a prosperity which would ultimately absorb the expenditure involved. In fact, this enterprising programme was in its essentials to be put into execution a few years later in America in the shape of President Roosevelt's famous New Deal.

Nathan strove hard to put over Lloyd George's ideas in his speeches at this time. 'Unemployment is the Black Death of the twentieth century,' he would say, 'and the tragedy about unemployment is that it creates more unemployment. Trade has a very delicate constitution. It shuns instinctively countries stricken with the plague of unemployment. The men outside the employment exchanges advertise our poverty, few will buy in shops that look poverty-stricken. Now Mr Lloyd George has told the country that he can end it. "We can conquer unemployment" is the message the Liberal Party bring to the electors.'

Lloyd George had always been a man of action rather than theory, and it is doubtful whether he fully understood all the ideas put forward in his name. The same might be said for many of the other Liberal candidates, who did not belong to the Asquith following which was faithful to the conventional economics of Gladstone. The new Liberal programme had been largely prepared in secret, and when its details were made public in the handbook there was not sufficient time to convince the nation of their soundness or at least to persuade the country to try the experiment. Added to this there was a massive feeling of distrust for Lloyd George and the impression that if he were to become Prime Minister again he would behave like a dictator, as he had done in the war, and there would be no Liberal government in the ordinary sense. At all events, both the Conservatives and the Socialists brushed aside the Liberal New Deal, and the country as a whole refused to endorse it at the polls.

The General Election, which took place in May, 1929, brought Labour back to power, but still as a minority government as in 1924. In the result Labour won 288 seats and the Conservatives 260, with the Liberals in third place holding the balance between the two major parties. Although the Liberal vote went up by over two million, this was due to the increased number of Liberal candidates in the field; the percentage of Liberal votes in contested elections declined, so that the actual Liberal strength in the new House of Commons was only 59 as compared with 40 in the old House. The 19 Liberal gains included North East Bethnal Green, where there was a three-cornered contest. Besides Nathan, the new young Liberal M.P.s included Megan Lloyd George, Leslie Hore-Belisha and Frank Owen, who at 24 became the 'baby' of the House.

From the outset of the campaign in North East Bethnal Green it was clear that the real struggle for victory lay between the Liberal candidate and the former sitting Labour Member. The intervention of a Conservative, Captain J. A. Bell, was a source of considerable worry to Nathan, since he felt that this might split the Liberal vote and let Labour in again. Had it been a straight Liberal–Labour fight as in 1924, it is likely that Nathan's majority would have been in the region of 2,000 or more instead of a little over 500. The actual voting figures were as follows:

Major H. L. Nathan (L.)	11,690
W. Windsor (Lab.)	11,101
Captain J. A. Bell (C.)	1,908
Liberal majority	589

Nathan had achieved his ambition of becoming an M.P. by the time he was forty. Unfortunately, so far as further political hopes went, he belonged to a party whose fortunes were rapidly declining in spite of all its 'back room' thinking.

4

Meanwhile, Nathan's industry in politics, which had secured his election to Parliament, had been equally well matched in the professional sphere. During the decade following the end of the war, he had succeeded in considerably expanding and consolidating his solicitor's practice. Alfred Mond, who, as we have seen, early sought him out, was followed by other wealthy clients, who enabled him to develop large-scale commercial and financial professional interests, particularly in the international field. Because of the peculiarly confidential relationship which exists between a solicitor and his lay clients, it would not be proper generally speaking to discuss their affairs in a book of this kind. However, the situation is otherwise where the client himself subsequently makes a detailed public disclosure of them. Mr M. A. Novomeysky, whose name has already been briefly mentioned, was one such client.

Moses Abraham Novomeysky was a highly knowledgeable industrial chemist and mining engineer, who had been born of Russian-Jewish parents in Eastern Siberia, where he had been brought up and had worked for some years. As a young man he had twice visited Palestine in the days of Turkish rule and had been struck by the possibilities of extracting salts from the Dead Sea for use as raw materials in industry. After the Bolshevik Revolution he left his native Siberia and succeeded in crossing the Gobi Desert and eventually made his way to Palestine, where he made his headquarters in Tel-Aviv, then a small township of some 14,000 inhabitants. Indeed in the whole of Palestine there were barely 700,000 people, less than that of the province of Galilee in the time of Christ. Like other Jewish immigrants, who were encouraged under the British mandate to settle in the country in accordance with the Balfour Declaration, he bought land, in his case on the shores of the Dead Sea, where he proceeded to make preliminary experiments. To go further it was necessary to obtain a licence or concession to exploit minerals from the British Government as the Mandatory Power, and it was this which first brought him to London in 1921, and led him to instruct Herbert Oppenheimer, Nathan & Vandyk to act for him.

Nathan was the partner who took charge of Novomeysky's business, and soon, according to Novomeysky, he became more than his legal adviser. 'Before very long,' wrote Novomeysky afterwards, 'he had made himself my wise and enthusiastic general counsellor and guide. Together with him I was to forge my way through a jungle of vicissitudes, and always he was of inestimable service to me. Moreover as solicitor to Sir Alfred Mond, he was later of great help in my talks with the founder of Imperial Chemical Industries. He enjoyed Sir Alfred's full confidence, as well as mine, and in my conferences with Mond he played more the part of a common friend and arbiter than of a solicitor.' It should be added that Novomeysky was to prove a most demanding client. For instance, he thought nothing of telephoning Nathan at three o'clock in the morning and inviting him to come along to his hotel and discuss some knotty legal point which had arisen.

The jungle through which Moses Novomeysky had to forge his way with Nathan's help was both dense and tortuous; it included the legal complications of the old Turkish administration having previously granted a concession to another party which was thought to have lapsed but was unexpectedly revived; there were several giant American trusts such as Du Pont and General Motors which tried to squeeze out Novomeysky; there were the troubles over putting the concession out to tender and seemingly interminable meetings and arguments with the Colonial Office; there was an anxious search for approved backers and finance before the grant of the concession was finally made to Novomeysky and his British partner Major T. G. Tulloch, and there was a powerful campaign in Parliament against the grant of the concession which had to be overcome.

In 1924, after Novomeysky had submitted three reports on the results of the experiments he had made, he was invited to appear and give evidence before the Dead Sea Mineral Resources Committee which the Government had set up under the chairmanship of the Chief Crown Agent, Sir Henry Lambert. Nathan accompanied his client to the meeting, which lasted about two hours.

Sir Henry Lambert opened the proceedings. 'We have received your reports regarding the exploitation of the Dead Sea waters but have not yet studied them,' he said to Novomeysky. 'We do not know whether your scheme is a good one or not. But tell me, please, who the hell is going to live there? According to our information, only negroes could stand it, not white men.'

To this forthright and unconventional question, Novomeysky replied that he himself had been born in a very cold climate, but since 1921 he had spent a great part of every year at the Dead Sea— and he was still very much alive! He then explained that, owing to the dryness of the atmosphere and the constant pleasant breezes (dry north wind by night, moist south wind by day), residence there was quite possible. The only real drawback—and on the face of it a very considerable one—was the existence along the shore of large breeding grounds of the malaria-carrying anopheles mosquito. But, Novomeysky pointed out, he had already made it clear in his reports that his proposal to turn these marshes into systematized evaporation pans would completely eliminate the disease. (This indeed was what eventually happened.)

Novomeysky was then questioned at considerable length by an expert chemist, who was a member of the Committee, about the methods of separating the various salts, for example, potash from bromine. He obviously knew what he was talking about, and when he and Nathan left they were fairly optimistic about the outcome. But they were to experience many reverses and setbacks before the Deed of Concession was eventually signed five years later, since in addition to the British Government it was also necessary to secure the assent of the Governments of Palestine and Transjordan, as well as the Zionist Organization.

That the concession was not granted to the American group, which was represented by Sir Josiah Stamp, was largely due to Mond's intervention. The Americans were only interested in the bromine and not in the potash, whereas Novomeysky was willing to extract both and to make the bromine commercially available. On December 16, 1924, Mond wrote to Stamp:

> It would seem to me both wasteful and uneconomical to deal with only one of the contents and leave the potash untreated. As President of the Economic Board of Palestine, a society formed at the request of the Palestine Government to consider and advise that Government on all economic questions affecting the country, I would certainly use what influence I possess against such a proposal being entertained.
>
> You will readily understand that the matter is of more than mere industrial significance. The Dead Sea represents the only important mineral wealth of Palestine, and those of us who are interested in establishing there a National Home for the Jews cannot contemplate with equanimity the control of this passing into the hands of an American group, who are not interested in the economical development of the country. The Zionist Organization is the Jewish Agency under the Mandate, and will undoubtedly have to be consulted and have to give its agreement. The Organization has, as you probably know, the right to refer such a case to the Mandate Committee of the League of Nations.
>
> Under all the circumstances it appears to me that a reasonable way of dealing with the matter would be for some arrangement to be come to between the various parties interested. I have no doubt that Mr Novomeysky's group wishes to work in harmony with the important interests you represent, and I see no reason why this should not be achieved.

This is, broadly speaking, what happened. At one time Mond's great Imperial Chemical Industries undertook to sponsor the enterprise financially, and although their terms were relatively generous, Novomeysky felt that they must eventually jeopardize his independence and he preferred to form his own company with financial contributions outside I.C.I. But this did not affect his relations with Mond, but for whose friendly interest and support, prompted by Nathan, the whole venture might well have come to nothing.

The attacks in the House of Commons came mainly from a backbench Conservative M.P., Colonel Howard Bury, who disliked foreign Jews and thought that the concession should be entirely in British hands. On one occasion he denounced Novomeysky in the House of Commons as a concessionaire who was 'hunting around to find money, but his terms are so ridiculous that no one will accept them'. What little money he had been able to raise, said the Colonel, came from the Kali Syndikat, the German potash monopoly. Both these statements were blatantly untrue, and had they been uttered outside the House, Novomeysky would have had a good claim for damages for libel. As it was, all that Nathan could do was to send Bury a strongly worded solicitor's letter.

In the Upper House there was a good deal of anti-Semitic feeling expressed, notably by the Duke of Buccleuch, for whom Lord Birkenhead offered a somewhat lame apology on behalf of the Government. 'The noble Duke animadverted unfavourably upon Mr Novomeysky's name,' observed Lord Birkenhead in regard to this personal attack. 'It is not a name with which I am particularly enamoured or desire to bear, but the only argument which the noble Duke used was in the first place that he was a Jew.'

Nathan was in the gallery of the House of Lords with Novomeysky during this debate. A day or two later they called at the Colonial Office. 'It was very wrong of Lord Birkenhead to speak like that,' a Colonial Office spokesman remarked to them, adding that he was sure Novomeysky must have felt very offended by Lord Birkenhead's words.

Novomeysky tried to reassure him. There was, as he saw it, no need for Lord Birkenhead to expect to be enamoured by the name Novomeysky. 'It happens to be my name,' he said, 'And I am quite happy with it. Nor, may I add, has it ever occurred to me to change *my* name.'

This shrewd hit went down well with the Colonial Office. Before his elevation to the peerage, Birkenhead had been plain Mr Smith!

The matter was raised again in the House of Lords by Lord Templetown, who attacked both the Rutenberg and Novomeysky concessions. 'Whoever holds the Dead Sea holds the key of the Middle East,' said Templetown on this occasion. 'It might be said that Haifa harbour, the electrification and irrigation of the Jordan valley, and the Dead Sea, constitute a unique industrial trilogy, which can unlock to the world great beneficent powers and revive again an active civilization from the River Nile to the River of the Euphrates. In a situation so complicated, permanent British control becomes essential.... The Rutenberg concession, which gave a Russian Jew a stranglehold on the economic life of Palestine and Transjordania for 70 years, indicates the undue influence of Zionists and international financiers.'

Lord Templetown was followed by another peer from the back woods, Lord Danesfort, who said he could not understand why the League of Nations mandate to govern Palestine excluded British control.

This brought Alfred Mond, by then Lord Melchett, to his feet. 'My Lords,' he said, 'I should not have intervened in this debate had it not been that perhaps I know more about the Dead Sea and about the chemical industry than some of the noble Lords who have addressed the House.' He went on to castigate these peers for the ignorance of the subject they had shown, particularly in attacking Rutenberg and Novomeysky on baseless grounds, because they were not British subjects. He dealt admirably with the attempt to create prejudice against the two men, particularly Rutenberg.

> I happen to be a director, with the noble Marquess opposite [Lord Reading], of a company formed to supply Palestine with cheap electricity. Why was that concession given to that gentleman [Mr Rutenberg]? It was given because he happens to be a very competent electrical engineer, who applied for it. The

noble Viscount, Lord Templetown, cannot know the years of difficulty we had to find the necessary capital, and cannot know how Mr Rutenberg was thanked by three successive High Commissioners. I think he might withdraw the kind of expression he used.

Might I ask whether *no* Palestinian subject is to have a concession in Palestine—because both Mr Rutenberg and Mr Novomeysky are Palestinian subjects? To have a concession in Palestine you must apparently be a subject of another nation. Surely such a claim cannot be substantiated. *It is time people recognized that there is such a thing as a Palestinian nation.* It is not true to say that Mr Rutenberg is a Russian Jew. He is a Palestinian Jew. I must enter a protest against the endeavour to create prejudice against men who have gone to Palestine, and have become Palestinian subjects.

This debate took place in March, 1929. A month later the Novomeysky concession was signed, and within twelve months the Palestine Potash Company Ltd had been formed with a mixed English, American and Palestinian Board, Novomeysky being Managing Director and Lord Lytton Chairman. The Company was established in London, which was to remain its headquarters, Nathan's firm acting as its solicitors from the beginning.

The choice of a suitable chairman presented a problem. Novomeysky was anxious to obtain the services of Lord Allenby, who had captured Palestine from the Turks. This choice was warmly endorsed by Dr Chaim Weizmann, the Zionist leader, but Allenby felt he must decline it. 'I appreciate the offer as a very high honour,' he told Weizmann, 'but I regret I am unable to accept it. I have no business experience, and I am now too old to undertake affairs which entail the acquisition of expert knowledge and call for close application and great energy.' Nathan then suggested Lord Winchester, the premier Marquess of England, but Novomeysky did not take to this candidate, and the negotiations, which had begun with a private luncheon at the Savoy, quickly broke down. The eventual choice was an ideal one in every way and proved a great success, since Lord Lytton was *persona grata* with both the British Government on account of his distinguished record of service overseas and with the Jews on account of his connection by marriage with Lord Balfour.

Much hard work had to be done to put and keep the new company on its feet, since everything had to be built up from scratch; there were few scientists and skilled workers available in the early stages; and there were no industrial amenities of any kind available at the Dead Sea. But within a year of commencing operations, the company's first product, a quantity of bromine, was on the British market. Production steadily rose, and, during the Second World War, Palestine Potash supplied half the demand for potash in Britain, and four-fifths of that of the Commonwealth, apart from Canada. By the time of the outbreak of the Arab–Jewish war in 1947, over one million tons of potash had been extracted from the Dead Sea by a mixed body of Jewish and Arab workers numbering 2,000. The original works at the northern end of the Dead Sea were destroyed in the fighting, but fortunately subsidiary works had been developed at the southern end, on the site of the ruined Biblical cities of Sodom and Gomorrah, so that production continued uninterrupted, though on a reduced scale. The latter area was also developed as a health resort, where the curative properties of the waters gradually turned the place into a second Lourdes—childless women have testified to becoming pregnant after bathing there.

Thus Nathan and his friend Novomeysky lived to see the fulfilment of the Biblical prophecy of Ezekiel concerning the Promised Land, that 'the miry places thereof and the marshes thereof . . . shall be given to salt'.

5

In June, 1929, Ramsay MacDonald became Prime Minister for the second time, with Arthur Henderson as Foreign Secretary and Philip Snowden as Chancellor of the Exchequer. J. H. Thomas, who wanted the Foreign Office, was made Lord Privy Seal with special responsibility for unemployment. By agreement with the Conservative Opposition, the Liberals were allotted the first two benches below the gangway in the House of Commons. But as these two benches could not accommodate the whole of the parliamentary party, the Liberals decided to appropriate a third bench immediately behind the other two. The only method of insuring this was for a group of Liberals to place their cards on the bench when the doors of the Chamber were opened at eight o'clock in the morning of the first day of the session. To make certain that the places on the third bench would not be taken by Conservatives, it was necessary for the Liberals to sustain an all-night vigil outside the doors. For this purpose Nathan arrived at the House shortly before midnight and waited with a handful of colleagues, including Major Gwilym Lloyd George, son of his leader, and Percy Harris, who had been returned for the other division of Bethnal Green. The corner seat on the front Opposition bench below the gangway was reserved for the Liberal leader.

The new Member for North East Bethnal Green lost no time in making himself known to the House. He walked through to the House of Lords with the usual throng of Members to listen to King George V read the traditional Speech from the Throne which his Ministers had prepared for him. As soon as it was over, Nathan returned to the Commons chamber and, along with Percy Harris, put down an amendment to the motion of thanks on the Order Paper regretting that the Speech contained no mention of education, a strange omission on the part of a Labour Government. In the event the amendment was not called, but it was noted and commented upon in the newspapers. Next Nathan busied himself with parliamentary questions to Ministers. His first questions were on the subject of electricity undertakings and unemployment. One was addressed to the Minister of Transport, Mr Herbert Morrison, and asked whether, in connection with the Government's unemployment plans, steps would be taken to construct an electric railway from Liverpool Street, via Bethnal Green, to Leyton and Waltham Cross, and to Ilford and Hainault Forest in Essex. The Minister replied that the underground railway companies, which at that time were private concerns, had been asked to suggest schemes of development of this kind, and that he was not yet in a position to say precisely what schemes were likely to be carried out. As a matter of historical interest it may be added that the Minister's main scheme was that of a public corporation for transport within the metropolis and surrounding suburban area. This was to develop into the London Passenger Transport Board, while Nathan's proposed extension of the existing underground railways was eventually incorporated into the general pattern

Within a few weeks of taking his seat, Nathan made his maiden speech, always a trying ordeal, since this performance can make or mar the speaker's subsequent reputation in the House. On the whole, Nathan came out of it well and was warmly congratulated on his performance afterwards. He chose for the occasion the debate on the financial resolution in the committee stage of a Bill authorizing the Treasury to guarantee loans of £25 millions for schemes of public utility. It was a hard-hitting speech asking for details of what the Government proposed to do with this blank cheque in the Lord Privy Seal's favour. In particular he wanted to know on what basis the money was to be distributed. For instance, there was the Liverpool Street electrification project on which he had already asked a parliamentary question. It was easy to solve the unemployment in one locality by increasing it in another locality, and he hoped that the unemployed in the East End of London would be absorbed in the works scheme before occupation was found for men outside that area. 'When a man is drowning,' he said, 'you cannot enter into elaborate contracts for the provision of a suitable rope for rescuing him; you have to take the first thing that comes to your hand. More than one million men are drowning, and they look to this House to throw them a lifeline and to throw it immediately. I do not think there can be any doubt about the Liberal position in relation to this problem. We are with the Government in every well-devised attempt to grapple with this grim problem. All we ask is that they will tell us what they are going to do—at the present time we know nothing—that they will press forward with vigour, determination,

foresight and courage, and, above all, that they will do it quickly.'
He ended with a neat quotation from *Macbeth*.

> If it were done, when 'tis done, then 'twere well
> It were done quickly.

'Where is the bloody dagger?' Nathan's colleague Leslie Hore-Belisha jokingly asked him in the lobby afterwards. Hore-Belisha, who supplemented his income from journalism, later wrote in the *Daily Express* of Nathan's peroration and the general impression he gave.

> He is a dark man, and he made a sombre speech ... No Lyceum hero ever got more savour out of the excruciating words. Poor Mr Thomas was the Banquo of the piece, and was mercifully outside the Chamber. Otherwise the public view of his agony might have been unbearable. ...
> Major Nathan is one of the intelligentsia of the Liberal Party—the party which, as he put it, 'did its thinking years ago'. He has written a book on Free Trade, and published one or two collections of addresses on the problems of the day.
> All this is very remarkable, for Major Nathan is one of the busiest City of London solicitors. Nor are his political achievements confined to the mental sphere. He swept Socialism out of Bethnal Green, which now enjoys the isolated, yet splendid distinction of having, I believe, all its councillors and guardians, as well as its two members of Parliament, adherents of the Liberal faith—or perhaps, I should say, sect.
> Consequently the House was expectant when he, who had done so much behind the scenes, appeared for the first time on the stage. It found a determined, deliberate, self-possessed, heavy-featured man, who, as it were, sharpened the cruel steel of each syllable before he thrust it home.

Back in Bethnal Green, Nathan warned the Socialists that their proposals for tackling unemployment were not radical enough. 'Office seems to have equipped the Labour Members with smoked glasses,' he declared. 'They once saw the gravity and magnitude of the unemployment problem in all its hideous reality. Through the windows of Whitehall I can only suppose that it appears blurred and indistinguishable. For if they saw on the Treasury bench unemployment as clearly as they saw it when they were in Opposition, their conscience would never let them bring forward their paltry schemes. The Liberal party is not going to acquiesce tamely in the supine attitude of the Government before the tragedy of human suffering that the unemployment figure express. We are going to goad the Government into doing something drastic.' Finally he issued a stern warning. If there were no bold measures to grapple with unemployment and other problems by the next autumn session, the Liberals would have no alternative but to cut short the life of this Parliament and to give the electors a fresh opportunity of securing a Government that would do things.

These were brave words indeed. But they could only be put into effect if the Liberals had been a united party, as for instance the Irish Nationalists had been when they held the balance between the two main parties and could dismiss the minority government in office whenever they wished. Unfortunately for the Liberals their titular leader, Mr Lloyd George, was anxious to discredit the Labour Government without discrediting himself, while at the same time he hoped to take the credit for their successes which united Liberal support could insure. But he was unable to carry his party with him—one group led by Sir John Simon tending to vote with the Conservative Opposition, while another group holding to the pure milk of Liberalism, personified in Sir Herbert Samuel, as often as not abstained from going into the lobbies when the division bells rang. For a time there was a rumour that Lloyd George was flirting with the idea of a Liberal–Labour coalition, and this so alarmed Nathan that he was moved to speak his mind when he addressed the Council of the National Liberal Federation on the eve of the autumn session. 'If there be any section of our forces who want to sue for peace with the Labour Party—for that is what an alliance would mean—they will do it without me,' he said. 'I will not go along that road, and I will dissociate myself with those who do. . . . Liberalism, to survive, has got to keep to its own track, however dark and difficult may be its present progress.'

Thus the Liberals in the 1929 Parliament could not bring themselves to turn out the Labour Government as they had done with its predecessor in 1924. Nor could the Government carry through any really bold and imaginative measures to cure unemployment, handicapped as it was by Snowden's financial orthodoxy at the Treasury in insisting on balanced Budgets. In the period of a little more than two years that the second Ramsay MacDonald Government held office, jobs for only 60,000 workless were found, not an achievement to be proud of. The only member of the Government to rise to the challenge, oddly enough, was the aristocratic Oswald Mosley, a recent recruit to the Labour ranks, whose nominal task was to assist J. H. Thomas. His plan, which called for the systematic use of credit to promote economic expansion, was quite beyond the grasp of his chief, while it was naturally anathema to Snowden, who succeeded in securing its rejection by the Cabinet. In the end, it was the mounting pressure of external economic events which terminated the Government's life and not any adverse vote of the Liberals in the House of Commons.

During this Parliament Nathan attended regularly and played an active part in the day-to-day business, sitting on committees, drafting amendments to Bills and the like. Indeed he made a point of being the first Member to appear at Westminster for each new session and did not seem to mind the all-night vigil which this entailed. Occasionally he made a mistake, as every new Member does. When a private member's Bill for the abolition of corporal punishment was introduced, he accidentally voted in the wrong lobby, with the Noes instead of the Ayes as he had intended, and he learned to his disappointment that this error could not be rectified. In this instance, however, the mistake made no difference since the measure was defeated by a substantial majority.

One personal habit was commented upon widely in the press. He used to ride in Hyde Park for exercise in the early mornings and from time to time would trot over to Westminster to collect his mail and parliamentary papers for the day. He was the first M.P. on horseback who had been seen at Westminster for many years, and his use of the old mounting block in New Palace Yard attracted some attention. It is reported that he was careful to remove his spurs before entering Westminster Hall, since according to ancient tradition only county members could wear spurs, and the fact that Nathan sat for a London borough necessitated his appearing without these aids to equitation in the Members' Lobby.

As a faithful 'Lloyd Georgian', Nathan endeavoured to support his party leader, although this was not by any means easy in the light of Lloyd George's varying tactical manœuvres during this relatively short Parliament. Eventually the economic crisis which overtook the country in the summer of 1931 led to a temporary parting of the ways, when Nathan followed Sir Herbert Samuel and the other Liberals who supported the all-party 'National' Government headed by Ramsay MacDonald, the previous Labour Prime Minister. Actually the idea of a National Government originated with Samuel; it was endorsed by Baldwin and welcomed by the King, who had a high opinion of MacDonald. Lloyd George, the only other possible national saviour, was confined to bed, recovering from a serious operation, so that his participation was ruled out, although he did send his blessing to the new Administration, in the belief, generally shared at the time, that it was for the sole purpose of dealing with the emergency—that is balancing the budget and saving the pound—and that after it was over the political parties would resume their normal positions.

Curiously enough, Nathan only just missed being a junior Minister in the first National Government 'by the skin of my teeth', as he put it afterwards. He received a letter at the time from Samuel, saying that if an exclusively Liberal administration had been formed, Nathan would certainly have been included without question. As things were, however, there would only be a few posts available for the Liberals. One of these was the parliamentary secretaryship to the Ministry of Health. Samuel had already written to another Liberal M.P., Ernest Simon (later Lord Simon of Wythenshawe), who was abroad, offering it to him. If he declined or did not answer immediately, would Nathan accept? Nathan answered that he would—but unfortunately for him so also did Simon. 'So', as Nathan was to recall some years later, 'that opportunity slipped away.'

CHAPTER FOUR

National Defence and Army Welfare

AFTER THE IMMEDIATE FINANCIAL CRISIS WAS MET BY DEVALUING the currency and going off the gold standard in September, 1931, there was plainly much more to be done in the way of the economic reconstruction of the country. Early in October came the announcement of a General Election and the dissolution of Parliament. MacDonald asked for 'a doctor's mandate' for his National Government, with each Party putting forward its programme in the hope of general agreement within the new governmental framework and MacDonald acting as a kind of catalyst or at any rate honest broker, who hoped to reconcile the conflicting interests of protection and Free Trade in the light of the nation's economic ills. While the Conservatives were for a full-blooded policy of tariffs, the Liberals were divided, one group led by Samuel remaining faithful to the party's Free Trade principles (Liberal Nationals) and another group led by Sir John Simon (National Liberals) favouring a Protectionist policy. The latter was soon to become Conservative in all but name.

In North East Bethnal Green the going was easier for Nathan than it had been in 1929. For one thing he had no Conservative opponent to reckon with, while at the same time his former Labour opponent had dropped out and there was another Labour candidate, a newcomer from the Midlands named William Barrett who was a stranger to the constituency, although widely known as a shoe manufacturer in Northampton, where he employed 1,000 workers. (He had started his career as a shop assistant in Islington and had married on 22s 6d a week.) Nathan, on the other hand, was well known and popular, particularly through his free legal aid scheme which he claimed had dealt with two thousand cases since he had introduced it. During his campaign he pledged general support for MacDonald and his colleagues in the task they were trying to do, but at the same time he made it clear that he opposed a policy of Protection which he felt must lead to dearer food prices for the housewife.

I support the National Government in every step they take to put the national finances on a proper basis [he said], but nobody can claim that proposals which would mean the taxation of food and other necessaries of life are going to save the situation. You cannot get more trade by putting tariff barriers round this country. What is wanted is not a tariff policy but a world round-table conference to discover the best and quickest way of getting rid of present-day tariffs. If there were any danger of a complete collapse of our currency, if we could not find money to pay for food and raw materials, then I would be ready to look into means for keeping out non-essential goods. But prohibition is my method—not tariffs.

I am more of a Free Trader than I ever was—and the applause this statement draws at my meetings convinces me I am right.

During this campaign Nathan was the victim of an example of particularly blatant political misrepresentation on the part of his Labour opponent. Lloyd George in a broadcast had advised Liberals to vote for the Labour candidate if he was a Free Trader and *if there was no Liberal candidate*, or if there was a Liberal candidate and he was a 'wobbler' on Free Trade. Mr Barrett endeavoured to turn this statement to his own advantage by placarding the constituency with the legend that 'Mr Lloyd George advises Liberals to vote for the Labour Free Trader.' This subterfuge incensed Nathan, the more so since he possessed a letter from Lloyd George warmly commending him to the Liberals of North East Bethnal Green on account of his Free Trade principles.

His meetings were also the target for some rowdyism, but on nothing like the scale he had to contend with in 1924. Most of the interrupters were youths who had not reached voting age and who tried to break up the meeting by throwing stink bombs among the audiences. 'But this doesn't hurt me,' the candidate remarked. 'I am too well known in the constituency. And most people here have a strong sense of fair play. The effect of this rowdyism will certainly be to win me votes.' When hecklers at one meeting tried to drown his oratory by singing 'The Red Flag', he seized the chance to inquire, 'What is this dismal tune? It sounds like a funeral march, and that is what it is—the funeral march of the working classes!' As usual in his election campaigns Nathan was served by a wide range of voluntary helpers, including members of his office staff, regardless of their personal politics, and former members of his old territorial battalion.

When the votes came to be counted, it was seen that Nathan had increased his majority by more than 2,000, although the total poll was smaller than in 1929. The figures were as follows:

Major H. L. Nathan (L.)	... ...	13,135
W. Barrett (Lab.)	... ...	10,368
Liberal majority	... ...	2,767

In the aggregate returns the Liberals were split three ways—the 'pure' Liberals or Liberal Nationals led by Sir Herbert Samuel, who got 33 seats, the 'National' Liberals led by Sir John Simon, who got 35 seats, and finally the Lloyd George family party, consisting of himself, his son, his daughter and son-in-law, who preferred to sit as an independent group. Thus the Conservatives, with their 13 National Labour and 35 National Liberal allies, won 521 seats, a situation which made Ramsay MacDonald and his handful of National Labour colleagues virtually prisoners of the Tories. The moment he saw the completed election returns on that autumn afternoon in October, 1931, Nathan realized, as he subsequently admitted, that the 'National' Government was already dead. 'More than 460 Conservatives had been elected,' he reflected afterwards. 'It was not in the Conservative nature to refrain from exacting the full price for their overwhelming dominance. Within three weeks there were 300 Tories clamouring for a whole hog Tariff policy; within three months Great Britain had become a complete Protectionist country. Mr Ramsay MacDonald, from being Premier, had become prisoner.'

There followed for Nathan a time of growing exasperation with the Liberal Party. From a Government that had declared for economic Nationalism, the Liberals ought in his judgement to have severed all their moorings. Instead the Liberal leaders, headed by Samuel, although opposing tariffs, remained in the Government that sponsored them. They not merely acquiesced in but they supported what Nathan called 'that grotesque subsidy to the wheat farmers in the form of wheat quotas and a suicidal tariff war with Ireland that to me was a violation of every fighting principle of Liberalism'. He fought the Import Duties Bill all along the line, and during the committee stage moved amendment after amendment designed to exempt specific goods and commodities from the proposed tariffs. Within four months of the General Election he was describing the National Government in a speech to his constituents as a bitter disappointment, 'a disappointment, that is, to those who believed that party differences would be sunk, and party programmes postponed, in a common effort to rehabilitate the national credit'. In his view the National Government had simply defrauded the electorate. 'The National Government is not a National Government in any true sense of the term at all,' he declared in March, 1932, 'but merely a Conservative Protectionist Government under a false alias, and the policy it has used its majority to inflict upon the country is indistinguishable from the policy which it would have put forward had it been by name as well as in fact a Conservative Protectionist Government.'

He was disgusted by the conduct of the Liberal leaders, with whom he became extremely unpopular, not merely for his criticisms but for going out of his way to take the chair at a meeting welcoming Lloyd George back to public life, an occasion which was studiously boycotted by all the Samuelites.

   With Ottawa the Tariff ring became complete.* But though the Liberal leaders removed themselves from the Treasury Bench, it was only into neutrality on the Government side of the House. They made hostile speeches, but they would not back them up with votes of censure. They were ready to wound but they dared not strike. I could stand it no longer, and at the beginning of February, 1933, I moved a resolution at a Party meeting that the Liberal Party should join Labour in opposition. I could secure no support for it. . . .

There was only one course open to Nathan in the circumstances, and that was to cross the floor of the House and to sit in future on the Opposition benches. 'I realize that this step involves, to my unfeigned regret, dissociating myself for the time from the Liberal Parliamentary Party,' he wrote to Samuel on February 7, 1933. 'Nevertheless the course I am adopting is to my mind imperative for those who would make the Liberal standpoint and Liberal policies living actualities. . . . Judged by every objective test—the state of trade, unemployment, the well-being of the people—this Government has been a disaster. Its policy of economic nationalism at home and in the Empire, its failure to promote real disarmament, and the weakness of its international policy, no less than its discouragement of reproductive work, have jeopardized the prestige of the country abroad and the prospects of recovery at home. All this you yourself have said, and I feel bound to follow your argument to its irresistible conclusion. By remaining on the Ministerial side of the House and thus giving the semblance of support to the Government, the Liberal Parliamentary Party is in my opinion denying the beliefs and policies of Liberalism and—which is more important—confusing the public mind and doing disservice to the national interest.'

* As a result of the Imperial Conference held at Ottawa in the summer of 1932, a series of agreements was worked out which had the effect of shifting British trade away from foreign countries to the Dominions and colonies.

It only now remained for the dissentient Liberal to perform the physical act of crossing the floor of the House. This he did with some ceremony three days later, choosing a moment during Question Time—whether by accident or design is not clear—when the Chamber was unusually crowded. He entered and stood for a few minutes at the Bar, chatting with apparent unconcern to Captain Margesson, the Government Chief Whip, a spectacle which caused some hilarity on the nearby benches among those who knew what was afoot. After Captain Margesson had gone to his own seat, Nathan paused a minute or two longer, and then to the accompaniment of cheers and laughter solemnly walked to the Table and, bowing gravely to the Speaker, turned sharply to the right to make for the third Opposition bench below the gangway. The corner seat was occupied by Mr David Kirkwood, a well-known 'Clydesider', who kindly moved along to make room for him. There was more cheering and ironical counter-cheering as he sat down. In the words of the *Daily Telegraph's* Lobby Correspondent, who witnessed the scene from the Press Gallery, 'Sir Herbert Samuel and the attenuated Liberal party watched with the stolidity in which Liberal adversity had schooled them.'

2

For the time being Nathan sat with the small Lloyd George family group on the Opposition benches, a group increased by the accession of six Welsh Liberal Members who followed Nathan's example in crossing the floor of the House shortly afterwards. Now began a lonely and difficult time for Nathan, since he was cold-shouldered by many of his old Liberal colleagues, although his constituency association in Bethnal Green endorsed his action. At the same time, he was not part of the official Opposition. He did have a talk with the Labour Opposition leader George Lansbury, with a view to immediately accepting his leadership. But although they found themselves in agreement on all the principal political questions of the day, Nathan came to the conclusion that he ought to wait for a time and see how far he was able to co-operate with Lansbury and his followers in the everyday work of the House of Commons before taking any further action. The result was that during the next eighteen months, when he sat as an Independent Liberal, there was not one important question on which he did not feel able to give the Labour Party his wholehearted support.

The process began barely a week after Nathan had crossed the floor, when he strongly backed Lansbury's proposal that the Government should impose an embargo on the sale of arms to Japan when that country invaded Manchuria. He made a bold bid to secure the immediate adjournment of the House to debate the question, but the Speaker refused to entertain his motion on the ground that it was not sufficiently urgent within the definition of the Standing Order of the House. Thereafter he joined with the Labour Opposition in 'its protests against the swelling armament expenditure, its exposure of the successive tariff ramps, its fight for the unemployed through the long hours of debate on the Unem-ployment Bill,* its demands for a more searching regulation of industry and the Banking system, its indignation at the monstrous provisions of the Sedition Bill',† and much else, supporting the Opposition in the division lobby and often in debate.

On the eve of the summer recess, in July, 1934, Nathan decided that he must take the plunge. First, he consulted his political mentor Lloyd George. He told him that he was thinking of joining the

---

* This measure, which became law in 1934, completely changed the old conception of unemployed relief, with its hated 'means test', by removing its administration from the public assistance committees of the local councils with their party political overtones and entrusting it to a statutory Unemploy-ment Assistance Board, with its own offices and staff throughout the country.

† The Incitement to Disaffection Act restored general search warrants, unheard of since the time of John Wilkes in 1765, as a precaution against Communist propaganda in the armed forces. As first drafted, the measure proposed that the warrants could be issued by any magistrate, but this was later restricted to High Court judges. Although in fact the power was to be sparingly exercised, nevertheless it represented a serious encroachment upon civil liberties.

Labour Party but that he would not do so if Lloyd George felt that it would be 'desertion'. Lloyd George told him that if he took this step Nathan would still retain his confidence. 'If I were a young man, I should join the Labour Party myself,' he added. 'But I'm too old now. I was born a Liberal and a Liberal I shall die.'

Next Nathan informed Sir Herbert Samuel and the Liberal executive in North East Bethnal Green of his decision and that he intended to apply for the Opposition Whip. 'For several years,' he said, 'I have found that the policies I was advocating were indistinguishable in their central features from those put forward by the Labour Party. The policies of the Labour Party, indeed, are the inevitable outcome of Liberal policies carried to their logical conclusion.' He elaborated this view in a speech to his constituency party executive when he said:

> For eighteen months I have been in isolation from the Liberal Party, and from my position of detachment I have been increasingly aware of its tragic ineffectiveness. The country wants to return to the two-party system. Minority government has not worked. The last two Labour governments showed that. It was for them office without power. It meant bargaining and compromise and weakness. The electors would not tolerate it a third time. Whatever the complexion of the Government they want it to govern. The Liberal Party as an organized political force is doomed.
>
> Today the issues are crystal clear. There is internationalism and there is nationalism. There is disarmament through the League of Nations and there is rearmament in isolation. There is the policy of the open door and there is economic self-sufficiency. There are those who oppose any change and are timid and reactionary, and there are those who believe that our whole economic life needs reorganization and reorientation, and are consequently bold and far seeing.
>
> That is the gulf in politics, and I know which side I am on, and I think I know which side you are on, too. Let us therefore keep together in the future, as we have done in the past. Only a name separates real Liberals from Labour today. Let it not stand between us any longer. Parties were made for men

and not men for parties. There is something greater than
loyalty to parties and to men, and that is loyalty to ideals.

These words were received by the 120 members of the Liberal
executive in North East Bethnal Green with mixed feelings and
not unnaturally some indignation. In a statement issued on behalf
of the executive immediately afterwards, the chairman observed
that the members had had no previous indication of the purport of
Nathan's statement, which had therefore come 'as a complete surprise'. The chairman went on to say that the chief officers of the
Association were 'outspoken in their criticism of what they did not
hesitate to term a betrayal of the Liberal cause'. Later the executive
passed a formal resolution expressing regret and disapprobation
of their Member's action.

Nathan was undismayed. 'The talk about my betraying the
Liberal cause is, of course, nonsense to anyone who knows the
facts,' he remarked afterwards. 'No one had the effrontery to make
that statement in so many words to my face. How could he? For
the Liberal executive, at a meeting some eighteen months ago,
warmly and unanimously supported my action in leaving the Parliamentary Liberal Party, crossing the floor of the House of Commons and going into Opposition alone. Since then I have worked,
voted and spoken with the Labour Party sitting by their side in
the House. My action during this time has met, from time to time,
with the expressed approval of the Liberals in Bethnal Green.
When I made my speech to the executive, the passages most
warmly applauded were those in which I told of the action I had
taken in co-operation with Labour and in contradistinction to the
action taken on the same occasions by the Liberal Party.'

Nevertheless, while the renegade M.P. was given a warm welcome by the Labour leaders into their Party ranks, he had to endure
a good deal of snubbing and backbiting from his old political
friends. In particular, he was the subject of a bitter personal attack
at the next Liberal Summer School at Oxford, a gathering which
he had helped to build up and to which he had frequently contributed in the past. 'Exultant friends we do not mind,' said one

speaker there, 'deserting friends are another matter. There are few things more despicable than to adopt a new faith and still wrap yourself in the mantle of the old. . . . Major Nathan must be un-leavened bread to state dictatorship.'

During this summer Nathan had the misfortune to be involved in a minor motoring accident when he was driving a party of friends from his house at Churt to the Military Tattoo at Aldershot and collided with another vehicle. As a result, he received a summons for careless driving. The case came before the Farnham Magistrates' Bench shortly after Parliament reassembled in the autumn, and the errant motorist was fined £5 and ordered to pay costs of £2 17s 6d. The case was widely reported in the press, *The Star* coming out the same evening with the headline:

M.P. ON WRONG SIDE OF ROAD

When he appeared in the Members Lobby and Smoking Room of the House of Commons, the new Labour convert was subjected to some banter, not all of it devoid of malice. One newspaper lobby correspondent wrote:

Wrong Side of Road

The defection of Major Nathan from the Samuelite section of the Liberal party to the Socialist party has created for him a number of not very sympathetic critics. They were disposed today to make some fun out of the fact that the major had been involved in an expenditure of £7 17s 6d for being on the wrong side of the road. I heard it suggested that it would probably cost him a good deal more than that sum for having gone on the wrong side of the political road. He had already been received into the Socialist party, and the other day attended his first meeting of Socialist M.P.s in the House of Commons. Where he will fight at the next election is not yet known, but the division which he sits for—North East Bethnal Green—will not know him as a Socialist candidate at the next election. A Socialist nominee is already in the field, and the major will have to find a new place. I have no doubt whatever that it will be found for him, and, knowing him as well as I do, I am confident that wherever it is he will fight with the determination to win. This is one aspect of Major Nathan which stirs the admiration of political friends and enemies alike.

Personal attacks were not confined to Nathan's erstwhile Liberal friends. When the Air Estimates were next before the House, Nathan moved to reduce the strength of the Air Force by 2,000 men on the ground that the Government had shown no justification for its proposed increase in R.A.F. personnel. ('The only defence against air armaments is an agreement to abolish them. Yet the Government insists on the right to use bombs from the air.') The motion, which Nathan insisted on carrying to a division, was heavily defeated, but not before some harsh things had been said about the mover. One Conservative backbencher, Edward Doran, who represented Tottenham, expressed his contempt for the mover by describing him as a 'sewer rat' who had scuttled into the underground shelters during the war.

This grossly defamatory allegation was, of course, protected by parliamentary privilege, and Nathan chose to ignore it. But among those who chanced to read of it was an anonymous ex-service man in Tottenham who had served under Nathan in the Royal Fusiliers. He wrote to his local newspaper in defence of his former commanding officer, and the sincere and dignified language he used deserves quotation.*

In 'C' Company of a certain territorial battalion in September, 1914, was a lieutenant. The battalion went overseas in February, 1915, and heavy training on poor food, which had been ruined by almost tropical heat, caused such irritation as to provoke the beginnings of a mutiny. By a kindly act, which endeared him to the whole battalion, this lieutenant put the matter right. Promotion to captain soon followed, and so to that death-trap, Gallipoli.

Death, wounds and disease rapidly reduced the number of senior officers until the captain, now promoted major, assumed command of the battalion. Many of your readers will recall the blizzard which decimated our Gallipoli troops towards the

---

* *Tottenham Weekly Herald*, April 5, 1935.

end of 1915. The major still carried on with the remnant of a battalion until Suvla Bay was evacuated. Then round to Cape Helles to help others to get away from there. In 1916, westwards to France, where the remaining few were disbanded and, bad luck, lost their major. I heard, towards the end of the war, that the major had 'stopped a bad one' but was glad to know that he had survived.

To Mr Doran, M.P., I say that the above are the facts about the life of Major Nathan, M.P., during the first two years of the Great War. Does such a record give Mr Doran justification for classifying the major as a 'sewer-rat'? I think not! Mr Doran says he watched people 'scuttling' into underground shelters. Major Nathan was at that time more usefully employed O.H.M.S.

My old commander will never know who wrote this letter if I have my way.

Yours, etc.

'SIG TWO ONE'

Although some good friends came to Nathan's defence in the face of such scurrilous attacks at this, there is no doubt that some of the mud thrown at Nathan during this period stuck. His transfer of his political allegiance also injuriously affected his law practice. In the 1930s a Labour solicitor in the City was unlikely to be consulted by leading bankers and industrialists, such as those whom Nathan had previously included among his clients. Nor was his popularity in the City enhanced by the stand he took in the House against the attempts by City speculators to corner certain commodities on the market, such as pepper, shellac and tin, with their ramifications in Government and financial circles.

Speaking in the debate initiated by a Labour colleague, George Grenfell, on this subject, Nathan gave an elaborate description of the abuse of the Companies Act by a network of City companies which were nominally distinct and separate but were really controlled by a dominating personality, in this instance a certain Mr John Howeson, whom he referred to as 'the presiding genius and adviser of the tin-control committee', and he supported Grenfell's demand for a public inquiry. 'If you look at the records of some of the companies involved,' he said, 'you will find they are scattered as with pepper out of a pepper pot with the names of bank nominees and shadow men and shadow women. It would be impossible for anyone except with the most serious, acute and prolonged inquiry to determine who precisely are the really important shareholders in a great number of these companies.'

Replying to the debate on behalf of the Government, Mr Walter Runciman, the President of the Board of Trade, defended speculation in 'futures' as the only way in which the big staple industries in the country could get their supplies of raw materials at a fair and equal price. So far as the individuals whom Nathan had mentioned, the Minister admitted that he was not much interested in them. 'I am more concerned with maintaining the reputation of the City of London for clean dealing,' he said. However, he did promise that an inquiry should be directed specifically into the transactions in the City, to which Nathan had drawn attention, and this should be carried out by the Official Receiver, a judicial official with wide powers. As a result a number of individuals, including Mr Howeson, were charged with various offences under the Companies Act and subsequently convicted at the Old Bailey.

With the prospect of an approaching General Election, Nathan was now faced with the problem of finding another constituency. There was no question of his fighting again in Bethnal Green, since there a Labour candidate had already been adopted, Mr Dan Chater, an ex-M.P. who had lost his seat in 1931, and he not unnaturally refused to stand down in Nathan's favour, although some pressure was put upon him to do so. Through the Labour Party Head-quarters at Transport House, Nathan's name was sent to two constituencies, Romford and Sunderland, which were looking for candidates. But in both these divisions there were other aspirants; and although Nathan got on to the 'short list' in each, he did not relish the prospect of a preliminary contest before another Selection Committee after he had been turned down in Romford. While he was considering what to do, he heard that the prospective Labour candidate in another constituency, Cardiff South, had suddenly retired on account of ill health and that there was a good chance of his unanimous selection there if he acted quickly. So he withdrew from Sunderland, journeyed down to Wales, was interviewed by the South Cardiff Selection Committee, and made such a favourable impression that he was adopted on the spot.

At the same time the Committee left him in no doubt about the nature of the struggle ahead. Except for the short 1929 Parliament, Cardiff South had always been represented by a Conservative. The sitting M.P., Captain Arthur Evans, had won the seat in 1931 with a majority of nearly 6,000. What was more, he was a well-known Welshman, who was Vice-Chairman of the Welsh Conservative Parliamentary Party and was identified with various Welsh national institutions. Nathan, on the other hand, was a stranger, an Englishman and a Jew, without Welsh associations of any kind.

As soon as the news of Nathan's adoption had been officially announced, Captain Evans addressed a letter to the local newspaper, *The Western Mail*, earnestly appealing as the sitting Member to the electors of Cardiff South, in the coming General Election, 'for a clean, straightforward contest on the policy of the Socialist party on the one hand and the continuance of the National Government on the other—*to the total exclusion of unnecessary personalities and side issues*'. (The italics were those of Captain Evans, whose anxiety was due to the fact that he had recently become involved in divorce proceedings, a fact not calculated to endear him to the Welsh nonconformist voters.)

Unfortunately for Nathan, this appeal was to be flagrantly disregarded at a crucial moment in the election by the very journal which had published it, as well as by some of the Conservative candidate's more unscrupulous supporters.

3

The celebration of the Silver Jubilee of King George V's reign in the summer of 1935 was followed by two changes in the personalities of the political scene. First, the ageing and decrepit Ramsay

MacDonald retired from No. 10 Downing Street, giving way to the Conservative leader Stanley Baldwin, who thus became Prime Minister for the third time. Secondly, the Labour Party leader, George Lansbury, resigned after the annual party conference and his place was taken as Leader of the Opposition by Major Clement Attlee, a middle-class Labour 'intellectual', who had fought in the Great War like Nathan and, like him also, had considerable experience of social work in the East End of London. So far as the Government went, where Baldwin had reshuffled several ministerial posts, the new Prime Minister might have carried on until the following spring or even later, but he preferred to seek a fresh mandate from the electorate with the minimum of delay. Accordingly he got the King to dissolve Parliament on October 29, so that the voters could go to the polls on November 14.

It was a curiously apathetic Election, with none of the drama and excitement which had characterized the electoral contests in 1924 and 1931. In the field of foreign affairs the only issue was how to treat Italy for her wanton invasion of Abyssinia in disregrad of her obligations to the League of Nations, and on this Conservatives and Labour were broadly in agreement that all sanctions should be applied short of war. At home, housing and unemployment were the main questions, and on these Nathan concentrated in the straight fight he had with Captain Evans, for there was no Liberal or other candidate in Cardiff South. But if the fight was a straight one, it was unfortunately not a clean one, or at least not as clean as the Conservative candidate had publicly expressed the wish at the outset of the campaign that it should be.

Nothing of any consequence happened until the actual day of the poll. But on the morning of November 14, *The Western Mail and South Wales News* came out with an extraordinary story under the following headline:

WHERE IS MAJOR NATHAN'S ROLLS-ROYCE?

After describing Nathan as being classed among the 'wealthy candidates' of the Socialist party in this election and referring to his town house in Wilton Crescent and his country house at Churt, his membership of two London clubs, the Reform and the National Liberal, several of his references to the Socialists when he was a Liberal ('One is fawned upon and flattered' and 'What we have to aim at is not a watery Socialism but a full-blooded Radicalism'), the account went on to quote a political commentator who wrote that 'with the accession of Major H. L. Nathan,' the Socialists 'once more have a Rolls-Royce at their disposal'. It concluded with these words:

> Major Nathan brought his Rolls-Royce to Cardiff and put it into storage. He favours a hired car—useful, but less pretentious—for his electioneering campaign.

At the same time, *The Western Mail*, which incidentally was a Conservative organ, then owned by Lord Kemsley, issued a newsbill which was displayed throughout the constituency repeating the words of the headline and asking where was Major Nathan's Rolls-Royce.

The statement about the Rolls-Royce was completely untrue, as the newspaper subsequently admitted when sued for libel by Nathan. When the matter came before the courts, Nathan's counsel said with reference to the newspaper statement which had appeared on polling day:

> There could be no doubt that that allegation, published on that day and in that form, was intended by the defendants to damage Major Nathan's prospects of success in the election by holding him up to the voters in his constituency as a hypocrite who desired to conceal from a working-class electorate the fact that he was a person of substantial means, by pretending that he could only afford a hired car, whereas he actually possessed but kept concealed a car of a very expensive make.
> The moment chosen by the defendants for the publication of the statement rendered it impossible for Major Nathan to obtain, before the poll closed, equal publicity for the true facts, which were that he did not possess a Rolls-Royce, that he did possess an Austin, that he had brought it to Cardiff, where it

was continually in use throughout the election campaign, and that he had only hired another car because one was insufficient for his own and Mrs Nathan's needs in getting about the constituency.

It is impossible to say how many votes Nathan lost as a result of the defamatory statement. He himself thought that they were enough to deprive him of victory. As it was, Captain Evans only just scraped home, his six thousand majority dropping to five hundred. The actual figures were:

Captain A. Evans (Conservative) ...	14,925
Major H. L. Nathan (Labour) ...	14,384
Conservative majority	541

If a parliamentary candidate has once been 'in' as an M.P., there is no more morale-shattering news when the Returning Officer announces the result which shows that he is 'out' by no matter how narrow a margin. In Nathan's case, the news was all the more galling since there was a definite swing to Labour throughout the country, the Party recovering the votes of those who had abstained in 1931. This brought a hundred or so gains to Labour, which thus secured 154 seats in the new House of Commons as against 432 supporters of the National Government. The Liberals fared worse than ever before, dropping to 20, of which 4 represented the Lloyd George family party. The National Government, now wholly Tory in complexion, had got its mandate for rearmament.

On his return to London from Cardiff, Nathan issued a writ for libel against *The Western Mail*. As might be expected, the case was settled, since there was no possible defence on the facts or in law. The settlement was announced on June 9, 1936, in open court before the Lord Chief Justice, Lord Hewart, who gave leave for the record to be withdrawn.

'Major Nathan had been long enough in politics not to be unduly sensitive to attacks,' said the plaintiff's counsel, Lord Reading, K.C., son of the former Lord Chief Justice and Viceroy of India, 'and he was naturally prepared for his opponents to make all possible capital out of his change of party, but he deeply resented the suggestion of bad faith contained in the words of which complaint was now made.'

Counsel continued:

> Nevertheless, although Major Nathan believed that his defeat, which was only by a narrow margin, was due to the circulation of the damaging statement, he did not desire to be vindictive, and he was prepared to accept the defendant's assurance that they published it in good faith and on information which they believed at the time to be correct, although they now agreed that the allegation was wholly baseless and untrue. He had accordingly agreed to a settlement of the action, which involved the defendants making a public apology in that Court, indemnifying him in respect of costs, and paying a substantial sum by way of agreed damages, which he had no intention of retaining for his own profit.

On behalf of *The Western Mail*, Mr Trevor Hunter, K.C., said that the defendants associated themselves wholeheartedly with the statement made by Lord Reading, and they greatly regretted that they published the statement complained of, which they now admitted to be wholly without foundation. 'They now wished to make it clear that Major Nathan did not store any car owned by him while at Cardiff and hire a less pretentious one for the electioneering campaign.'

Meanwhile Nathan remained without a winnable seat. The constituency Labour party in Cardiff South would have been glad for him to continue to nurse the division, but he could not afford to spend the time away from his law practice in London that this would have entailed, particularly since in the normal course of things the new Parliament might be expected to last for the best part of five years. What he wanted was a constituency nearer home, preferably a London one. Here indeed he was to have a considerable piece of luck, or rather two pieces of luck.

In the first place, a vacancy among Labour candidates suddenly became available in Wandsworth Central. Nathan put his name forward and he was adopted at the beginning of August, 1936. As in Cardiff, he knew that he would have to work hard if he was to gain the seat, which was represented by a popular and respected Conservative baronet, Sir Henry Jackson, with a majority of over 4,000. But Labour was already making headway in Wandsworth, where the Party had two members on the Borough Council. Of its two members on the L.C.C. one was Labour, and there were high hopes of capturing the other seat from the Conservatives at the next local government elections. These hopes were to be realized when Eleanor Nathan went forward as she had done in Bethnal Green, blazing the trail for her husband with a triumphant return to County Hall in March, 1937.

As soon as the holiday season was over and political meetings began again, Nathan was introduced to the division and set up a party headquarters. His faithful and efficient agent, Mr Alan Herbert, who had served him in Bethnal Green and Cardiff, was now appointed Labour agent for Central Wandsworth. During the next few months Nathan addressed a series of meetings with the object of getting to know the constituency. He is not on record as having expressed himself on the constitutional crisis, which marked the closing weeks of the year 1936, and led to the abdication of Edward VIII, but he spoke on a variety of other political topics, including the Spanish Civil War ('If we send armaments to a duly constituted Government in Spain, I cannot see how in logic we could refuse to send arms to Hitler and Mussolini if and when they are placed in a similar position'), the 'loud-mouthed propaganda and quasi-military uniforms' of the Mosleyite Fascists ('Mosley's antics are a treason against democracy, and the same severity should be meted out to them as treason against the King'), and the 'shambling, sorry, shabby affair Mr Baldwin makes of democracy' by playing straight into the hands of Sir Oswald Mosley ('How can we hope for leadership from men of this kind with a political squint?'). He even attacked the Government for what he considered to be its misguided physical training programme.

I have every sympathy with the Government's intention to introduce measures to improve the physique of the nation. But

At a National Defence Public Interest Committee Luncheon, 1941.
Left to right: Hugh Dalton, M.P. (Minister of Economic Warfare), Peter
Fraser (Prime Minister of New Zealand), Lord Nathan (Chairman
N.D.P.I.C.), Ivan Maisky (Soviet Ambassador in London)

With Ernest Bevin during 1945 General Election. Lady Nathan is
seated on the right

Outside No. 10 Downing Street after a Cabinet meeting, 1945. Left to right: Lord Alanbrooke (C.I.G.S.), Admiral Lord Cunningham (First Sea Lord), Lord Nathan (Under-Secretary for War)

The Old Kiln, Churt, Surrey

what is necessary first is to improve the diet of the nation. Four and a half million people are living below the minimum scale regarded by the British Medical Association as necessary for elementary well-being.

What is the good of telling boys and girls, who for years have suffered from the evils of undernourishment, that what they want is a course of physical jerks? Nurse them into health before you teach them the best way of using their health.

But a policy of improved nutrition costs money. The Government, apparently, cannot afford it. Owing to the failure of the Government's foreign policy, the money that might have been used to feed the children has, of necessity, to be used by the defence departments to feed the guns.

Nathan's second piece of luck was the unexpected death of the sitting Conservative Member, Sir Henry Jackson, which occurred in February, 1937, during the L.C.C. election campaign, and necessitated a parliamentary by-election. As Nathan recalled in a tribute which he paid to Jackson at the time, they had both been Members of the 1931 Parliament and had met habitually then. 'His was a cheery spirit,' Nathan remarked, 'and I suppose scarcely a day passed when we did not exchange greetings. In the camaraderie among the Members of the House because they are Members of the House and irrespective of their politics—a camaraderie which is one of the pleasantest and most notable characteristics of the House of Commons—there existed between us, I like to remember, a feeling of mutual liking and regard. With those who have for years been his constituents here in Central Wandsworth, therefore, I share the feeling of shock and regret at his sudden death.'

Two other seats fell vacant at this time, both, like Central Wandsworth, previously held by Conservatives. The Government consequently decided that all three by-elections should take place on the same date, after the L.C.C. elections had been held. Polling Day was fixed for April 29. Nathan entered the fray heartened by two considerations. The first was the success of his wife in getting back to County Hall in March. The second was the choice of his

Conservative opponent. The Central Wandsworth Conservative Association did not select a local man or at any rate one who knew the constituency. Instead they adopted as their standard bearer a forty-three-year-old accountant from Sunderland named Roland Jennings, who was a complete stranger to Wandsworth; he had sat for the Sedgefield Division of Durham in the 1931 Parliament, in which incidentally he had seldom opened his mouth, and had lost his seat like Nathan in 1935. Since his adoption only took place on the day before the writ was moved, Mr Jennings had barely three weeks in which to campaign, a definite handicap in spite of the majority he had inherited from the late Member.

Both candidates indulged in what today would be called 'gimmicks'. Nathan's slogan was 'Let Wandsworth Wake the Government Up!' and to start his meetings, which were mostly held at street corners in the open air, an alarm clock was let off before the microphone in the Labour candidate's loud-speaker van.

As he had the reputation of being a comparatively wealthy man for a Socialist, Nathan was naturally asked some questions about his background. It was even suggested that he was interested in arms manufacture. This he denied indignantly. 'I am neither director nor shareholder in any armament firm, nor do I act for them in my professional life as a solicitor,' he declared. 'I am an Englishman who is a Jew, and a Jew who is an Englishman, and I am proud to be both. I am a Londoner born and bred, educated in a London school, mobilized, served and wounded with a London regiment. I married a London woman and always lived and worked in London, and represented a London constituency in Parliament. My wife is a member of the L.C.C.'

The Conservative candidate, on the other hand, made the most of the fact that the Tories were the patriotic party by exploiting the Red, White and Blue colours in the shape of posters and leaflets and the general Coronation Year sentiment, since George VI was due to be crowned in a few weeks' time. But Nathan stole a leaf out of his opponent's book when his agent issued a leaflet in red, white and blue on 'The Parable of a Busy M.P. and a Lazy M.P.', possibly suggested by Hogarth's famous cartoons of the Industrious Apprentice and the Idle Apprentice.

From 1931 to 1935, the leaflet pointed out, the Busy M.P., who was of course Major Nathan, made 97 speeches in the House of Commons, asked 211 questions, and played his part in debate to the extent of 212 columns of Hansard. The Lazy M.P., by contrast, made one brief speech in the same period, asked ten questions, and over the three years from July, 1932, to October, 1935, when Parliament was dissolved, *said nothing whatever*. Mr Jennings attempted to explain this unimpressive record by saying that when he was first elected Mr Baldwin called the Conservative M.Ps together and told them that 'the Government had such a large majority that it would be a mistake for us to spend our time sitting about at Westminster and that we'd better go out and work in our constituencies. So I took his advice.'

Although the Conservative candidate was handicapped by his newness to the constituency and his previous record of parliamentary inactivity, Nathan suffered from the fact that before his arrival on the scene there had been an almost total absence of Labour organization in what was essentially a working-class constituency, but one where many of the working-class voters had previously been faithful to the Conservative tradition. There was also the question of how the 4,000 Liberals in the division would vote, where there was no Liberal candidate in the field. In an attempt to capture their support Lloyd George and his daughter Megan both addressed eve-of-poll rallies when they asked the Liberals to come out for Nathan. Everyone agreed that it was going to be a close run thing, and so it proved.

At the General Election the Free Church and Liberal vote had gone heavily for Sir Henry Jackson in the belief that he would support a firm policy of peace and collective security abroad and reconstruction at home. Disillusioned by the Government record during the past eighteen months and evidently dissatisfied with the answers given by Mr Roland Jennings, these powerful elements transferred their support to the Labour candidate. This action was decisive—but only just.

The votes in Central Wandsworth were counted immediately after the poll closed, and the result was declared late the same night as follows:

Major H. L. Nathan (Labour) ...	12,406
Mr Roland Jennings (Conservative)	11,921
Labour majority	485

Although he had won by less than five hundred votes, Nathan had succeeded in turning over 5,000 compared with the General Election poll. It was the first time that Labour had won the seat by a clear majority, and Wandsworth had indeed woken the Government up. Four days later Nathan was formally introduced into the House of Commons, his sponsors being William Paling, the Labour Whip, and Ernest Thurtle, an old East End friend, who sat for Shoreditch.

4

Like other M.P.s, Nathan was awarded the King's Coronation Medal in May, 1937. At the same time he received another distinction, which made him particularly proud, when he was appointed Honorary Colonel of the 33rd (St Pancras) T.A. Anti-Aircraft Battalion, Royal Engineers, which later became the 300th Royal Regiment of Artillery in the Territorial Army. He used to say that he was the only Coronation Colonel on record; certainly it was a fitting recognition of close on thirty years' service as a 'Terrier'. Thereafter he devoted his energies to the attraction of recruits for the T.A., notably after Hitler's invasion of Austria in the spring of 1938 brought the menace of war appreciably nearer. Nathan's old Liberal colleague, Leslie Hore-Belisha, who had become a National-Liberal in 1931, was now War Minister, and Nathan had several talks with him, following which he became chairman of a committee, known as the Territorial Army Public Interest Committee, to promote recruiting for the Anti-Aircraft Division responsible for the ground defence of London against air attack.

The recruiting campaign was opened by Nathan in May, 1938, during the intermission in the public performance at the Odeon Cinema in Bromley. He spoke briefly and to the point:

> I am here tonight with the full knowledge and approval of the Secretary of State for War. Never was it more necessary than now that the Territorial Army should be brought swiftly up to its full strength. Few of you probably realize that to the Anti-Aircraft Division of the Territorial Army there has been entrusted the task of providing the sole defence of London from the ground against attack from the air. In that regard, therefore, the Territorial Army is in the forefront: it is the first line of defence. We have been given a job of work to do. If we are to perform our task effectively, we must be fully manned at once, for adequate training takes time.
>
> The Territorial Army are civilians in uniform, indeed, but we are not just dressing up to play at soldiers. Those who, like myself, have experienced war and the filth and turmoil of it all, know that war is loathsome, but, because we all hate it, we must not, in the world as it is today, fail to recognize that it may come, and if it comes and we are not prepared for it, God help us! The attack may never come. We all pray that it never may. But it is much less likely to come if the world knows that it is certain to fail if it does come. And it is for us to make it certain to fail.

The Territorial Army Public Interest Committee was the outcome of a gathering in the House of Commons, to which Nathan invited M.P.s of all parties representing constituencies where there were T.A. unit headquarters to meet Major-General Sir Frederick Pile, the Anti-Aircraft Divisional Commander. The War Minister was present and he gave his blessing to the setting up of the committee. It was a small working committee, which included in addition to Nathan as chairman and Sir Fredrick Pile, Major-General Liardet, the first Territorial officer to be appointed to the command of a Division, Lord Nuffield, Mr Oscar Deutsch, the chairman of

Odeon cinemas, who agreed to put his theatres at the disposal of the committee, and Mr Sydney Walton, a well-known public relations consultant. During the 'interruptions' at the cinema performances, the local Territorial unit would send a detachment with their band to play on the platform, while the Mayor attended to give the appeal the blessing of the civic authority and thus, in Nathan's words, 'to make it clear that the Territorial Army is in truth the Army of the citizen in uniform'. Either Nathan or some other member of the committee would address the audience, 'the object being not so much to obtain immediate results in the way of recruits as to create an atmosphere of encouragement for the Territorials and to bring into existence and maintain a sound public opinion.... We feel strongly that the Territorial Army, which works without advertisement, must be brought out of its obscurity and, in a word, be made "fashionable".'* In addition, military displays were held in Hyde Park, and on Hackney Marshes and Clapham Common, and were attended by members of the Army Council and other military leaders.

Early in 1939, the committee, which was serving the needs of the Auxiliary Air Force as well as the T.A., was further extended to include civil defence. This was done at the request of Sir John Anderson, the Lord Privy Seal, and an outstanding administrator, who had recently been brought into the Cabinet to take charge of this service. He wrote to Nathan: 'You can hardly at this juncture press one particular service without reference to the other services for which volunteers are to be invited to come forward. I should, therefore, be very glad of any help that you and your committee can give in respect of the present campaign.'† Thus, in addition to Air Ministry nominees from the auxiliary bomber and balloon squadrons, Anderson's department was also represented on the committee, the latter's name consequently being changed to the National Defence Public Interest Committee (N.D.P.I.C.). Before Anderson took over air-raid precautions, the Home Office had been responsible for A.R.P. and had fallen down badly on the job, as the

* *The Observer*, June 26, 1938.   † *The Times*, February 8, 1939.

pathetically inadequate preparations at the time of the Munich crisis in September, 1938, had shown. Indeed, Nathan had been hammering away at the Home Office ever since his return to the House of Commons, and six months before Munich he had stated in a letter circulated to the Press that he had repeatedly tried to find out without success regarding A.R.P. what he should do 'as an M.P., a householder, a considerable employer of labour, and chairman of a hospital in London'. (He had recently been elected Chairman of the Infants' Hospital, Westminster, now known as the Westminster Children's Hospital, in succession to Lord Kemsley.)

Under the auspices of the N.D.P.I.C., Nathan arranged a series of luncheons and dinners where defence problems could be discussed informally and 'off the record'. One of these, which he gave in the House of Commons shortly before the outbreak of the Second World War, was expressly in honour of General Sir Walter Kirke, who had just relinquished the post of Director-General of the Territorial Army on his appointment as first Commander-in-Chief, Home Forces. Nathan recalled the occasion some years later (1943) in a letter which he wrote to his son, then serving in the army overseas.

To that dinner I invited all our leading Generals as well as a number of Members of the House of Commons. I think there were about 100 Generals there and it was said that the Parliament building saw a larger number of Generals that evening than it had done since Oliver Cromwell removed the mace from the Commons! At my table I had the various Commanders-in-Chief, and other senior Generals; amongst the former was Wavell and amongst the latter Alanbrooke. I suppose there were ten or a dozen Generals at my table, but it was quite obvious from the first that in personality and intellectual power Wavell and Alanbrooke towered above the rest.* After

---

* Archibald Wavell, later Earl Wavell, who had been on Allenby's staff in 1918, became successively Commander-in-Chief, Middle East; Commander-in-Chief, India; Supreme Commander, South-West Pacific; and Viceroy of India. Alanbrooke, later Viscount Alanbrooke, became Chief of the Imperial General Staff.

NATIONAL DEFENCE PUBLIC INTEREST
COMMITTEE

[signature]

Luncheon

to

The Right Honourable
PETER FRASER
M.P.

PRIME MINISTER
of
NEW ZEALAND

[signature]

IN THE CHAIR:

COL. THE LORD NATHAN OF CHURT
Chairman of the Committee.

[signature] J. Maisky

MENU

[signature]

La Petite Salade Printanière

L'Eminée de Volaille Dorchester
Les Choux Fleurs au Gratin

Le Triffle au Sherry

DORCHESTER HOTEL   25th June, 1941

132

the dinner I went straight to Hore-Belisha, who was Secretary of State for War, to tell him that I was certain that the two men that the War Office ought to keep their eye on were Wavell and Alanbrooke. It was not a bad judgment as events have shown.

I was reminded of this when I went to the Trade Union Club the other day to meet and hear Wavell. He remembered this dinner well and reminded me that at it he had been placed next to Arthur Greenwood. When I recalled it afterwards to Arthur Greenwood, he had forgotten all about it. Curious, I thought.*

After the outbreak of war, the N.D.P.I.C. was kept in being by Nathan as a convenient means of entertaining leading Commonwealth personalities as well as foreign heads of state and representatives of countries which had been attacked and overrun by Hitler's forces. These occasions took the form of fortnightly luncheons in the Dorchester Hotel and provided an excellent platform for the pronouncement of official policies by these different personages. They were open to the public at the controlled price of five shillings a head, and they proved an effective means of boosting civilian morale, particularly for evacuees and other victims of the 'blitz'. The official guests of the committee included King George of the Hellenes, Crown Prince Olav of Norway, Prince Bernhard of the Netherlands, the Grand Duchess of Luxemburg, Dr Edward Benes, President of Czechoslovakia and M. Jan Masaryk, Foreign Minister in the Provisional Government, M. Pierlot, Prime Minister of Belgium, M. Maisky, the Soviet Ambassador in London, General de Gaulle, then commanding the Free French Forces, and the Prime Ministers of South Africa (J. C. Smuts), Australia (Robert Menzies), and New Zealand (Peter Fraser). It was useful publicity for the individuals and countries concerned, since the Press were invited and the proceedings widely reported. In addition, all the Cabinet Ministers were invited as guests of honour to the luncheons,

* Arthur Greenwood, Deputy Leader of the Labour Party, was an ineffective member of the War Cabinet, from which he was ejected by Churchill in 1942.

which, according to the *Daily Telegraph* in March, 1940, 'now enjoy
a popularity rivalling those at which Miss Foyle used to produce
literary lions'. At the end of the first year of these luncheons,
Nathan and the rest of the committee were entertained by the
supporters of the luncheons and Nathan was presented with an
album of photographs of the Cabinet and ex-Cabinet Ministers who
had spoken on these occasions. Commenting on Nathan's reply to
the toast of his health, *The Star* remarked that 'he has that not-so-
common virtue of always speaking briefly'.

In August, 1939, in recognition of the committee's work in
attracting recruits to the Auxiliary Air Force, the Air Minister
announced Nathan's appointment as Honorary Air Commodore of
No. 906 (County of Middlesex Balloon) Squadron, and some
months later he received the thanks of the Prime Minister and the
Defence Ministers for his work on the N.D.P.I.C. The Prime
Minister wrote:

10 Downing Street,
Whitehall.
24th November, 1939

My dear Nathan,
   I am glad to hear that your National Defence Public Interest
Committee is continuing its work in War-time. I know that it
was very successful in stimulating public interest in the Defence
Services, both fighting and civilian, during the pre-War
period, and that the demonstrations it organized and the visits
to Camps and Training Centres it arranged had a marked
effect on recruiting.
   Today we are faced with a different problem. In what I have
called 'this strangest of wars', we must see to it that the public
morale is sustained. People are sometimes apt to get a little
restive when, as they put it, 'nothing happens'. So I welcome
these War-Time Luncheons you are arranging, at which
Members of the Government and other leading figures will
speak. They will, I am sure, have a steadying effect on morale
on the Home Front, which will be most valuable.
   I am particularly glad that you are inviting representatives
of the Press of the Dominions and of the United States and of

other neutral countries to attend them. Important as it is to inform our own people of what we are thinking and doing, it is of just as much importance to tell our neutral friends.

I told you once before that your work had my warm support. Your present activities are at least as important as those you have carried out during the past two years, and I hope you will increase and extend them.

Yours sincerely,

NEVILLE CHAMBERLAIN

In Parliament Nathan now alternated between khaki and air force blue, since, as the *Evening Standard* observed at the time, he could turn his own searchlights on his own balloons. Speaking at one of the N.D.P.I.C. luncheons a little later, Sir Archibald Sinclair, the Air Minister, jokingly remarked that Harry Nathan was entitled to wear more uniforms than anybody other than a member of the Royal Family—always excepting Field-Marshal Goering! There was indeed some truth in this jest, for besides his military and air force uniforms, he could don the black robe of a solicitor, the scarlet robe and plumed hat of a Deputy Lieutenant of the County of London, and finally—for he had just been created a peer—the scarlet and ermine of a baron.

Nathan's departure from the Commons for the Upper House came about in this way. Clement Attlee, who continued to lead the Opposition until he joined the War Cabinet under Churchill in May, 1940, was anxious in the early months of the war, as he put it, 'to reinforce the scanty representation of Labour in the House of Lords'. He had been favourably impressed by Nathan's work for the N.D.P.I.C. and also for army welfare following his appointment as Director of Welfare in Eastern Command and London District, as described later in this chapter.

Some time in the spring of 1940, Attlee approached Neville Chamberlain, who was still Prime Minister, and asked him to recommend Nathan for a peerage. Chamberlain was agreeable, but before the recommendation could be implemented, the Chamberlain Government fell and Churchill formed his Coalition. Attlee then brought the matter to the new Prime Minister's attention. Churchill also agreed, there now being an additional reason in the need to find a seat in the House of Commons for Ernest Bevin, the powerful Secretary of the Transport and General Workers' Union, whom Churchill wished to bring into the Government as Minister of Labour and National Service. On June 13, it was officially announced from Buckingham Palace that the King had been pleased to confer a Barony on Colonel Harry Louis Nathan. A few days later Bevin was unanimously adopted as Labour candidate in Central Wandsworth, and as an electoral truce had come into operation between the three political parties the new Minister of Labour was returned without a contest.

Nathan took as his title Baron Nathan of Churt in the County of Surrey. He is believed to have been the first practising solicitor to have been made a peer. He was formally introduced into the House of Lords on July 3, 1940, his sponsors being Lord Snell and Lord Strabolgi. As a Jew it was noted that he kept his cocked hat on while taking the oath, which he did on the Old Testament. Suitable headgear had also to be provided for his daughter Joyce, who had come with her mother and various family friends and relations to witness the occasion. Since the rules of the House of Lords require that ladies in the gallery should be 'covered', and as Joyce had arrived without a hat, she could not be admitted until an attendant had found her a beret.

Gossip had it at the time and afterwards that Nathan was deliberately 'kicked upstairs' to make way for Ernest Bevin in the Commons. But it was not true. The matter had been agreed in principle with Chamberlain before there was any question of Bevin coming in. As Attlee was to put it with his customary dry brevity, 'fortuitously this provided a seat for Mr. Bevin.' However, when the new peer duly obtained a grant of heraldic arms, he showed a certain wit in choosing as his motto the Latin words *Labor nobilitat*, which may best be translated literally as 'Labour ennobles.'

5

More than a year before the outbreak of war and the calling up of many civilians, Nathan had realized that these men would undoubtedly be confronted with a variety of personal problems in regard to such matters as mortgage repayments, insurance premiums, hire purchase contracts, school fees and the like. In addition there would be anxiety that their wives and families might suffer as the result of being bombed out of their homes while they themselves were on active service elsewhere. Except for very limited funds for the provision of a few sports and recreation grounds, there had been virtually no public finance available for welfare for the Regular Army between the two World Wars. Certain welfare services and amenities, it is true, had been provided through regimental and kindred agencies, but generally speaking there had been relatively few occasions when soldiers of the Regular Army had required skilled assistance in the solution of their domestic and legal problems.

With the drastic change in the situation brought about by the events of September, 1939, Nathan believed that urgent action was necessary, and during the next few weeks he had a series of conferences with the War Minister and other War Office chiefs such as the Adjutant-General and Commander-in-Chief Home Forces. This resulted in the creation of a new Army Welfare Service to be based on voluntary and unpaid workers and to be linked with the various Territorial Army Associations. Command Welfare Officers, as they came to be called, were to be chosen by the various Home Commands with the approval of the War Office, and at the same time each County T.A. Association was to appoint a Social Welfare Committee with a County Welfare Officer of influence and independence, and also a number of Area, District and Local Welfare Officers with sound local knowledge who could serve the troops within their respective geographical areas. No public money was to be made available to these committees, which had to raise the necessary funds by appeals within their counties. The Command Welfare Officers were charged with the duty of carrying out the social welfare policy of the Commanders-in-Chief and of co-ordinating the activities of the County Welfare Officers.

'Welfare is an essential part of a soldier's life,' said the War Office, 'and must be planned to dovetail in with all his activities.' The objects of the welfare scheme, which was operating by the end of October, 1939, were officially described as being

(a) to strengthen the morale of the men by making the fullest possible provision for the needs of their spirits, minds and bodies, so that they may be at all times fighting fit, ready to fight, and able and willing to give their best; and

(b) to link officers and men together in a bond of mutual friendship and respect, which will not only stand the hardest tests of war, but will be strengthened by them.

At the urgent invitation of the Army Council, Nathan became Command Welfare Officer with the style of Director of Welfare for Eastern Command and London District, where thousands of members of the armed Forces had their homes and civilian occupations, and where inevitably large formations of troops would be stationed. Since the Treasury was not prepared to sanction an Army Welfare Service with paid officers and appropriate quarters, Nathan perforce had to find his own accommodation. This he did by persuading his law partners to agree to the partition of the firm's offices in Finsbury Square, fifteen rooms of which were put at the disposal of his headquarters staff. Unfortunately these premises were completely gutted by fire in the heavy Luftwaffe raid on London on the night of December 30–31, 1940, which destroyed all the army welfare records as well as all the office files of the law firm. Luckily his clients' title deeds, leases, wills and other original documents had been moved to the country and were safe, but every other scrap of paper in the offices was lost, including a valuable library of law books, a wide range of political correspondence with well-known individuals such as Lloyd George and Herbert Samuel, including Samuel's letter offering him a ministerial post in 1931, and a complete set of Hansard's Parliamentary Debates going back to

1906. Temporary accommodation was quickly found at 25 Buckingham Gate for the army welfare work and also in Donington House, Norfolk Street, off the Strand, which served as temporary offices for Herbert Oppenheimer, Nathan and Vandyk.

Perhaps the most important welfare problem was caused by the soldier's anxiety on account of enemy air action against his home town. In London Nathan made it a matter of top priority to deal with 'the anxious soldier', so that wherever he was stationed he could apply for information regarding his family and home. Wives and other next-of-kin were asked to carry in their identity card a note bearing the name, regimental number and other unit particulars of their soldier relatives. 'I am still convinced that the greatest trouble of a soldier is worry about his home,' said Nathan at the end of three and a half years as the Army's principal Command Welfare Officer. 'Some welfare workers emphasize the importance of providing entertainment, sport, books, and so on. These are important, but to my mind the really vital thing is to relieve as much as possible the anxieties of a soldier about his family, his job, his home.'* With quiet and characteristic efficiency Eleanor Nathan took charge of the 'Anxious Soldier' Section at Command Headquarters. For instance, when a bomb fell in the neighbourhood of a soldier's home, she would immediately find out the effect of the damage and whether his family was safe and would then relay the information to the soldier affected.

The other Command Welfare activities included advice on legal and domestic problems, the provision of hostels and canteens for soldiers on leave, entertainments, sports and games, gardening, talks, music, and an Information Bureau in Trafalgar Square staffed by welfare personnel. At this Bureau, as well as at a number of welfare centres and Service Clubs in London, any man or woman of the British and Allied Forces on leave and in uniform could buy a special ticket for a shilling which could be used on all underground railways, buses and trams in the metropolitan area. The tickets, which were Nathan's idea, were available from 10.30 a.m. until the

* *Evening Standard*, April 1, 1943.

last trains and vehicles had stopped running. The talks included one on cricket by Sir Pelham ('Plum') Warner, the famous M.C.C. Captain, and another on astronomy, which was much appreciated by the searchlight units. An elderly lady offered to give some readings from the works of Dickens to a small unit in the country. At first regarded somewhat askance by the men, these Dickens readings soon proved most popular. Equally successful was the provision of good music for the troops in the form of specially arranged concerts.

As Director of Music Nathan appointed his old friend from Malta days in the First World War, Captain Graham Carritt, an accomplished and dedicated musician. The idea was to provide for better music than the ordinary barrack-room type of concert usually produced. A beginning was made in December, 1940, with three experimental concerts at which Oda Slobodskaya sang Russian and Spanish songs, and Kathleen Moorhouse and Desirée Macewen played works by Fauré, Chopin and Bach on the cello and piano, accompanied by Val Drewry. These went down so well that a large public concert was next given in the Wigmore Hall in March, 1941, at which the same artists performed, with the addition of Maurice Cole (piano) and Leonard Hirsch (violin). A representative committee was thereupon formed by Sir George Frankenstein, the former Austrian Ambassador, to appeal to music lovers for funds to provide further concerts in adequate halls with the best available performers. These were subsequently given in different parts of the Eastern and London Commands. One fund-raising public concert was given at the Albert Hall and attended by the Princess Royal, with Myra Hess and Harriet Cohen, and Sir Malcolm Sargent conducting, and this concert raised the satisfactory sum of £1,800. As Nathan put it in a few words he spoke during the interval at the Wigmore Hall concert, a man might go back to do his job all the better for an hour of such detachment. 'Such music,' he said, 'can give a man the sense of still possessing a private life, the loss of which is one of the greatest hardships which Army life entails.' As one who has a vivid recollection of one of these war-

Royal conversation piece at County Hall, London, 1947. Left to right: Lord Nathan, Queen Elizabeth, Princess Elizabeth, King George VI, Princess Margaret, Lady Nathan (Chairman L.C.C.)

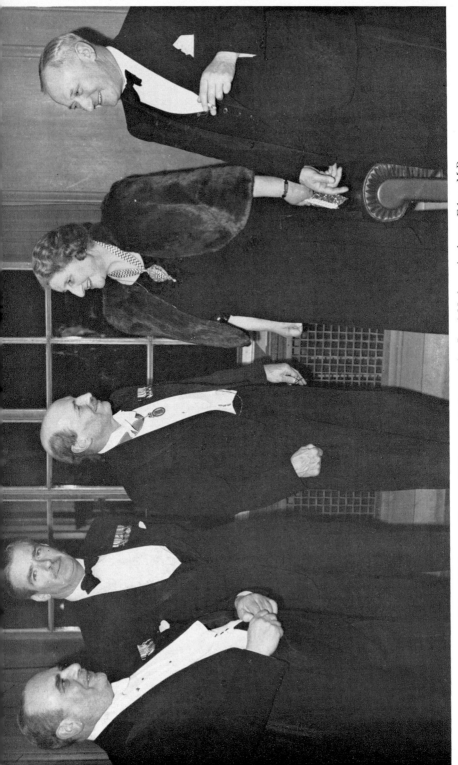

Prime Minister at County Hall, 1947. Left to right: Lord Nathan, Anthony Eden, M.P.,

time concerts, when Mozart's Clarinet Quintet in A (K.581) was most beautifully rendered, the present writer is in a position to endorse the truth of this remark.

As a means of raising funds to defray the expenses of these various welfare activities, Nathan hit on the idea of organizing two luncheon parties in St James's Palace, where H.M. Gentlemen-at-Arms kindly made their Mess available for the purpose. Nathan persuaded the Earl of Athlone to take the chair on each occasion and appeal to the influential and well-to-do guests who had been invited for their financial support. As a result £20,000 was immediately subscribed.

Nathan liked to describe himself as 'Scrounger-in-Chief to the Army'. By May, 1941, through his welfare officers in Eastern Command alone he had 'scrounged' over 100 pianos, 50 billiard tables and unknown quantities of books, gramophones and sports gear. 'For what?' he asked. 'To ease the lot of the civilian soldier, particularly in the isolated units, of which there are many. The welfare officer today is a vital link between the soldier and the civilian. He keeps each in touch with the other. And if welfare is important now, how much more important will it be when the war ends and the demobilization of the troops sets in? We are already studying problems of demobilization and planning to meet them. Welfare is educating the soldier, not by formal classes, but by talks and discussions. It is stimulating his interest in music and the arts, in craftsmanship, in literature, in history and economics. And it will not be the fault of welfare if the soldier is not a better citizen when he comes out of the Army than when he went in.'

Welfare amenities were also provided by Nathan's directorate for the women's Auxiliary Territorial Service (A.T.S.), members of which were employed from the beginning of the war as storewomen, cooks, drivers, clerks and orderlies, and later at anti-aircraft sites. There were liaison officers at headquarters too, to act with the Dominion troops and Free French forces. Hospitality for men and women on leave was another matter in which Nathan interested himself, supplying those willing to be hosts and hostesses with the names of lonely service personnel, particularly at Christmas. Nathan made a point of sending a personal answer to every letter he received, from the officer who wished to know how he could claim for kit lost at Dunkirk to the private soldier who wrote asking, 'Could you find me a refugee girl who is willing to marry?' Incidentally, many of Nathan's replies to these correspondents were dictated on to an early dictaphone from the basement of his house in Wilton Crescent, while the bombs of the Luftwaffe were falling overhead.

As already mentioned, Eastern Command and London District were originally treated as one Command for welfare purposes. But by 1941 the immense volume of welfare work in London made it necessary to appoint a separate Command Welfare Officer for each of the two Commands. Accordingly Nathan continued to act for London District only, while Brigadier (later Sir) Frank Medlicott took over the other Command. As a proportion of the funds he had raised, Nathan was able to let Brigadier Medlicott have over £4,300 to start him off in his new job.

In March, 1943, the Army Council decided to put welfare in London under a whole-time paid staff officer with the status of Assistant Adjutant General.* This was an inevitable step in the process of recognizing welfare as an essential part of contemporary Army life. It involved the relinquishment by Nathan of his appointment as unpaid Director of Welfare for London District, and in the next District Orders the G.O.C. expressed 'on his own behalf and on behalf of all ranks within and beyond the London District, who have derived benefit from the Scheme, appreciation of Lord Nathan's initiative, energy and unremitting work for the welfare of the Forces'.

This sentiment was echoed by the first Director-General of Welfare at the War Office, Lieutenant-General Sir John Brown, in a letter which he sent to *The Times* and which was published on April 2, 1943. 'When welfare started,' he wrote, 'it was a vague, amorphous thing, ill-defined because it was impossible to define,

* Colonel Sir Ronald Ross, Bart., M.C., M.P.

142

and many were more than a little suspicious of it. Lord Nathan played a large part in both defining—and widening—the boundaries of welfare, and also in breaking down the quite natural fear on the part of many that welfare might come between the officer and his men. Today welfare is an essential part of the Army, and that in three and a half years it has achieved this position is a credit to Lord Nathan and the band of loyal helpers which he built up, first in the Eastern Command and London, and later brought to its present high efficiency in London. Well may the official announcement of his going say that he has played "an outstanding part in welfare work and was indeed the pioneer of that work". Well may the Army Council thank him "for his most valuable contribution to service welfare during the past three and a half years".'

CHAPTER FIVE

Labour Peer in Wartime

THERE WAS ONLY A HANDFUL OF LABOUR PEERS ABLE TO ATTEND the House of Lords during the war. The Party leader was the septuagenarian Lord Addison, formerly Dr Christopher Addison, who had served as a Liberal Minister in the Lloyd George Coalition during the previous war, when he was the first to hold the newly created post of Minister of Health. The Labour Chief Whip was the Earl of Listowel, and the only other Labour member of the Upper House in the Coalition Government was Lord Snell, who was Deputy Leader of the House of Lords. Besides Nathan the most vocal Labour peers on the back benches were probably Lords Noel-Buxton and Strabolgi (formerly Lieutenant-Commander J. M. Kenworthy). Later during the war they were reinforced by Lords Wedgwood, Stansgate and Winster, all of whom, like Nathan and others, had once been Liberals. But the effective Party representation in the Upper House was always relatively small, barely a dozen in the war years. Once a week when Parliament was sitting, Addison, Listowel and Nathan, who acted as an Assistant Whip, attended the Labour Party meeting in one of the committee rooms in the Commons to keep abreast of policy, and the Labour peers would also have a weekly meeting among themselves to decide who should speak on what subject, if necessary expressing the official Labour Party view. 'We receive every courtesy,' said Lord Addison at this time. 'We are a very small Party but speak regularly in the ample time allotted.'

144

One of the first measures on which Nathan spoke officially on behalf of the Labour Party in the Lords was the War Time Adjustment Bill, which was introduced by the Lord Chancellor, Lord Simon (as Sir John Simon had now become), its purpose being to permit the revision of contracts, leases, mortgages, rent and other obligations, to enable debtors to carry on instead of being made bankrupt. Nathan, in welcoming the measure as equitable to both creditor and debtor, referred in particular to its inclusion of hire purchase agreements, so that people should not lose the goods on which they had paid a good deal. He spoke on a wide variety of other subjects during this period, including national service, defence, food distribution, education, the provision of nurseries for mothers engaged on vital war work, the Press—he acted as legal adviser to the Foreign Press Association—and post-war planning. He combined with Lord Londonderry, a Tory peer who had been Air Minister in Ramsay MacDonald's National Government, in pressing the War Office to publish the despatches of General Lord Gort, commander of the British Expeditionary Force in France and Belgium under the French General Gamelin in the months preceding Dunkirk. Much had already been written about the campaign by war correspondents and others, and there had been some strong criticism of Gort, who had refused to attack southwards towards Amiens in May, 1940, when the greater part of his forces was already engaged against the Germans on the Scheldte, and by so doing had saved the bulk of the B.E.F., although his action led to the breakdown of the Anglo-French alliance. For a long time the Government held out against publishing Gort's despatches, the only 'authoritative statement from the one who was in a position to make it', to quote Nathan. Eventually, after the matter had been raised four times by Londonderry and Nathan, the War Office gave way, and in October, 1941, the despatches duly appeared in print.

Nathan also initiated debates on several topics of moment by the traditional method used in the Lords of 'moving for papers'. One of these was in March, 1942, when he called attention to the necessity of maintaining the freedom of the Press as an essential element in the successful prosecution of the war. The most outspoken news-paper in its criticism of the War Cabinet and in particular of Winston Churchill, who combined the offices of Prime Minister and Minister of Defence, was the popular left-wing *Daily Mirror*. Matters came to a head when this journal published a drawing by the political cartoonist Philip Zec, which showed a torpedoed sailor adrift on a raft in a black, empty, angry sea. Underneath appeared the following caption:

> 'The price of petrol has been increased by one penny.' Official.

Tankers were being sunk by enemy submarines at an alarming rate at this time and the Government had just authorized an increase in the price of petrol. The purpose of the cartoon was to bring home to the public the fact that merchant seamen were dying in terrible circumstances, and to emphasize that the oil which was being trans-ported to Britain at a high cost in human life was being needlessly wasted. Unfortunately Zec's stark drawing was capable of a different interpretation, which was put upon it by the Cabinet, namely that the merchant seamen were risking their lives so that bigger profits might be made by the petrol companies.

This so enraged the Prime Minister that he wished to suppress the *Daily Mirror* altogether, under the Defence Regulations, and in fact the Home Secretary, Herbert Morrison, at Churchill's prompting, sent for the editor and bluntly threatened to do so. In his speech, Nathan described the cartoon as 'ill-conceived and deplorable', and he thought that the leading article which accom-panied it was 'false, abusive and unmannerly'. But if the *Daily Mirror* had offended against the law, he argued, let it be brought to the arbitrament of the law. Let it be warned and prosecuted under the law. On the other hand, he went on, 'the action which the Government has threatened is of vital concern to the whole nation, because it involves establishing a precedent in the control of the expression of opinion in the Press, and it carries a grave threat to our national liberties'. This produced a lively debate to which the

Lord Chancellor replied for the Government, making it clear that the Cabinet would certainly use the power 'if a matter arises in which it became necessary to do so'. The upshot was that Nathan withdrew his motion, whose object, he said, and that of his speech, was not to justify the *Daily Mirror*—he expressly repudiated it— but to draw attention to the choice of procedure on the part of the Government. The net result was that the threat of suppression was reduced to a solemn warning, and the *Mirror*, although it continued to criticize the conduct of the war, did so in terms which just managed to keep it within the law. Anyhow there was no further talk of suppression, and for this the newspaper largely had Nathan to thank, a fact incidentally which Mr Hugh Cudlipp in his 'astonishing story' of that journal (*Publish and be Damned!*) omits to mention.

The debate on post-war planning, which Nathan opened in December, 1942, was the occasion of considerable publicity by reason of the name which Nathan coined for the 'ordinary Briton' in the Forces, 'who wants to know what is going to happen to him, his family, his home and his job after the war'. Nathan called him 'Private Tom Snooks', and as a result Tom Snooks became the subject of extensive press comment. As *The Manchester Evening Despatch* remarked, why Lord Nathan should have chosen 'Tom Snooks' to typify the 'Tommy Atkins' of other days must remain his secret. Research revealed that there was no one of this surname in the London telephone directory, though apparently the name was not unknown in Wiltshire, Dorset and Somerset. *The Star* reminded its readers that 'Snooks' was a Mark Twain character and he also figured in a short story by H. G. Wells, *Miss Winchelsea's Heart*. Miss Winchelsea fell in love with 'a scholarly young man, gentlemanly and refined', whom she met on a conducted continental tour. When she found out that he was a Snooks, she decided that she did not like the name and finished with him. Snooks then married Miss Winchelsea's friend Fanny and he changed his name to Sevenoaks which, he said, was the original form of Snooks.

However that might be, Nathan publicly affirmed his 'passionate faith in the Snookses of the country. It is the wants and needs of the ordinary man—"Tom Snooks"—that is the real war aim.' In fact the name had suggested itself to him from the real Tom Snooks, who, it will be remembered, had been his orderly in Gallipoli and was the first man he had seen wounded in the fighting there. He had kept in touch with Nathan between the wars and came to see him again on account of the publicity his name had got in the news-papers. 'In the early days of Gallipoli,' Nathan recalled the incident in a letter to his son Roger, 'he was talking to me outside the dug-out when suddenly he fell into my arms, shot through the back. A Turkish sniper had got him, and if it had not been his back, it would have been my chest, so I have always felt particularly grateful to him. I well remember him being taken off in a stretcher and not hearing again of him till after the war. The last time I saw him was when he was home from a job in Nigeria, and the last time I heard from him was when he asked me if I could do something to get his A.T.S. daughter transferred nearer home, which incidentally I was able to do. It is always nice to keep in touch with the Tom Snookses, and I must say that all my Tom Snookses of the last war were extraordinarily good fellows and with many of them I have been in touch throughout. I hope the same will happen to you, because there is a confraternity arising from that kind of common experience and relationship which is quite unique.'

Roger Nathan, who had got his commission in the 17th/21st Lancers, went off with his Regiment to North Africa at this time, and for the next two years or more when Roger was on active service, his father wrote to him a regular account of his doings, from which it is possible to follow the elder Nathan's activities, experiences and thoughts on a wide variety of topics until virtually the end of the fighting. Some extracts from these letters follow:

London, May 31, 1943. I think I told you that there was some query as to the extension of my office as Honorary Colonel, owing to a new Army Order under which extensions are not to be granted except to members of the Royal Family or those who have attained the rank of Lt.-Colonel. Apparently the C.-in-C.'s office did not know my previous record. When I took the matter up with the War Office, it was put in order because in the last war I commanded my Battalion at Gallipoli as a temporary Lt.-Colonel and in this war have been for a considerable period an acting Colonel, so it is all right and I have been extended for three years. Also, by reason of my work as a Command Welfare Officer, the Army Council have given me the honorary rank of Colonel in the Army, so that I now hold the honorary rank of Colonel and the rank of Honorary Colonel—I imagine a rather unusual combination.

June 10. On Tuesday there was a rather important debate on the fall in population in the House of Lords, in which I took part, making a rather careful speech, because it is such a vitally important subject for the future of the nation. I coined the slogan: 'Make large families fashionable; make large families the thing,' and that, together with another slogan: 'The larger the family, the lower the rent', seems to have caught on because I find in my Press cuttings a good many headlines quoting it.

If Nathan got the headlines for this speech, he also received a heavy mail from those who had read his remarks.

June 15. It has brought me every kind of correspondence, and a great mass of it, some abusive, asking how we can expect people to have large families under existing conditions; some saying they cannot get on with their wives, so how can we expect larger families; some saying they cannot get on with their husbands, so ditto; others saying why don't the better-off people have larger families and set an example, and still others saying that houses are not built sufficiently strongly nowadays to stand the racket of children, so what about it?!! All these have got to be answered as a matter of courtesy, if not of interest, and in such a way that there is no come-back. So it is quite a job.

In the same letter, Nathan mentioned that he had broken off the Whitsun holiday to attend the Labour Party Conference.

Attlee spoke well and Morrison admirably. The general tone of the Conference was very sound and solid, better, I think, than I have known it before. There is no doubt of the complete unanimity in an all-out determination to carry on unitedly to win the war, and the suggestion that the electoral truce should be brought to an end was defeated by six to one. It is clear that one of the outstanding questions which is going to give rise to a deep political controversy is the control of monopoly and in that connection the extension, at all events for some time into peace, of the existing controls. Personally I think they will have to be continued on purely practical grounds, quite apart from any ideological preconceptions on the part of anyone. That is the view which Morrison put forward freely.

There has been a contest in the Party between Greenwood and Morrison for the Treasurership of the Party, in which Greenwood has been successful, though Morrison seems to hold a higher place at present in the public esteem, but he is not perhaps as well-liked as Greenwood in the Party, or considered so 'sound' from the Labour standpoint. Personally, I think he is very sound.

June 24. During the week we have had in the House of Lords a small but useful Bill dealing with Old Age Pensions, upon which I delivered myself of some observations, with which I was rather pleased because they seemed to go quite well, although they were not long, perhaps partly because of that, and it was another bit of practice in speaking spontaneously without notes. One gets rather into the habit of relying too much upon notes, and I think it is a good thing to speak without them when the opportunity arises.

Last evening we went to a show organized by the Labour Party in Central Wandsworth. It was at the Wandsworth Technical Institute. The last time I spoke in that hall was before the war and I remember very well that, ironically enough, it was at a meeting in support of the League of Nations. There were about 150 people there last night, I should think. There were half a dozen speeches, at least four too many, sweetened by a certain amount of choral singing and a violinist drawn from the membership, not too bad.

I spoke for about ten minutes on the change in the situation from the days when I was actively concerned as their M.P. I told them something about the Labour Party Conference, pressing the view, which received warm approbation, that after the war we should have nothing to do with the Coalition, but, win or fail, the Party must stand on its own feet. The best speech of the evening was made by George Tomlinson, Parliamentary Secretary to the Minister of Labour. He is a Lancashire man and a Trade Unionist, the Secretary of a Cotton Weavers' Union. It was remarkably humorous, made all the more so by the fact that he has a very broad Lancashire accent. His best phrase, I think, was that three years ago after Dunkirk all we could do was to pray. It is good to pray, but better to watch and pray, but best of all is to work and watch and pray. Our release from extreme danger after Dunkirk was providential, but Providence needs a helping hand and that is what we are giving.

He also paid a warm tribute to Ernest Bevin, as I had done previously. In fact, as I said, I think Ernest Bevin has done a very remarkable bit of work. Nobody but a man with Trade Union experience and a strong character could have done the job that he has had to do. When you come to think of the fact, it is amazing that in spite of the fact that his directing finger has pointed at almost everyone in the community and has dislocated millions of lives and homes, he nevertheless holds firmly the public confidence. The two people who have interfered most with the domestic life of the people are Bevin and Woolton* and it is a very remarkable thing that they are both looked upon as being perhaps the two most competent members of the Government. It is also a tremendous tribute to the British people that they recognize strong and firm and fair government when they see it, however harshly it may affect them individually.

July 6. When I wrote to you last, I told you that I was going to take Mummy's place and speak to the Women's Section in Central Wandsworth. I had a very pleasant meeting. It was the first time I had spoken there for a very long time. I did not know what to speak about, so on the spur of the moment I selected the House of Lords. I was a little doubtful as to how this would go down because there is a sort of inhibition in Labour circles generally with regard to the House of Lords. However, it went down very well indeed and I believe I left them with the impression, which it was my object to convey, that the House of Lords is performing a really valuable

* Lord Woolton had been Minister of Food since April, 1940.

service in the public interest, though the House of Commons is and must always remain sovereign and though (although I do not suppose you will be particularly pleased to hear this) I do not believe in the hereditary principle as far as legislators are concerned. It is one thing that a title should pass from father to son, though I feel that that is a little difficult to justify, at all events through an indefinite number of generations; but it seems to me impossible to justify the maintenance of a position in which a son, whether he has the qualifications or not, gets automatically a seat in the Legislature merely by reason of the fact that he is his father's son. My audience was, I think, much impressed; indeed they all expressed a wish to come and see the House of Lords in actual operation, but having regard to the limitations upon our space I had to say I could only manage a handful. . . .

I spent last Thursday night on the very uncomfortable sofa in Lord Addison's room in the House of Lords, fire-watching. It was fortunately a quiet night.

2

Nathan's comments on persons and events during this period, as reflected in his letters to his son, were shrewd as well as informative, and it is tempting to quote from them at length. For instance, there was Anthony Eden, the future Conservative Prime Minister, later Earl of Avon, and the speech he made at a mass meeting in the Albert Hall in honour of China and the completion of six years of the Sino-Japanese war. Eden was then Foreign Secretary. 'It is very curious about Anthony Eden,' remarked Nathan: 'he has a very good record; he is extremely good in personal contacts, I should think pretty resilient and resourceful as a negotiator; he is *en rapport* with the House of Commons; but I have never heard him make a public speech which was significant, either for its manner, substance or phrasing. Though I suppose that he would be the next Tory Prime Minister, I feel that doubts are increasing as to whether he is really of the stuff of which Prime Ministers are made. Certainly on this occasion his speech fell entirely flat.'

On another occasion, Nathan had an appointment with Attlee, then Deputy Prime Minister as well as leader of the Labour Party, in the Cabinet Offices. On his way there the air raid siren sounded, and when Nathan arrived he was told that he was wanted at No. 11 Downing Street, which Attlee occupied. 'I then proceeded to Downing Street in the face of some gunfire, though not too much, and when I arrived there was told "they have all gone down to the shelter under No. 10".' Nathan followed, hoping to find Winston Churchill there but did not. 'I found myself in a quite comfortable shelter along with the Deputy Prime Minister, with whom I had a very pleasant talk during the currency of the raid, after which we went to his room in No. 11 and had a cup of tea and a biscuit! It is an experience not to be forgotten to have spent an air raid in a shelter under No. 10, don't you think?'

July 26, 1943. Mummy and I dined with some people with a flat at 55 Park Lane. ... There we met two Frenchmen, one in the French Air Force and the other in the French Army, both of whom had recently come from France, one with false papers, and without too much difficulty, the other having to walk across the Pyrenees and having a pretty thin time in Spain. They were both, particularly the Army officer, in the underground movement in France, which, from what they told me, is far more organized than I had previously imagined, though I gathered from André Philip that there was quite a fair amount of cohesion. The fact that so many of the young men have been taken away on forced labour is, of course, an adverse factor, and the shortage of food has meant a real deterioration in health and strength. Babies in particular are born very weak, and so great is the shortage of ordinary domestic necessaries that the newly-born child is not wrapped in a towel or blanket but in a newspaper. T.B. is pretty rife, and the general debility may affect the physical fighting strength, but not the moral fighting strength. De Gaullism is generally a real force in France, widely spread, and is the cement which holds all the elements of the underground movement together. De Gaullism, however, is something bigger than and not necessarily identified with the personality of de Gaulle himself. It indicates the resistance movement rather than adherence to de Gaulle personally. That is rather important, because, with the inter-play of personalities, it is vital to have some cohesive force for the movement outside and beyond a particular person.

There is no doubt, I think, that de Gaulle, whom I have met and have had talks with on a number of occasions, is a very remarkable fellow. If he had not had the initiative and public spirit to set himself up at once as a rallying point for French-men outside France and for those who might escape, it may very well be that an underground movement for resistance would never have got on its feet. France and the United Nations owe him an enormous debt of gratitude. He has made a real contribution to world history. On the other hand, I think he has, or at all events at the beginning had, a rather rigid mind of an authoritarian complexion, and, whilst certainly a Radical as a soldier, he seems to have been rather reactionary as a politician; in fact, he probably did not know much about politics at all, and a military training naturally lends itself to authoritarianism.

During the latter part of the summer and autumn Nathan was laid up with a bad attack of sciatica which necessitated hospital treatment and he chafed at the consequent enforced inactivity. He spent some time recuperating in the New Forest, where he had a succession of visitors, including his daughter Joyce, who had just become engaged to Bernard Waley-Cohen, elder son of Sir Robert Waley-Cohen, managing director of the Shell Transport and Trading Company.

> *November 8.* Last Monday Mummy was here. She left on Tuesday morning to attend an L.C.C. meeting at which the White Paper on Education was under discussion. Tomorrow (Tuesday) she returns to me here till Friday. On Saturday Joyce and Bernard come till Monday evening, and also the Tyermans, husband and wife. He is acting Editor of *The Economist* and he has recently been appointed Political Editor of *The Observer*. They stop till next Tuesday evening, when Lord and Lady Addison come on the Friday, to be followed by Mummy again on the Saturday. So you see I am not much alone.
>
> Indeed, that is not the whole of the story, for this (Monday)

afternoon Lord Snell has left me after being here since Friday. He is a marvellous old boy, 77 years old, began life in an agricultural village in Nottinghamshire as a farm boy; today he is President of the University College of Nottingham, Deputy Leader of the House of Lords, and in that capacity, by a strange irony, Captain of the King's Bodyguard, a curious job for one who has all his life been in the vanguard of Socialist thought and practice. He is a grand fellow: broadminded, sound judgment, widely read, eloquent with a true literary flavour, deeply cultured, widely respected: in short, one of the most distinguished Englishmen of our time—a real tribute to the virtues of our own particular brand of democracy. . . .

Nathan greatly admired old Lord Snell, who died a few months later. 'Although he was a non-believer,' Nathan wrote on this occasion, 'he was a truly religious man. He was entirely selfless and devoted to the public good. I do not believe he had an enemy in the world, and he had many warm friends. Although he was a Rationalist and would have been amazed to have thought a Memorial Service would have been held for him in Westminster Abbey, yet so it was, and the Dean himself insisted upon there being a Memorial Service for the man whom he described, so it is reported, as the best Christian he had known.'

There is one rather disconcerting factor arising out of my illness. The Prime Minister is generally understood to be contemplating drastic reconstruction of Cabinet and of the Government generally including, it is rumoured, the disappearance of John Simon from the Woolsack (time will show). I don't know whether he proposed to appoint any Labour peer to the Government Bench. Snell is the only Labour peer now holding any office, and the opinion is held in some quarters that we ought to have at least one more peer in the Government. It may be—who can say?—that I might have had a chance, but I fear that this unfortunate illness of mine, which has involved, in effect, my absence from the House since early August, will, apart from any other reason, have put me quite out of court. Heaven knows whether or when another opportunity may occur again, so it looks very much as if an honourable ambition held and pursued since boyhood is unlikely to be fulfilled. After

all, there comes a time when it is too late to start what in substance is a new career.*

Joyce Nathan and her fiancé Bernard Waley-Cohen were
married in the New West End Synagogue on December 21, 1943,
shortly before the bride's twenty-fourth birthday. The union of
two well-known Jewish families meant that it was a big wedding,
to which over a thousand guests were invited. The bride and
bridegroom were both working as temporary civil servants in the
Ministry of Fuel and Power, so that it was appropriate that their
health should have been proposed by Sir Ernest Gowers, an old
family friend. In doing so, he unintentionally raised a laugh when
he said that he had been responsible for the bride's 'make up', so
that he had to explain that he meant not the make up of her face for
the wedding but her intellectual and moral make-up.

January 24, 1944. I saw Gilbert Frankau during the week.
He told me how very much impressed he himself had been by
the wedding. I had not seen him since then. It had made quite
an uncanny impression upon him, and indeed it is remarkable
from the letters we have had and the things we have heard,
first hand and second hand, the impression which this particular ceremony seems to have created. Everybody, even those
who had never been in contact with Jews before, was saying
that they wished they could have been married or their
daughters might be at a wedding which was as impressive as
this particular one. I must say that this was all very gratifying,
as I have not generally found these weddings impressive, although, as I think I told you, I did think this one was.

Anyhow, Frankau was so much struck by it that he said that
in the middle of the Service he got his theme for a new novel!
A Jew leaves the Jewish community, but after many years his
daughter becomes engaged to a member of the Jewish community and marries him, and he, the father, returns to the
Synagogue after a lifetime of absence and estrangement, in

---

* There was a minor reshuffle in which Lord Woolton, who had become
Minister of Reconstruction, entered the War Cabinet, and Lord Strabolgi
was promoted to the Front Bench in the House of Lords. Simon stayed on as
Lord Chancellor.

order to give his daughter away at her wedding. There is plenty of room for a psychological study here, and when I told Joyce (at a dinner at Kettner's on her birthday, after going to the Palace Theatre to see Cicely Courtneidge and Jack Hulbert's latest show), she said that it is something to feel that your wedding has inspired the plot of a new novel by a well-known writer!

'Gilbert Frankau is the only man I know who has had three wives and is keeping them all at the same time,' Nathan remarked in another letter. 'No wonder he has to work hard turning out books with little relaxation!'

At this time Nathan was much exercised in his mind about the future of Palestine and the relations between the Jews and the Arabs, since owing to Arab pressure Jewish immigration had been halted and Britain had abandoned the Balfour Declaration after twenty years of attempting to reconcile the irreconcilable. Nathan did not feel as indignant as might perhaps have been expected over Britain's broken promises had he been a more ardent Zionist.

One evening we had Dr and Mrs Weizmann to dinner and Joyce and Bernard were there too. He is an extraordinarily interesting fellow, quite the biggest man in Jewish affairs, but I think a disappointed man because nothing has gone as it was hoped. He is always well worth meeting and I think both Joyce and Bernard felt that they had met a really big man. There are not so many men who are built on the large monumental scale: Lloyd George is one of them and Winston another, and so was Lord Lothian. Weizmann is one of this limited class. The others were, on the whole, more virile in their attitude towards life, and perhaps Weizmann has fallen down a little by having something of a feminine rather than a masculine kind of mind. Anyhow there is no doubt that the intrinsic difficulties of the whole Palestine situation are enormous and I do not see any easy solution. . . .

I have always felt that it is in truth rather a far-fetched suggestion that the Jews, who left Palestine 2,000 years ago, are returning to their 'national home'. I clearly see that it is desirable that there should be a place of refuge for Jews who are unable to find suitable living conditions elsewhere and it may well be that Palestine is the natural and most suitable place for that purpose. Indeed, there is no doubt that the Jews who have settled in Palestine during the past 20 years or so have done a most magnificent piece of constructive work. The troubles have not been made by them, but by the 'politicians' and theorists. If the Jews who are doing the work were left alone, the problem would largely solve itself, especially as the influx of Jewish manpower and capital resources into Palestine has greatly improved the whole economic structure of the country, and perhaps most of all has vastly raised the conditions and standards of living of the indigenous Arab population. But there is no getting over the fact that, if the Jews have been out of Palestine for 2,000 years, the Arabs have been there for 2,000 years, and the Arab claim to Palestine is not one which can lightly be set on one side. They again have been bedevilled by the political standard-bearers of a United Arabia.

It must, however, be remembered that in the last War, as a deliberate act of policy on the part of the Allied and associated Powers, Palestine was offered to the Jews as a 'national home', if not in the political sense, at least in the sense that they could enter that country and settle there, not on sufferance, but as of right. That itself was a very great advance, and undoubtedly met many deep-felt Jewish aspirations. Weizmann has continually announced it as Jewish policy that the Jews do not wish to dominate the Arabs, though on the other hand they would not consent to be dominated by them. Against that, the British people, instructed by centuries of democratic organization, believe in majority rule. Indeed, was it not Disraeli who said, that no matter how good your arguments, what matters is the big battalions? And there is no doubt that the Arab population of Palestine is largely in excess of the Jewish. Compulsory transmigration does not seem to me a practicable proposition, and the Jews will not accept under any Constitution the position of a legalized minority. That is where the impasse comes.

There is talk of an Arab Federation or a Greater Syria, with a Jewish Palestine as a unit of such a Federation, but I have never really known what people mean by the term 'a Jewish State'. One of the great difficulties is that the Palestine which was in mind when the Balfour Declaration was made is a

different Palestine in its geographical frontiers from the Palestine to which the Mandate applies, because Transjordan was
cut off from the Palestine of the Balfour Declaration, thus
greatly limiting the area to which the Mandate applied and
therefore the boundaries within which, whilst still remaining
in their own Palestine, Arabs might find new homes and Jews
might settle.

Somehow or other, we have got to get this Arab–Jewish
problem settled by agreement; otherwise it will be settled over
everybody's head, perhaps by force of circumstances and not
in the least appropriate way. Weizmann is working very hard,
but, as I have told you before, he is really a disappointed and
very frustrated man. His world has fallen to pieces before his
eyes.

Nathan was now faced with the problem of finding new offices
for his law firm, since the landlord of the offices in Norfolk Street
wanted them back. 'It is a staggering misfortune that we have to
leave here,' Nathan wrote to his son. After a considerable search,
he and his senior partner eventually found other premises to which
they moved in 1944.

We have decided, having regard to the nature of the practice, not to go to the West End, but to return to the City.
There the destruction of so many offices has greatly diminished the space available, while a good many firms are optimistically inclined, like our landlords here, and are contemplating returning to their old haunts and accordingly will not
let their empty offices. I think, however, we may have found
some accommodation in Copthall Avenue, right in the heart of
the City. It is rather dark and the offices will be rather scattered
and on more than one floor, but on the whole it will not, I
think, be too bad, though it is a tremendous come-down from
Finsbury Square and also from here. They are certainly not the
offices we should choose if we had a choice, but, alas and alack,
we have not.

Mr Oppenheimer and I, like great twin brethren, are going
to have adjacent rooms. They are quite largish, but they look
out, at eight feet distant from the window, on a blank white-
glazed wall, and the rooms are so far from the top of the

building—they are on the first floor—that one cannot even get a glimpse of the sky, try as one will. It is a tremendous contrast from here, and indeed from Finsbury Square. It is true that I did not have much of a view from my room at Finsbury Square, but there was plenty of air about. It was a corner building and had Finsbury Square itself in front and the H.A.C. Parade Ground in the rear. It so happened that my room was not very well placed for a view, though I never felt any lack of air. What I shall do in the new offices I do not know.

Here I have been most happily placed, with a glorious view of the river and I shall greatly miss it, more especially as the iron bridge which shrouded the new Waterloo Bridge has now been taken away (designed, I believe, for Addis Ababa). It has left revealed the new Waterloo Bridge, which is quite shatteringly beautiful, entirely breath-taking, Rennie was a wonder-worker; Giles Scott has him beaten to a frazzle. . . . It is the air which I shall miss, and the constant movement on the river, and the quite extraordinary beauty of the shifting lights of riverside London, and especially when the mist in the early morning or evening makes Old London look like fairyland. However, said he, heaving a sigh, there it is, but what a fall, my countrymen!

3

From the Peers' Gallery in the House of Commons, Nathan heard the Prime Minister report to the Members on the opening of the Second Front with the invasion of Normandy in June, 1944, 'informing them that so far all had gone well, and indeed well beyond anticipation. He seemed, I thought, rather tired, but then he is getting an oldish man now. I sat between Woolton and Margesson. . . . I had earlier in the day followed Woolton, who as Minister of Reconstruction had opened the debate on the Education Bill. Butler, the responsible Minister, had a very uncomfortable seat on the steps of the Throne.'

That Whitsun Nathan and his wife spent their first week-end at Churt for more than two years.

Being rather short of things and just being by ourselves, we thought we would invite ourselves to tea with L[loyd] G[eorge], but he and Mrs L. G. (the former Miss Stevenson) responded by saying that they would prefer to come to us, so instead of having a quiet morning and then going off quietly after lunch to tea with the L. G.s Mummy had to set to and make cakes. She produced a marvellous sandwich cake and some little Madeira cakes, which went down like the Grace of God. I had not seen L. G. for upwards of 18 months. . . . He walks with a less firm step. That marvellous head of white hair, so vivid and alive, has now lost its gloss and life, and he has got rather thinner, but he still has the piercing eye and the magic voice and the fascinating laugh, and though he speaks slower, and I observed thinks slower, he is full of interest in what is going on.

He does not often go to the House now. He went the other day when Winston was going to make an important speech on foreign affairs. Apparently the old man, Father of the House, received a special cheer from Members. He told me that he was quite taken by surprise. He had not expected anything of the sort and it was 'so kind of them'. I thought that was rather nice of the old boy, who after all was the dominating figure in Parliament for so long.

Among other subjects, Nathan was interested in the future of Anglo-American relations. In August, 1944, he attended a meeting of the British Group of the Inter-Parliamentary Union in the House of Lords—he was a member of the Executive Committee— to hear Lord Halifax, who was on leave from the Washington Embassy. 'He really seems very little different now after a pretty long absence from what he was before,' wrote Nathan; 'a very simple, straight, honest, decent fellow, and he seems to have had rather a success in the United States, though he started rather badly and had to compete with the high reputation which Lord Lothian had achieved.'

I am not at all sure that one of the most formidable problems as between the United States and ourselves, with which we may be confronted after the War, may not be difficult discussions not as between Governments but individuals, as to the relative contributions made by our two countries to winning the War. Even after the last War, which they entered so late and with such light casualties, the Americans established a tradition among themselves that they had won the war, a tradition for which there was no solid foundation of any kind, although their help, somewhat belated, was most highly welcome at a critical moment. This time their contribution has been both on the Atlantic and the Pacific fronts a great deal more substantial, and both of a negative and of a positive character, negative in the sense that whilst not actively contributing towards the fighting forces they were providing much material and sustenance through lease-lend, and positive by the very large forces which they have furnished in the battle fronts in the two zones.

It is sometimes annoying to see in the newspapers so much reference to American troops, Canadian troops, Australian troops, Polish, Czech and other Allies, to say nothing of the Russians, who have done so marvellously, but all too little reference to British troops and the British contribution to the War, both in the industrial and economic sphere as well as in the three elements. I do not denigrate in any degree what others have done, but it does seem to me shameful that even our own reporters from the Front and our own newspapers should give so little prominence to what the British have done and are doing, and so much to what has been and is being done by others. All this I fear may have a political repercussion after the War, and it will be widely felt in other parts of the world that we have done precious little, and they will point to our contemporary newspapers as supporting evidence.

The plain truth of the matter is that the effort of this country, both martial and industrial, has been quite stupendous, and proportionately to our population the greatest of any of the allied nations. But how many are there who realize that? Few I fear indeed, and it is largely our own fault. I am pretty certain that one of our prime tasks for the future must be to make it clear how large is the contribution we have made to the War, and how tremendous have been our sacrifices compared with other people's. The plain fact of the matter is, of course, that neither Russia nor the United States came into the War until they got pretty heavy kicks on the backside, and if they hadn't had those kicks on the backside it is very doubtful whether either would have come in. We, on the other hand, had no kicks on the backside, but entered the War in one sense in complete altruism, although I must confess that it was to our own national interests to do so; but it was actually in fulfilment of a pledge given to a small nation which we could not even reach physically. I think we have a splendid record in all these matters, and it is painful to reflect on how little it is appreciated by other people who are so much better at advertising than we are. We shall have to employ some American publicity agents to put Britain over!

Towards the end of 1944, Nathan was shocked to read in the newspapers of the death of Philip Guedalla, then serving in the R.A.F., since he regarded him as his 'earliest friend' from the days in North Kensington when they used to play together as children.

I had not seen a tremendous amount of him of recent years because our paths diverged. The last time I actually met him was after he had returned from his 20,000 mile trip to the Middle East as a Squadron-Leader, when he came to lunch with me to meet President Benes, and the last time I heard from him was when, a few months ago, I heard from him asking me to a meal, but I could not accept because I was then having one of my illnesses. He was just my own age within a few weeks.

He has written some brilliant books, although whether he has made a permanent name as a historian time alone can show. I think his principal works which have any chance of a continued life are his *Palmerston* and his biography of Wellington. He had great political ambitions in the Liberal Party and stood as a candidate on five occasions without success in any. I always thought it unlikely that he would be successful as a candidate because he was rather exotic in appearance and manner and a little sarcastic and recondite in speech, but if he had been elected to Parliament I think he would have put up a very good show.

I went to the Memorial Service [at the Spanish and Portuguese Synagogue], where there were a number of interesting people like Rose Macaulay and Victor Gollancz, the latter of whom is very active now in political circles and I think contemplates standing for Parliament as a Labour candidate.

A fortnight later there appeared the news in the New Year Honours for 1945 that Lloyd George had been created an Earl.

A good many people feel an affectionate regret that he has not remained to the end the Great Commoner. On the other hand, there are many precedents for a former Prime Minister taking an Earldom. He is by tradition entitled to that honour if he cares to claim it. Disraeli, of course, became an Earl and so did Balfour and Asquith. Mr Gladstone, on the other hand, never took a peerage, but remained just 'Mr Gladstone' to the end. I do not quite know what the factors were which influenced Mr Lloyd George's mind, but he must have been affected by the fact that this was something which he could do for his wife. I doubt very much whether at 82 and no longer in robust health he is likely to take any active part in the proceedings of the House of Lords. I have told you previously that they came to see me at Churt when I was convalescing. It was obvious from what he said to me at the time that he had the possibility of taking an Earldom in his mind, but I did not know, of course, whether he was going to pursue the matter seriously.

Anyhow, the occasion of his leaving his constituency, which he has represented for well over 50 years, was marked by articles on his career in most of the newspapers. They were almost in the nature of obituary notices. It is not often that a man has a chance of reading articles of that kind about his life and achievements. 'Lord Lloyd George' does not sound very euphonious to me and I am quite certain that he will go down to history—for go down to history he certainly will as one of the greatest of our Prime Ministers—just as 'Mr Lloyd George'.

Lord Lloyd George did not live long to enjoy his honour. Less than four months after its announcement he was dead. It fell to Nathan, in the absence of Lord Addison, to speak the customary tribute in the House of Lords on behalf of the Labour Party. ('It was a difficult job, and I am not very satisfied with the effort, but there it is—I did the best I could.') To his son he was able to write more freely.

For almost the whole of the twenty years we were neighbours. I was the recipient to a quite exceptional degree of his friendship, and confidence: for several years I was very much his 'blue-eyed boy'—and I knew him really well. To be in his presence was to know that you were in the presence of greatness—greatness without trappings. There was nothing about him of pomposity or pomp. He lived, as you know, quite simply. In his home there was nothing marking out very particularly that it was the home of a most remarkable world figure. True, he had in his sitting-room some of the caskets containing the scrolls bestowing on him the Freedom of many cities, and that he had about him photographs of old colleagues and friends, such as Wilson, Clemenceau, Foch, Asquith, Milner, Balfour and Bonar Law; but it was not these, it was not even the autographed photographs of King George and Queen Mary, that had the place of honour in his home. In the place of honour, he had hung the portrait of an austere-looking bewhiskered old man, his uncle, the village cobbler, who had brought him up from childhood, and of whom I never heard him speak save in words of tenderest affection and indeed reverence. . . .

He had the peculiar quality of making those with him feel better, more confident men than they probably were in fact. He admired above all courage, vision, drive and resourcefulness, and he himself was the exemplar of all these qualities. I never went to see him feeling a bit 'down' on personal or public matters, but I came away refreshed and reinvigorated with a restored courage and a new optimism. People have often spoken of his 'magnetism'; there was magnetism and, consciously or unconsciously, he could exercise it with equal ease over the public or the individual. I have seen him sway great audiences at will: I have seen him turn hostility in private persons into devotion.

His crucial error was not to have resigned after the last War, an error which, despite the example, Winston looks very like repeating. He often told me—though perhaps it was not the whole of the truth—that he had wanted to resign, but those around him said: 'Prime Minister, you can't resign; the country needs you now more than ever; you have got the country through the perils of war—only you can now pull her through the perils of peace. It's your duty to carry on.' And then he would go on to say: 'But they weren't really thinking of the country—they weren't really thinking of me—they were thinking of *themselves*; for if *I* went *they* went.' But he allowed himself to be deceived at the time and it was his undoing. I can see history repeating itself in the not too-distant future and under very much the same circumstances.

When I first knew him, he had fairly recently ceased to be Prime Minister—his mind was on the preparation of new policies for Britain and the reintegration of the Liberal Party. But the chasm was too deep—try as he would, the old enmities persisted, not so much arising out of differences in policy as out of personal hostility, on the part of those displaced in 1916— they never forgave.

Yet the country owes much to L. G. for his work after the War, which led to the Liberal Yellow Book (in which I had a part, albeit a small part) and the pamphlet, *We Can Conquer Unemployment*, with which, again, I was concerned, and which was the central feature of the 1929 General Election. It is noteworthy that now, years later, the policies for which L. G. was then responsible, and for putting forward he incurred every kind of contumely, are the politics which the Conservatives (a little less) and the Labour Party (a little more) are putting forward for the coming General Election. The Government's White Paper on Full Employment is scarcely more than a gloss in Treasury English on the 1929 pamphlet *We Can Conquer Unemployment*.

It is difficult for my generation to think of L. G. as dead: it is difficult perhaps for me. The last time he came here (Churt), I said to Mummy that we should never see him again. The step that has been so long and swift was a little halting now, the vivid white hair was a little less vivid, almost yellowing with age, but the head (the finest I have known save perhaps only C. P. Scott's of the *Manchester Guardian*) had all its beauty and grandeur, the eye that had so truly reflected the turbulent spirit within had acquired serenity, the deep-throated gurgling chuckle had become a rather tired and wistful smile, the magic voice had gained a new gentleness, though it remained as clear as ever and had lost none of its sweetness: L. G. was an old man, and when we shook hands to say 'good-bye' I felt it was indeed 'good-bye'.

It is difficult to appraise him. That he was one of the world's great men History will no doubt declare. Indeed one of the greatest. That he matches where he does not surpass the greatest names in English History, almost all agree. I think myself that the true measure of his greatness may be found in a comparison with Churchill. Churchill is without doubt a very great man: he is an outstanding leader of men. But with Churchill war—this War and the last War—is his life. Take away these two Wars and what have you? With L. G., who dominated the world as Churchill never has, who was in the last War all, and more than all, that Roosevelt or Stalin (or the two together) have been in this, the War was but an episode. Men will long argue whether his true greatness arose because of his leadership of the People in War or his earlier leadership of the People in Peace: either would have gained him the accolade of greatness: together they are incomparable. . . .

He lies where he wished to lie, 'washed by the river, warmed by the suns of home'. He might, of course, have been buried in Westminster Abbey: he chose otherwise. . . .

Scarcely was this over when we were all shocked to hear of Roosevelt's death. A great shudder went through the nation. The blow was as shattering as it was sudden. I have never seen people so moved by the death of any public figure overseas. Both in the Press and in Parliament, parallels have been drawn between Roosevelt and Lloyd George: more nearly than anyone Roosevelt in this War has been to the peoples of the world what Lloyd George was in the last. He personified the virtues of the common people, and voiced their hopes and aspirations. Like L. G., but in the face of harsh physical disability, he was a man of boundless courage and uncanny insight and immense strength of will. He wanted 'the right things' and it will be more difficult to attain them now that he is gone: that is the pervading thought in all men's minds. L. G. (who certainly wanted 'the right things'), when upbraided about some of the terms of the Versailles Treaty, used to reply, speaking of Wilson and Clemenceau, 'But what could I do, with a man on one side of me who thought he was Jesus Christ, and a man on the other who thought he was Napoleon?'

4

Nathan paid a short visit to Paris at this time in order to see a client, Lady Mond, the elderly French widow of Sir Robert Mond. He had continued to look after her affairs since the fall of France, but, of course, without being able to tell her what he was doing or had done. When they met, the first time for five years, she had some amazing experiences to recount. Her château at Dinard was successively the Headquarters of the German Generals Von Paulus and Rommel, while her house and farm elsewhere in Brittany had also been requisitioned by the Germans, who had billetted 400 men there ('Some house!' remarked Nathan), while she herself had been relegated to a couple of rooms in one of the farm buildings.

April 20, 1945. By birth she is, as I think you know, French, and has a house—as well as the Château at Dinard and the flat in Paris—at Belle-Isle-en-Terre in Brittany, where she was born and all her home folk live. In the early days of the invasion of France, she was in Dinard and the last communication I had from her was one Sunday when we were at Churt; suddenly the telephone rang and there was Lady Mond speaking from Dinard, telling me that she had heard that the enemy were approaching Paris and should she try to get there before them to bring away her '*précieuses*' from Paris? Naturally I had to tell her that from here it was quite impossible to judge the situation, and I often wondered what had happened.

When the evacuation took place, she had the chance, as a British subject (by her marriage to Sir Robert), to get away to England, but, courageously I think, she refused it, preferring to remain with and be helpful to her own people at her home. After the over-running of France, the first I heard of her, and it was purely negative, was a telegram from a nephew-in-law in Bordeaux, asking if I had heard and could tell him anything of his aunt (Lady Mond) or his wife and child. But I had no information, and except for a few Red Cross messages, which each time took many months from the time I sent mine off till I received the reply, I had no direct communication with her until Paris was freed, when she immediately wrote to me—but she couldn't of course tell much in a letter.

From what I heard from various sources while in Paris, the occupying Germans were very 'patchy' in their behaviour. In some places their conduct was entirely 'correct'; in others indescribable. It depended not only on where they were, but who they were. The ordinary soldiery do not on the whole seem to have been anything like as bad as the Gestapo and the S.S., who were everywhere abominable.

Lady Mond always had Germans not only billeted in her large house, but also quartered in the small one, into which she had removed herself. Whoever they were, she called them, indiscriminately, Fritz. Fritz used to be fairly assertive and demanding. If the electric light went off—as on occasion it did—Fritz would come to her and ask her to have it put right. She would reply, rather courageously I think, that as they had commandeered the house, they must get it put right: 'I'm not an electrical engineer.' When the water gave out, because something had gone wrong with the well, and Fritz came to ask her to see that water was forthcoming, she replied: 'I'm not a spring.' This answer, 'I'm not a spring,' seems to have gone the rounds of Brittany as a good joke and aroused admiration for her boldness. On one occasion they brought her before the 'Beak'—I'm not quite sure what for—and she was sentenced to four months' imprisonment, but on the doctor's certifying that that would be the death of her *and* on her paying 200,000 francs, the sentence was remitted.

Later, however, she was less fortunate. This time she was actually sent by the Gestapo to prison. She had to share a cell with three or four others—with a urinal in the corner—only cold water to wash in and not much of that, and had to sleep in what she described to me as the drawer of a chest of drawers! Not very amusing for an old lady of 75, rather ailing, and used to all the comforts of wealth. And she had to exercise so many kilometres a day in the restricted prison yard. Somehow or other—I don't understand how or why—she seems to have been allowed to have food brought in, so in that respect she did not fare too badly. She says that the janitor in this instance was not an altogether bad fellow, unlike some of his comrades.

Apparently the worst thing was to have to listen to the cries and shrieks of those who were elsewhere in the prison under torture, and then to see them brought back along the corridor shattered, even if alive. The Nazis were, some of them so brutal in the neighbourhood that, for instance, passers-by along the road had observed some movement of the soil along the verge, and then discovered it to be the feeble motions of a hand. They set to work to dig, and discovered a pit with 17 bodies in it some of whom had been buried still alive. The tales she had to tell from her own experience bear all too close a family resemblance to the horrors of Buchenwald, Belsen and the rest, which are now being disclosed in the Press and which this weekend a Delegation from Parliament has gone off to see for themselves. They are unspeakable—these Huns—and have done the unforgivable things.

Ultimately one evening they told the old lady that next day she was to be moved from the prison. Not unnaturally she thought she was going to be deported to Germany and that it was all U.P. with her—but in the end they said they were going to release her (she doesn't to this day know why) and where would she like to go? She answered, 'Home to Belle-Isle,' but they told her she was much too formidable to be allowed to return home there, but could be taken elsewhere if she would say where. So she said Paris. She was taken there under guard of two S.S. men, and ultimately deposited in her flat—where she at once retired to bed (small blame to her!) from which she resolutely refused to budge until, a few weeks later, Paris was liberated!

The remarkable thing about the flat was that it had been left absolutely *untouched*: everything was there as it had been when I was last there in April, 1940, and when I went in at the front door five years later it was as if I was back again in April, 1940 —everything just the same. Doubtless this was, partly at least, due to the fact that she had a maid and her husband living there throughout, so that the flat was never empty. But the Germans (17 of them) were billeted in the flat above, and Lady Mond asked me to imagine (as I easily could) what it felt like to be listening to the B.B.C. surreptitiously each night, with Germans in the room above. For to be discovered would in all likelihood have meant out of bed and back to gaol. However, she said the risk was worth it, for she simply *had* to hear the news and the B.B.C. was the only source that could be trusted.

During these five long years, her family and friends in London had naturally been worrying about her and imagined that she knowing of the bombing, etc., in London, would equally have been worrying about them. Not a bit of it! When I said, 'You must have been very anxious about all of us in London,' her reply was: 'I'm bound to confess that I never thought about you at all. I was much too busy trying to keep alive and hold my end up here.' That I think, is an indication in some degree of the kind of experiences which she must have had.

However, she has come through it all now, not too bad in health and in tolerable good spirits, and with her indomitable courage and power unabated—a very remarkable personality.

Nathan was very well treated as Lady Mond's guest, with a suite consisting of a bedroom, sitting room and bathroom to himself. 'As she has five servants, I was well cared for,' he noted. 'Owing to the fact that the French have been nothing like fully mobilized either for the Forces or for industry, there is no dearth of domestic help, so markedly different from us at home!' He was also well served in the matter of food, since his hostess was able to have things like chickens, cream, eggs and butter sent up from her farm in Brittany. 'So there was plenty to eat at the flat, and very good it was. Also a fair modicum of wine, for her pre-war cellar was untouched.' On the other hand, there was a real shortage of food for many people, in spite of a flourishing black market. 'Even pretty well-off people, like a prosperous lawyer I met, may not have had meat for three weeks, and milk is practically unobtainable, even for babies. . . . It is not so much that, regarded globally, there is not enough food in France—French agriculture is probably more prosperous than ever—as there is not sufficient means of shifting the food from the place where it is produced to where it is needed for consumption.' The only time he went out for a meal was to the British Embassy when the Ambassador, Duff Cooper, invited him to lunch. 'We had a very simple lunch at a small round table in the corner of the Embassy dining-room waited on by two Tommies. The high note of the lunch was some Brie cheese—which I had not seen since 1939!'

The Embassy itself was entirely untouched and similarly the gorgeous Rothschild mansion next door.

I was only in Paris for three days, so I did not have much chance of a real look round. I was much impressed, however, by the fact that to all outward observance Paris (by which I mean the central parts which the visitor usually knows best) is almost completely untouched. On a spring day, with a blue sky and a shining sun, Paris has always seemed to shimmer in the light, and with its dignified buildings and broad boulevards, and spacious public gardens and squares, is in such a light extraordinarily beautiful. So it was on this occasion—scarcely a stone displaced or a window broken—so very different from poor old London as to give one a sensation of shocked surprise, and with the shops displaying quite a variety of goods of one kind and another. The streets were very full of people, and there was a good deal of motor traffic, not much less, if at all, than London, but no public conveyances such as taxis, buses or trams; the only method of transport being by Metro or, very expensive, a fiacre drawn by a half-broken-down horse or a push bike with a basket-trailer arrangement for passengers. I ventured with some misgiving in a fiacre, but I refrained from the velocipede, thinking that with my weight I should break the rider's heart!

The people in the streets looked fairly well-dressed, and not unhappy; the clothes are perhaps a little drab. There is a lack of leather for shoes, so that the girls wear sabots, but the Parisienne has such a style about her that even the sabots have been made to look smart; and voices were quiet rather than boisterous, but there was no obvious sign of unhappiness—only they are all perhaps a little sombre.

5

The war in the West was almost over. A fortnight after Nathan's visit to Paris, the Germans surrendered unconditionally on all fronts. Next day—May 8, 1945, otherwise VE-day—Churchill announced the news in the House of Commons and Lord Woolton in the Lords, and the two Houses proceeded to St Margaret's Church and Westminster Abbey respectively, where they gave thanks for victory.

In our House the announcement was made by Woolton, who was leading the House in the absence of Lord Cranborne at the San Francisco Conference. So rigidly traditional is the House that, notwithstanding this momentous announcement, we had first to proceed with the ordinary routine business set out on the Order Paper for that day, e.g. the Second Reading of the Pontypool Gas Bill and other routine matters. Then when Woolton had made the formal announcement in the same terms as the Prime Minister to the Commons, he moved that the House do now adjourn during pleasure ('*ad libitum*') and proceed to the Abbey Church of Westminster, there to give thanks to Almighty God for His Majesty's Victory over the Germans. It is thus—and thus only—that this historic moment is recorded in the Journals of the House—interesting, I feel, and rather moving.

So off we went in procession, through a considerable crowd, across the road to the Abbey, where there was a large congregation. . . . The Peers sat in the Canonical Stalls; it was a most impressive Service, made more so by the emotions that flooded the mind as we reflected on all that had happened during the harsh years of war, of what might have happened, and what the event signified for us and the world. Ultimately we 'processed' back to adjourn formally for a few days, when a Vote of Congratulation was to be moved—as it was—to the King on his Victory. Some good speeches were made, but, on the whole, I felt that the occasion was too big for any speeches to be adequate to it.

The Loyal Addresses of Congratulation were presented to the King in person, who attended for the purpose, with the Queen and the Princesses in the Royal Gallery at a joint meeting of Members of the two Houses. The King, whose defect in speech is much improved, made an admirable and clearly spoken Reply, and then Winston, raising his top-hat in his hand, called for 'Three Cheers for the King and Queen'—and we cheered! How we cheered!

It was some weeks after their happening that Nathan found time to write of these events, in fact, after the General Election had taken place but before the results were declared.

There was, of course, on VE-Day, as you will have read, a great amount of celebration—vast concourses of people in the

Mall, outside the Palace, and in the main thoroughfares like Piccadilly—but the crowds were astonishingly quiet and orderly—little or no rowdyism—though there was no doubting their feeling of intense relief that at long last it was all over. The Monarch had a magnificent reception at Buckingham Palace, where with the Queen and Princesses he appeared that night and on succeeding nights on the balcony, and so did Churchill—in both cases rightly so, for both have rendered services to the Nation which are unsurpassed, and will go down gloriously in History. The Monarchy, I feel sure, is more firmly established than ever, and Churchill's name and fame will be safe with posterity, though I fear that for the moment, as the result of the Electoral struggle, it is somewhat tarnished. But in the long perspective of History that will be wholly forgotten and only his achievements will be remembered, the manner in which more than any man and in a way and to an extent quite unique he sustained the spirit of the People through unprecedented misfortunes until we could feel a measure of reassurance once more. He has been a superb Leader, and has led us from the Abyss to the Heights.

What most people enjoyed at this time more than anything else was the end of 'the blackout' and the turning on of the lights again. 'I must confess that after the habit of the last five years,' Nathan admitted, 'I still feel rather guilty when I put the light on without drawing the curtains, or when I go into a room, put on the light and find it blazing into the open. However, this is a mental attitude of mind from which it will not take long to recover. It is a curious psychological effect of all that we have been through since September, 1939.'

CHAPTER SIX

In the Government

'IT LOOKS TO ME NOW VERY MUCH LIKE A GENERAL ELECTION in July,' wrote Nathan on the eve of VE-Day; 'but I think it will be a pity, as it will smack rather too much of the 1918 Khaki Election. On the other hand, it may be thought that to wait till October is to ask too much. However, the future will in this respect soon reveal itself.' Nathan's surmise was correct. Ten days later, Churchill proposed to Attlee that either the Coalition should continue until the end of the war with Japan or else there should be an Election straight away. But Attlee, primed by the Labour Party's annual conference then in session at Blackpool, was not anxious to have a rushed Election fought on an out-of-date Electoral Register. On the other hand, he would only agree that the Coalition should go on until October and that the Election should be held then. Churchill would not have this and insisted that, if there was to be a General Election, it should be held as soon as practically possible, which was early July. The Prime Minister's Conservative colleagues and party officials wanted the Election soon, since they saw—or thought they saw—the chance of exploiting Churchill's personal popularity in the wake of the military victory in Europe as an electoral advantage. So Churchill resigned on May 23, and came back to Downing Street to form a 'caretaker' Government of Conservatives and National-Liberals, with one or two Independents like Woolton and Sir John Anderson, which was to carry on until the election results were announced two months later. Meanwhile the former inter-party battles were resumed with their old intensity. The actual date of the Election was fixed for July 5, to be followed by an interval of three weeks before the declaration of the polls so as to allow time for the services overseas to vote.

Nathan strongly criticized Churchill's conduct of the Election and what he called the 'disingenuous ultimatum' which preceded it and which he attributed, with good reason, to the pressure brought to bear on him by the Tory party.

> *July 16, 1945.* From the consultations to which I was a party before the Labour Party's Conference at Blackpool, I knew that it was the understanding that the Election was to take place in the autumn, and that the Party Leaders went to Blackpool with the idea of 'putting that over'. Churchill's ultimatum came therefore as a bombshell: there never was any real question of the Election being postponed and the Coalition being kept together till the end of the Japanese War, but only when exactly the Election should be held now that the German War was over—i.e. this side of the summer on the defective Register, or in the autumn on the new Register. The ultimatum, which in the light of what had gone before, looked like a 'slick Alick' manœuvre, instigated by Beaverbrook or one of the other 'chaps' who had so baleful an influence on Churchill, altered the whole temper on both sides in which the Election was approached. The Tories knew that an attempt was being made to put over a fast one, while the Labour and Liberal Parties thought it was cheating.
>
> The Labour Party had been determined, and had publicly announced that, as far as it was concerned, the break-up of the coalition should be dignified and in a friendly atmosphere and that the Election which would follow should be conducted soberly between two different points of view, on which the Nation must pronounce.
>
> The unfortunate atmosphere created by Churchill's ultimatum was darkened still further by his most unfortunate first broadcast. This came as a great shock to Tories no less than to the other Parties. It was wholly unworthy of the Churchill we have known during the War. He seemed to have lost all sense of balance and responsibility. In that single moment he

ceased to be the National Leader—'fallen like Lucifer, never to rise again'—and disclosed himself as a reactionary Tory, the henchman of Lord Beaverbrook. Worse, he left the impression of insincerity. For in imputing to the Labour Party motives and prophesying all kinds of fantastic results—Gestapo, risk to the people's savings, and all that—he must have known full well that he was giving currency to ideas quite alien to the whole Labour thesis and practice. This involved him, directly and indirectly, in turning savagely upon those from the Labour Party who had supported, sustained and nourished his strength.

The British people does not care much for those who turn round and bite the hand that fed them. That is what Churchill has done, and I hold no doubt that he and his Party will live to rue the day. That first broadcast of his really set the tone of the Election as far as the Tories are concerned, but I am proud to think that throughout the Labour Party refused to be drawn into that kind of wrangle and conducted the Election with a fine sense of public duty, with dignity, leaving person-alities to the other side, and themselves, like the Liberal Party, seeking the suffrages of the people on the footing of Principles, Plan, Programme.

It is only fair to the Tories to say that vast numbers of them were as shocked and disgusted by Churchill's broadcast as were the other Parties; it was difficult to believe that the great War Leader had overnight become a mere Bogey Man. Nor did he greatly improve his position in his subsequent speeches and broadcasts—it was noticeable that of the ten broadcasts allotted to his party, Churchill himself took four—apparently not trusting any Tory at the microphone save Eden (who was good) and Brendan Bracken, the others being Independent, e.g. Woolton and Anderson. Moreover he tried to conduct the campaign as if it were a fight between himself personally and the Labour Party, putting forward no programme beyond the compromise White Paper policies earlier produced by the Coalition, with an appendix of abuse of the Labour Party.

It is true that Harold Laski* made a foolish and ill-considered

---

* Churchill had invited Attlee, as Leader of the Opposition in the House of Commons, to accompany him to Potsdam for the talks he was about to have with Marshal Stalin and President Truman. At this time Laski was Chairman

remark about Attlee's position in going to the Big Three Conference, but that was magnified by Churchill and Beaverbrook
out of all proportion till in the end it simply bored people.
Anyhow there was nothing of substance in it. In all the meetings
I attended it is significant that not once was Laski or his statement mentioned, and I am told that at Tory meetings it was
much the same, if questions are any guide to what interests the
electorate. It was just a stunt, and a poor stunt at that.

It is significant that, throughout, Churchill had little
support in the Press save from the 'mongrel' Press—*Express*
(which has run the stunt to death), *Mail* (which has said ditto
to the *Express*), *Telegraph* (which has been nauseating, without
being even amusing, much less convincing); all the respectable
Press, *Times*, *Manchester Guardian*, *Economist*, has been
highly critical. Never has a Tory Prime Minister been so
castigated by the journals of opinion and authority, both for
what he said and the nasty way he said it.

In the whole of Churchill's campaign—speeches, 'pro-
gresses', etc.—there were intimations that, as I think Lord
Acton said, 'power corrupts' and that Churchill has been bitten
by the Fuehrer virus. His whole campaign—except for vulgar
abuse of the Labour Party—was egocentric. Somebody with
a good deal of perception said that he was conducting the
Election on the basis of a struggle 'A Man versus a Plan', on
Churchill against the Rest. . . .

How this great man (for he is, intrinsically, a great man)
came to sink so suddenly so low is a problem only to be solved
by psychoanalysts. Let us hope that it was only a temporary
aberration, due perhaps to overwhelming fatigue, or to the evil
counsels of evil advisers. Let us hope, as I believe, that this was
a mere temporary aberration (though its consequences may be
serious for the country and the world) and that with rest he will
recover his old powers. I still think that his name will be remembered in History when this horrible and painful campaign
is forgotten, just as L. G. will be remembered in History
despite the folly of the 1918 Election.

---

of the Labour Party and his declared reaction to this invitation was that Attlee
should go to Potsdam as an observer only, and that if he did so, 'Labour and
he should not accept responsibility for agreements which on the British side
will have been concluded by Mr Churchill as Prime Minister.'

Like the other Labour peers, Nathan put himself at the disposal of Transport House as to where it was thought he might be most useful as a campaign speaker, though he made it clear that he felt that his first obligation must be to Ernest Bevin in his old constituency. In fact, he concentrated there, although he did speak in a number of other London constituencies, including Attlee's in Limehouse as well as several outside London. One of the latter was the Canterbury Division. On the way by car, Nathan stopped at an hotel in Maidstone for lunch. Here he ran into the local Conservative candidate, Alfred Bossom, later Lord Bossom, whom he had known in his own House of Commons days. They had some general talk about the Election, and the question arose as to the likely result of the Election as a whole, as distinct from Maidstone where Bossom was confident of getting back. 'Doubtless he will,' noted Nathan at the time. 'If Maidstone is not a safe Tory seat, what is?'

Bossom went on to say that, if Churchill was returned to power, as he (Bossom) expected he would be with only a small majority, it would in his view be a patriotic duty for the Labour Party to stand behind him and give him complete support. Did Nathan think they would? Knowing Nathan was 'a person of moderate views and exercised a moderating influence', Bossom was sure that Nathan would work to that end.

Nathan replied that, before answering that question, he would like to ask Bossom a question. Supposing that, contrary to anticipation, not Churchill, but the Labour Party was returned with a small majority, would Bossom and the Tory Party consider it the patriotic duty to stand behind the Labour Government and give it complete support?

Bossom's reaction to this question was dramatic. His eyes bulged and went all bloodshot, his cheeks were suffused with blood until Nathan thought he was going to have a stroke. 'Support Labour!' he said. 'Never!'

Nathan's daughter Joyce happened to be with her father at the time, and as he noted afterwards, it made her realize the difference between the Tory Party and Labour. 'That rather interesting little conversation, as I thought it, is indicative of much in our politics today,' Nathan added. 'The Tories have the impudent effrontery to feel, and even assert, that they have a monopoly of public spirit and patriotism; they actually degraded the Union Jack by turning it into their Party colours—the Union Jack which is the flag not of one Party but of us all. When, however, it comes to the point, though there are many upright and honourable individuals in the Tory Party, that Party as a whole is an unblushingly selfish and egocentric Party—selfish and egocentric in the sense that it is not the country they think of so much as of themselves, "the governing class". If *they* can't govern, no one shall govern: that is their philosophy.'

Nathan developed this view in one of his letters to his son at the time:

A. J. Balfour said in the days of the great Liberal Adminis-tration in the early part of the century: 'Whatever Party is in office, we are always in power'—the reference being to the Tory complexion and overriding veto (as it then was) of the House of Lords. Gladstone had said years before: 'The principle of Toryism is mistrust of the people, qualified by fear.' There can be no doubt, as one sees pretty clearly in the years that have passed since, that the economic blizzard, bad as it would have doubtless have been anyhow, was hastened and made worse—if not engineered, and even welcomed, as it was certainly, as a means of discrediting the Labour Party, by the Tory Party and those interests which it has become the main concern of that Party to protect. During the twenty years between the Wars, for so much the greater part of which the Tories were in power by overwhelming majorities, there can be no doubt that politi-cal power became increasingly concentrated in the hands of a few leading members of that Party, and their acolytes, and of a relatively small number of great industrialists. . . .

These few, politicians and industrialists, are now thoroughly frightened and will go to all lengths to retain their power as long as possible, though they know that the public's eyes are now opening to a realization of the true facts and the public con-science is fast becoming alert to ensure that this comparatively novel and thoroughly mischievous position cannot be allowed to remain as it is. Charming and amusing, attractive and very often intelligent as individual Tories for the most part are, as a Party Tories collectively are quite incredibly unscrupulous, as their forcing an Election both now and in 1931 (in face of their published assurances to the contrary) abundantly proves.

During the three weeks which elapsed between the casting of the votes and the declaration of the poll, there was much speculation about the outcome. Nathan and many others like him felt that, in spite of the manner in which Churchill had conducted the campaign, the Conservatives would nevertheless win by a majority of fifty or so. The unpredictable element was the Services, and in the light of what happened it is now thought that they must have voted overwhelmingly Labour. On the evening before the results were known, Nathan gave a small men's dinner party in Brown's Hotel, to which he invited a number of distinguished individuals. They included Ernest Bevin, who told them of his ambition, if and when Labour came in, to be Chancellor of the Exchequer; Lord Catto, Governor of the Bank of England, who said he would not be a bit alarmed if the Bank were nationalized, 'for that would merely be applying the formalities of the existing facts' and he recognized it was inevitable sooner or later; Sir Walter Layton, the Liberal economist, later Lord Layton, who expressed surprise that Labour had not 'claimed' the Election, for all the indications were to his mind that Labour would have an independent majority; and Brigadier Andrew Clark, K.C., Conservative candidate for the new constituency of East Barnet, who was sure that he was 'in' by thousands—he was in fact 'out' by hundreds—and was prepared to bet any money that Churchill would have a majority of at least 100. 'An interesting company,' Nathan noted at the time, 'and in its way, as things turned out, a bit historic. Bevin towered in intellectual vigour and imaginative vision far above the others, eminent though some of them are, and they all agreed when he had gone that he is a giant among men, and that with him in a position of real power, everyone might feel a steady confidence if, contrary to their, and my, anticipation, Labour was in a majority. The opinion was also expressed that, if Labour was returned, the City would react badly for a short time, but that markets would quickly recover, and events have now shown that that prophecy was correct.'

Next morning on his way to Transport House, Nathan happened to see the Tory Marquess of Londonderry, and Londonderry offered him a bet of five shillings, which Nathan took, that Churchill would have a majority of 70. ('The 5/– is now mine!') 'It's a land-slide,' was the comment of George Shepherd, the Chief Labour Agent at Transport House, 'where the results were shown on a screen as they came in, and you can imagine that as the astounding victories were recorded there was more than wild enthusiasm'. From Transport House Nathan went on to the Reform Club, once a Liberal stronghold, where he had arranged to lunch with his son-in-law, Bernard Waley-Cohen. There, 'instead of enthusiasm there was quite definite glumness, especially among the older men, many of whom muttered imprecations beneath their breath, and more vocally expressed the conviction that the only thing for them to do was to emigrate to the United States! There was no comforting them. The Reformers have become most of them, anyhow the older among them, hard-bitten Tories. The only cheers were at the defeat of Ernest Brown and of Duncan Sandys who seemed to be their pet abominations. Naturally there was much astonishment at the collapse of the Liberal candidature.'

The result in the aggregate was a striking Labour victory—393 Labour M.P.s, 213 Conservatives and allies, 22 independents, and 12 Liberals—which gave Labour a majority over all the rest combined of nearly 150, although, owing to the peculiar character of the electoral system which favours the winning Party, Labour obtained only 47.8 per cent of the total votes cast.

Nathan's final comment on this remarkable election concerned the virtually total eclipse of the Liberals as a parliamentary Party.

There is no doubt that the Liberal Party put forward what in point of quality was a fine body of candidates, but they had nothing particular to say, and what they had to say was said much more effectively by Tories on the one hand or Labour on the other. The country does not like balancing Parties—there was never any chance of the Liberals forming a Government—and it wants to get back to the Two Party System with a strong Government, whatever its colour, and in this I'm sure the country is right. Since the Asquith–Lloyd George row in 1916, the Party has been in a pretty bad way, and each Election has confirmed this. The last great effort, to which so much energy and enthusiasm was given (by myself among others), was, as those in the inner circle realized at the time, the Liberal Party's last throw. Since then its position has increasingly deteriorated, and I feel no hope of its revival and little of its maintenance.

The plain fact, in addition to the Two Party complex, which is really a condition of a vigorous parliamentary system, is that the Labour Party now answers the requirements of those who would but for the Labour Party be Liberals. The Liberal Party was doomed from the moment that the Labour Party became a really effective and well-organized Party, and its doom was sealed when Labour attracted to itself candidates representative of every phase of the national life and ceased to represent one section of the community only. The Liberal Party has a magnificent record—it has produced great measures and been the protagonist of most fruitful ideas and policies—but its mantle has now fallen on the shoulders of the Labour Party, which stands in 1945 where the Liberals stood 40 years back, as the Party of Progress and Reform. I'm sure that the best thing for the country, for clarity in politics and for the parliamentary system, is that right-wing Liberals should frankly join the Tories and the left-wing Liberals the Labour Party.

2

Churchill resigned in the late afternoon of July 26, 1945, and advised the King to send for Attlee. Within half an hour Attlee was Prime Minister, at the head of the first majority Labour Government in Britain's history. In the process of Cabinet making, Bevin did not become Chancellor of the Exchequer, as he had thought and as Attlee originally intended that he should, but went to the

Foreign Office, while Hugh Dalton, who had been originally cast for the Foreign Office became Chancellor—a last-moment change round said to have been suggested by the King and apparently designed to keep Bevin and Morrison apart. Nathan expected to be offered a junior ministerial post, and in this he was not disappointed. He received a summons to Downing Street, where the new Prime Minister asked him to go to the War Office as Under-Secretary of State and also to answer in the House of Lords for the Ministry of Labour and National Service, since this department would have a prime responsibility for demobilization along with the War Office. Attlee added that the new Secretary of State was to be Jack Lawson, in the Commons, a former Durham miner, who had been Financial Secretary to the War Office in the brief 1924 Government. Nathan, who had already thought over the possibility of office and had in fact discussed it with his senior partner, immediately agreed to serve.

The reasons which prompted Nathan to accept the Prime Minister's offer he set out in a letter which he wrote to his son at this time.

> To have been all these years in the House of Commons, and then in the House of Lords, has been an infinite satisfaction to me and, at least as regards the former, the fulfilment of an ambition held since boyhood. Whether from the professional point of view it has advantaged me or the reverse is a moot question: had I been a Tory it would have undoubtedly been an asset, but having regard to the political complexion of the sort of people who are our clients, it is perhaps doubtful whether membership of the House as a Labour Member—or even as a Liberal—may not be, on the whole, a disadvantage, at least in times of real political excitement. It is difficult to assess the influence one way or the other—but I can say at least that the practice must be pretty robust, because, despite the fact that during the war we have only just 'ticked over' (i.e. actually carried a loss but scarcely more, which was a great blow after a long series of pretty good pre-war years), the clientele has been maintained and even increased, and during the past few months the practice has shown definite signs of an

upward grade towards pre-war standards. It is unfortunate in a way that it should be just at that moment that this unexpected situation should arise when I have had to choose between the office offered me, or refuse, and in the latter event be of course dished for ever from the political standpoint.

It was only after grave consideration and many consultations that, with the warm and most cordial concurrence of Herbert Oppenheimer, who has been very good indeed in his attitude,* I decided to accept whatever might be offered. It will possibly have some effect in the practice when I am no longer there, though my absence is only, of course, an interlude. But we all feel that any diminution caused by my absence is likely to be offset by the additional prestige of the firm of having a partner in a Ministerial Office and the considerable *réclame* that brings with that, and that, when I return, it is likely to prove a great asset to the firm to have a partner who has been a Minister and to give great confidence to clients and perhaps attract as clients those who might not otherwise come to us. The short view, therefore, is that there *may* be a temporary falling away but that in the long view there *will* be a definite advantage. . . .

Inevitably my taking office involves a financial sacrifice because I shall have to readjust, for the period I am away, my financial relations with my partners to my detriment, since it is not reasonable to expect them to work at an increasing and more exacting practice while I am away on an entirely different job. I don't anticipate any difficulty in arranging an amicable adjustment, but it will certainly, and seriously, affect my pocket in comparison with what, after all the lean years of the war, I might have expected as compensation from the years of expansion now to all appearances ahead of us.

But I have to think not merely of the private and financial aspects but also of public duty. If—indeed, since—it is thought that at this critical time I can be helpful to the public interest, it would be churlish to hold back, and I should neither be forgiven by others nor, even more important, could I forgive myself, if having been invited, I held back. Moreover, I think that my refusal to make the sacrifice in the public service would have on clients an even worse effect than my acceptance.†

---

* Particularly so, since Oppenheimer was strongly anti-Labour in politics.
† The salary of an Under-Secretary at this time was £2,000 a year, and he could not undertake any outside business or professional work.

The appointment was announced with others in the newspapers on August 4, thirty-one years to the day on which Nathan was called up as a territorial subaltern on the outbreak of the First World War. By virtue of his office he now became Vice-President of the Army Council, the Secretary of State being *ex-officio* President. As the latter went off almost immediately on a tour of the Far East to inform the troops personally in that theatre of the demobilization arrangements Nathan found himself in the chair at the meetings of the Council for the next month or so. Fortunately he knew enough about army affairs to hold his own, and indeed more than his own, with the professional soldiers at the council table. These included Field-Marshal Sir Alan Brooke (later Lord Alanbrooke), Chief of the Imperial General Staff, General Sir Ronald Adam, Adjutant-General to the Forces, and Lt.-General Sir Archibald Nye, Vice-C.I.G.S. Nathan was still Under-Secretary eleven months later when the equable 'Brookie' was replaced by the more controversial 'Monty' as C.I.G.S. Montgomery had never previously served in the War Office, and it was to prove an interesting experience both for himself and his political masters, of whom his Pauline contemporary Harry Nathan was one. The other junior Minister was F. J. Bellenger, the Financial Secretary, who was eventually to succeed Lawson as Secretary of State.

Nathan was welcomed to his private office, looking over the Horse Guards, by the Permanent Under-Secretary, Sir Eric Speed, who proved an experienced and trusted counsellor. 'If you want anyone who is not on the Army Council, *send for him*,' Speed would say to a new political Under-Secretary. 'If you want to speak to the S. of S., find out if he can see you and *go to him*. If you want to speak to anyone else on the Army Council, ask if you can look in for a minute. You will find they will come to you.'

'What about Monty?'

'Well, there is no rule about. But if I were you, I would go to him—usually but not quite always.'

Of the many messages of congratulation which Nathan received on his appointment, three in particular are worth mention. The first was from Lord Londonderry, the Tory peer and coal owner and former Air Minister, who had lost his bet with Nathan about the outcome of the Election. 'You will certainly have a great deal to do,' he wrote from Wynyard Park, his seat in County Durham, 'and I hope you will be able to reform the W.O. in many ways. It is badly needed and I am sure no one is better qualified than yourself to establish what I call business lines which seem absent in more than one contact I have had with the W.O.' Although they belonged to opposite political parties, Londonderry had formed the greatest respect for Nathan as a lawyer and he had asked him to become his solicitor. Thus it fell to Nathan's firm to act for him in the negotiations consequent upon the nationalization of the coal mines, which was foreshadowed in the King's Speech at the opening of the new Parliament.

The second letter was from Brigadier Chichester Cooke, who commanded the territorial regiment of the Royal Artillery, of which Nathan was Honorary Colonel.

Headquarters. 40th A.A. Brigade. 6th August 1945.
What very splendid news! I know that the whole Regiment will be delighted, and will want me to offer our congratulations, and best and confident wishes for a great success. I am delighted at such a sequel to such hard, and unrewarded, work for the Army.

The whole country owes you so much that it may well grow to owe some more, and the Army will benefit widely from your intimate knowledge of its affairs and difficulties. It is going to need that very much, especially in its reorganization for the future, which will be a major task. It may well fall to you, also to save the T.A. from being snuffed out. . . .

The third letter was from a sergeant in the Durham Light Infantry named Herbert Garfield, who had served his articles as a solicitor with Nathan's firm—he was later to become a partner—and was now with his unit in Germany. He enclosed a souvenir of considerable interest.

Berlin. 11th August 1945. . . . I need hardly tell you with what enthusiasm the result of the election and the composition

187

of Mr Attlee's administration was received by the troops here.

I do not know how many 'souvenirs' of the Reich capital you already have in your possession, but I am enclosing a *Commentary on the Nuremberg Laws* which I extracted from amongst the rubble of what was once Hitler's private study in the Reich Chancellery when I entered Berlin with the first British troops. I am assured by Russian experts that this was the Fuehrer's personal copy and that he must have made the annotations himself.

I venture to hope that the book may be of some interest; I meant to send it to you some time ago, but somehow I felt that if I waited a few days I might have cause to add a word of congratulation.

Nathan accepted the gift gladly, which he assured Garfield would be placed amongst his 'trophies' as one of the most interesting and valued of them. 'It is, as a matter of fact, the only one I have had so far from Berlin,' he added, 'and I think it is most unselfish of you to have parted with it.'

The new Minister plunged straight away into the 'unaccustomed work' of a government department. 'I have been kept very busy,' he wrote at the end of his first month in Whitehall, 'working most nights until 2 o'clock and sometimes as late as 4 in the morning! However, it is all very interesting. It has some of the excitement of novelty, and I hope it is a useful job that I shall be able to do.'

3

The first task of the Labour Government was to finish off the war against Japan, and it was generally thought that this might take a considerable time, since a large part of South-East Asia had been overrun and occupied, and a further lengthy spell of jungle warfare was anticipated by the Cabinet. However, the situation was completely changed within a week of Nathan's coming into the War Office, when the Americans dropped atom bombs on Hiroshima and Nagasaki, and shortly afterwards the Japanese surrendered unconditionally. VJ-Day consequently came as a great relief, but it brought difficult problems in its wake. Instead of the gradual deployment of British forces from the Western to the Eastern theatres of war, the Government now had to deal with demobilization on a much larger scale than had been expected. Nevertheless, the Cabinet determined to adhere to the demobilization plans which had been worked out during the war largely under the inspiration of Ernest Bevin, the Minister of Labour. On the whole these plans operated smoothly in practice, in spite of Opposition pressure in both Houses of Parliament that the process should be speeded up— much better than the state of affairs at the end of the previous Great War when there were something like chaos and near mutinies. As the official Government spokesman in the Lords, Nathan naturally had to bear the brunt of the criticism that there was undue delay in releasing personnel from the Forces.

One of his duties after VJ-Day was to go down to Southampton with the Adjutant-General and welcome home the first ship, the P. & O. liner *Corfu*, bringing back some 1,300 former prisoners-of-war from the Far East. Nathan, who represented the Government, went on board to welcome the troops and read a special message from the King and Queen. Each officer and man was subsequently presented with a copy typed on Buckingham Palace writing paper and bearing the King's signature, as well as cigarettes, chocolates and other gifts, besides a pre-paid telegram form on which to send a personal message home—small but none the less thoughtful matters of detail for which Nathan, with a wealth of army welfare experience behind him, was responsible.

Both Germany and Austria were now under military government. So far as the British elements of the two quadripartite Allied Control Commissions were concerned, it soon became clear that the War Office could not continue indefinitely to be directly responsible for the administration of the civil population, and accordingly in October, 1945, the Cabinet decided to entrust German and Austrian affairs to a separate office under the immediate control of the Chancellor of the Duchy of Lancaster (Mr J. B. Hynd), subject only to the nominal aegis of the War Minister. At the same time Nathan had to answer for this new department in the Lords. The first time he did so was in reply to a debate on the subject initiated by Lord Vansittart, a former permanent head of the Foreign Office. Replying to the debate for the Government, Nathan made a number of interesting points. In German re-education particularly, the greatest difficulty was among youth, and more among girls than boys, he said. Books, even those of arithmetic, had to be rewritten, since the latter contained problems dealing with military matters. Likewise with children's fairy tales. Little Red Riding Hood, for example, was portrayed as a fine Nordic type and the wolf as 'a democratic plutocrat'. The young students were hotbeds of Nazism, but encouragement was being given to the formation of youth groups on a voluntary basis under strict supervision.

The British element of the Control Commission was anxious to encourage a healthy interest in politics and trade unionism, he went on, but the German people were completely apathetic to everything but food, clothing and warmth. All the interest was concentrated on the battle for the winter. Nevertheless there were observable effects of these processes of re-education in the desire for direction, and ideas of democracy were making headway. The best re-educator of all, Nathan added, was the private soldier.

In November he had to face a concentrated barrage in the course of a debate on demobilization and the turnover of factories to peace production. On this occasion he described the demobilization scheme as 'a model of efficiency', and to support his assertion that it was 'working extremely well' he gave figures to show that releases from the Forces up to October 15 had fallen short of the schedule by only one per cent—543,000 against the target of 548,000. He expected one million to be released by the end of the year, and that all the Services would have reached their demobilization targets by the middle of 1946.

Nathan's old leader Lord Samuel was foremost among the critics, and he illustrated his contention that demobilization was too slow by pointing out that one girl with a car could deliver the goods which a hundred women had to queue for and carry home. 'Seldom have so many borne so much to save so little,' said Samuel, parodying Churchill amid laughter and cheers. 'The service of many in the Forces is compulsory unemployment, and the pay is the dole in uniform.'

Nathan conceded that there were some flaws in the Bevin scheme in that there was an appreciable number of men awaiting release who might not be fully employed on military duties. 'But all men not on military duties are available for civil employment,' he added, 'and large numbers are doing it.'

This statement was greeted by several noble Lords with cries of 'What work?'

Amid considerable interruptions, Nathan replied that the men in question were assisting the Ministry of Fuel and Power in the delivery of coal supplies. 'Such work is required to be done as part of national service,' he added by way of explanation, 'and it is a method of using these men while preserving the Bevin scheme and also ensuring that these men are performing work of public service.'

So far as 'demobbing' property went, Nathan assured the House that all but 250 hotels and boarding houses would be freed within the next three months and that by the end of April, 1946, virtually all small flats, houses and schools under requisition would likewise be returned to their owners. Similarly 80 per cent of the land requisitioned was to be returned within the same period.

Another problem had a notable welfare aspect. This was posed by the numbers of Service marriages which had broken down or were in danger of shipwreck. By the spring of 1946, there were 48,000 petitions for divorce down for hearing in the courts, and it was estimated that a further 200,000 marriages were in jeopardy. The question was raised by way of motion in the Upper House by Lord Elton, who asked whether the Government was prepared to take steps to reduce the separation of members of the services from their wives which was now often 'excessively long'.

Speaking for the Government, Nathan said that, while separation was a central factor in the causes of the breakdown of marriages, it should not be exaggerated. This aspect of what was 'a social malady' was, he believed, only temporary. It was not a Service problem in the ordinary sense. It did not arise before the war, when the separation of serving men from their wives was a normal feature of life in the Forces. It was largely due to conditions produced by war, he pointed out, when a higher proportion of able-bodied men were in the forces and conditions at home were unsettled owing to changes of employment, environment, and association. However, he was able to promise several concessions—the reduction of the period of separation to three years (two and a half for the R.A.F.), better married quarters and barracks, and increased opportunities for wives and families to live abroad. By this date wives and families could join their husbands in any part of the world where the latter were stationed except Palestine, the Sudan and Germany. So far as the British Army of the Rhine was concerned, wives could now meet their husbands for short leave periods in Paris or Brussels, and Nathan hoped that arrangements could soon be made for wives and families to go to Germany. By the end of 1946, Nathan was able to assure the House, the bulk of the remaining non-regulars in the Army would be under the age of 24, and therefore the problem of the breakdown of marriages would not be very formidable.

By the end of July, Nathan was also able to announce in the Lords that the ban on marriages between British soldiers and German or Austrian girls had been lifted, two months earlier than after the end of the 1914–1918 war. At the same time the scheme for B.A.O.R. wives to join their husbands was put into effect. The first batch departed in the middle of August, and Nathan went to see them off at Folkestone and give the party an official blessing. 'You are pathfinders,' he told them. 'You are blazing the trail. We at the War Office, as well as the chiefs of the Army itself in Germany, have been at enormous pains to try to make things comfortable for you.' Not only that, but the Prime Minister had throughout taken an especial interest in the whole of this enterprise and had given personal directions that everything was to be done to make it a

success. Nathan went on to read out a message from the Prime
Minister:

> I know you will realize that each and every one of you has an
> important mission to perform on behalf of your country. The
> British soldier has been rightly called 'our best ambassador.'
> You can also do much to bring a wholesome influence to bear
> on the German people by your example. . . . .
> I hope that your stay in Germany will bring you happiness
> and that it will impress upon the minds of the Germans
> memories of a thoughtful, humane and generous people, whose
> way of life is one to emulate.

There was also the 'headache' of the repatriation of German and
Italian prisoners-of-war, with which the Under-Secretary for War
had to deal at this time. Controversy on the subject was sparked off
by the Bishop of Sheffield, Dr Leslie Hunter, in the House of Lords
in July, 1946. The Bishop reported that in the previous few months
there had been a change in the temper of the prisoners in Britain.
They were becoming sullen by reason of long separation from their
homes and families, and there was increasing bitterness among
men who formerly were reasonable. They were now losing hope,
and their hopelessness was being added to by the absence of any
clearly declared policy by the British Government. 'Ought not a
distinction to be made between reparations in the form of labour,
which was no doubt needed,' asked the Bishop, 'and the indefinite
detention of prisoners-of-war and their forced labour, which some
people found very hard to defend on moral grounds?'

Nathan did the best he could with a difficult brief. Prisoners-of-
war were used only on work of national importance, for which
suitable British labour was not available, he told the House.
338,000 German prisoners were so employed, half by the Ministry
of Agriculture as farm hands. Repatriation of the Italians was
practically complete, and of their numbers 1,200 were 'so apprecia-
tive of the treatment they had received that they are remaining
here'. The position with the Germans was not so easy. They were
classified politically as 'whites', 'greys' and 'blacks', the majority

being 'greys'. When specialists were called for by name or there was special need for particular service in Germany, such as miners for the Ruhr, 'whites' were repatriated. As to the decline in morale, the Minister stated that according to his information it was not of very significant dimensions and that it was reflected for the most part in a certain degree of apathy. So far as willingness, co-operation and discipline were concerned, there had been no decline at all.

The prisoners employed on the farms received 1s a day wages in addition to their bare subsistence, which yielded the Government a profit on each prisoner of 7s 6d. The cry that they were thus being used as slaves both in this country and the British zone of occupation in Germany in contravention of the Geneva Convention—Article 75 of which laid down that as soon as possible after the cessation of hostilities prisoners-of-war should be returned to their own country—was taken up in the House of Commons by Mr Richard Stokes, a Labour Member, who stigmatized Nathan's statement as 'sheer buffoonery and incompetence of the worst order'. However, it was not Nathan's fault that he had such a weak case to defend and that he had to shelter behind the Government's claim that repatriation was so slow because there was no Government in Germany with which it could negotiate, pending the signing of a peace treaty.

During his membership of the Army Council, Nathan had the interesting experience of working closely with the two great soldiers who held the post of C.I.G.S.—Alanbrooke and Montgomery. The former had wished to retire when the Japanese war was over, but both Lawson and Attlee had begged him to stay till the following year 'to see them through their troubles'. This he had reluctantly agreed to do, although he felt 'cooked and played out' after four years of arguing with Churchill. His successor's name was officially announced early in the New Year, but as Montgomery was not due to come to the War Office for some months, one of Alanbrooke's minor problems that winter was, as he put it, that of 'drilling into Monty how he is to behave when he takes over C.I.G.S.'. There was a foretaste of what was to come when 'Monty' met the Press and came out with such statements as 'Occupation must last another ten years at least' and 'You need have no fear, we shall export no food to Germany,' when the Cabinet had just decided to do so. Nathan could hardly suppress a chuckle when he had heard that his old schoolmate had been sent for by the Secretary of State and 'ticked off', by no means the first, or for that matter the last, reprimand which the intrepid Field-Marshal was to receive. ('Poor Monty!' was Alanbrooke's compassionate comment. 'He should have known by then the dangers of talking to the Press.')

Montgomery took over from Alanbrooke at the end of June. Although he had never previously served in the War Office and knew little about its organization or how it conducted its business, he was soon to learn about 'the great work it had done during the war', and before he left it in 1948 it is scarcely surprising that he had come to the conclusion that 'it was easily the best Ministry in Whitehall'. (He was once asked which was the worst and replied without hesitation: 'The Colonial Office.') Meanwhile the military and civil services side of the Army Council had been reconstituted in consequence of retirements—for instance, General Sir Richard O'Connor had succeeded Sir Ronald Adam as Adjutant-General.

At the first meeting of the Council which he attended, the new C.I.G.S. presented a paper on 'The Problem of the Post-War Army,' which Nathan heard him expound with his customary *panache*. Montgomery's fundamental concept was the need for agreement on the shape of the Army for the next fifteen years, which he said, as a balanced whole—Regulars and Territorials— must be adequately equipped to fight a major war, an operation of which incidentally it did not take him long to realize that 'there was in ministerial and military circles in Whitehall no clear conception'. He laid stress on the importance of a contented Army and the need to teach how to create high morale, as well as such matters as training, overall education, and scientific research and development. He also produced a memorandum on staff organization in which he urged the introduction of the Chief of Staff system in the

Army. He next submitted a paper on western strategy in a major war, advocating the establishment of a strong western bloc, 'so as to protect the peoples, territories and civilization of the western world against any invasion from the east', as well as the maintenance of a Corps H.Q. in the Middle East 'available to go off anywhere to handle an emergency'. The Council also agreed to the launching of a recruiting drive in the autumn. The C.I.G.S. had many other ideas which he was able to put into practice, though not by any means without a struggle frequently at Cabinet level. 'It's no good forgetting the politicians,' he used to tell his military staff. 'Never forget the politicians are *our masters*, and it is our duty to lead them —up the garden path!'

The Office was grateful for a breathing space in which to digest the Field-Marshal's innovations. This was afforded by his departure on a prolonged visit to Canada and the United States in the summer. By the time the C.I.G.S. returned in late September, Nathan's days as Under-Secretary were numbered, since Jack Lawson had tendered his resignation as Secretary of State on account of ill health, and Attlee consequently determined on a re-shuffle of ministerial posts, in which Nathan was to be involved.

Nathan's last public appearance before the changes were announced was on September 11, 1946, when he opened the recruiting drive for London district in the Mansion House in the presence of the Lord Mayor and other London Mayors, military members of the Army Council, and leading London citizens. It was a fitting swansong on the theme of the new Army, inspired in some degree no doubt by the absent C.I.G.S. 'We are determined that the Army's equipment shall be the finest which the experience of scientists and skill of craftsmen can make,' Nathan said. 'The soldier deserves to be superbly trained. He deserves to be superbly treated. It is our determination that he shall be. Many of the restrictions and petty annoyances of the past will be swept away. We shall require of the soldier strict discipline while performing his military duties. In his off-time we shall allow him, as his right, the same freedom as if he were a private citizen.'

4

The Government changes were announced from Downing Street on the eve of the reassembly of Parliament for the autumn session in October, 1946. Nathan was promoted to be Minister of Civil Aviation, in the place of Lord Winster, whom Attlee sent off to be Governor of the somewhat neglected colony of Cyprus. A new Parliamentary Secretary was also appointed in the person of Mr George Lindgren, M.P. (later Lord Lindgren), who had begun his career as a railway clerk and now had the responsibility of answering for the department of civil aviation in the Commons. Since he had attained senior ministerial rank, Nathan was immediately sworn in as a member of the Privy Council at Buckingham Palace.

A department of civil aviation had been created within the Air Ministry after the First World War, but it had only existed as an independent Ministry since 1944. Admittedly Nathan did not know very much about its work, although he had managed to pick up a few pointers from Lord Londonderry, a former Air Minister and enthusiastic amateur pilot. Fortunately, as at the War Office, he was served by a most experienced Permanent Secretary, Sir Henry Self, who was to prove an excellent adviser.

On coming into power, the Labour Government had nationalized British air transport, and by the Civil Aviation Act, 1946, had set up three state Corporations—British Overseas Airways Corporation (B.O.A.C.), British European Airways (B.E.A.) and British South American Airways Corporation (B.S.A.A.C.), the latter being merged three years later with B.O.A.C.* The existing privately owned airlines operating scheduled services were bought out and integrated with B.E.A. Privately owned air services were only permitted to continue as charter-flight operators. The directors of the three corporations were appointed and removed by the Minister,

---

* B.O.A.C. was of rather earlier origin, having come into existence in April, 1940, on the amalgamation of Imperial Airways and British Airways. The three corporations were initially headed respectively by Lord Knollys, Sir Harold Hartley, and Mr John Booth of the Booth Shipping Lines.

and the corporations had the exclusive right to fly scheduled services, subject only to the competition on international routes of the foreign airlines to which the Government gave landing rights under bilateral agreements.* At the same time, it was recognized that there would be an initial post-war period in which the state would have to subsidize the development of the air services—in other words, to begin with, the three corporations might be expected to operate at a financial loss. In fact, as will be seen, the loss turned out to be considerable.

Nathan's Ministry was situated in Ariel House in the Strand once the Gaiety Hotel. The Minister and his private office were accommodated in a suite of rooms at the head of the old hotel staircase in what had formerly been the Royal Suite in the palmy Edwardian days before the First World War. Nearby there were some narrower stairs leading direct 'back stage' to the Gaiety Theatre, which had been wrecked by a flying bomb in the Second War and as yet had not been rebuilt.

The new Minister had his first meeting with members of the senior staff of the department in his room overlooking the Strand on the morning of October 11, 1946. Present on this occasion were Sir Henry Self, the Permanent Secretary; Sir George Cribbett, the Deputy Secretary; Air Chief Marshal Sir Frederick Bowhill, the Chief Aeronautical Adviser; Mr (later Sir) James Dunnett, Assistant Secretary; Mr Peter Masefield, Director-General of Long Term Planning and Projects, and Mr Richard Poland, the Minister's departmental Private Secretary. As Peter Masefield was later to recall, Nathan appeared to those assembled to meet him on that wet October morning 'as very much the army officer in mufti, stocky, precise, direct, and—with better acquaintance—a sensitive and likeable and liberal man'.

'I am delighted to meet you, gentlemen,' said the new Minister introducing himself, when they had all taken their places at the

---

* This policy of exclusive rights was subsequently modified in favour of a limited return to private ownership. But the corporations still carry about 90 per cent of the scheduled traffic.

long table in the room. 'I don't know anything about civil aviation but I do know that in the future, when we get it sorted out, it's going to be very important, and I do know also that you have got to instruct me in what needs doing. One thing I am sure, too, is that we must have no compromise with safety. And as the Minister of Civil Aviation, I am determined to have a policy of safety first, safety second and safety third, although I certainly intend to take the air on all suitable occasions.'

Peter Masefield (later Chairman of the British Airports Authority) had just returned from a tour of duty as Civil Air Attaché to the British Embassy in Washington to take up his new post. He and the Minister were to see much of each other, particularly in the first few months, since Nathan asked Masefield to accompany him on many of his official visits. On several occasions they flew together in a small Miles Gemini aircraft belonging to the Ministry, with the result that various aircraft manufacturers, flying schools and gliding establishments were somewhat surprised to see the Minister of Civil Aviation, accompanied only by the Director-General of Long Term Planning, landing unannounced and otherwise alone in a tiny aeroplane at their fields during that spring and summer of 1946. Masefield has recorded that he found the Minister 'a lively and inquiring companion with a rich fund of stories as well as common sense, and a deep feeling for Britain'. Certainly Nathan was 'very much struck by the almost pioneering and very much formative stage in which he found so many aspects of early post-war civil aviation'. He summed this up one day when he remarked to Masefield: 'You know, the one fact I have discovered about civil aviation is that there are no facts, only opinions.'

The new Minister held his first Press conference in his room in the House of Lords. 'Nathan's the name,' he announced breezily as he bustled in, grabbing the hand of the first reporter he saw. 'I want to get to know you all. You can ask what you like and see what you like. I am absolutely satisfied that this new Ministry cannot be developed satisfactorily without frankness on both sides and the co-operation of the Press.'

He went on to explain his aims, of which the first was safety·
'After that I would put regularity, so that you may know when you
are leaving a certain place at a certain time that you will leave at
that time, and that you will arrive at your destination at the
scheduled time.' Other objects were comfort and adequacy, i.e
having enough aircraft and crews to carry the passengers and
freight, enough airports to handle the traffic, and enough adequately trained personnel on the ground to control the traffic in the
air and on the ground. To meet the requirement of adequacy, he
admitted, 'is going to be one of our very great problems'. He put
speed last, apart from his general aim 'to see British civil aviation
holding the place it should hold, whether from the point of view of
air commerce or in its international and, I can almost say, its
ambassadorial aspect'. His Ministry at Ariel House would also seek
to make the people of Britain air minded, and he hoped to encourage
flying clubs and similar organizations to which he 'attached great
importance'.

'I couldn't agree with him more,' said Mr C. G. Grey, the experienced editor of *The Aeroplane*, afterwards.

The big problem, as Nathan correctly foresaw, lay in the
adequacy requirement, and throughout his whole tenure of office
for the next nineteen months he was to be bedevilled by a long
series of disputes and differences of opinion on this aspect of civil
aviation policy. These were mainly due to the heavy losses incurred by the nationalized airlines owing to the employment of
uneconomic and unsuitable 'stop-gap' types of British aircraft, such
as the Avro, Lancastrian and York, and to the Government's 'fly
British' policy, by which Nathan was bound and which inhibited
the purchase of modern American aircraft. The Ministry of Supply,
the department responsible for supplying the corporations with
aircraft, generally tended to support the view urged by the British
aircraft industry that purchases of American planes for British air
services would be damaging to the industry's prestige and efficiency.
B.O.A.C., on the other hand, consistently advocated their view
that they, rather than any Ministry or the aircraft industry, should

decide the types of aircraft best suited to their commercial air services, irrespective of whether they were British or American. This particularly applied to long-distance routes on which foreign competition was most severe.

It was not long before Nathan's Ministry found itself at loggerheads with B.O.A.C. on the use of the Avro Tudor I, Britain's first post-war long-distance air liner, which had received a certificate of airworthiness from the Air Registration Board and, according to a Ministerial announcement on November 25, was 'intended to be used by B.O.A.C. on the North Atlantic'. The Corporation, however, subjected this aircraft to further flight trials, as a result of which B.O.A.C. did not regard it as airworthy, taking the view that its deficiency of performance effectively prevented it from operating the North Atlantic run. After further review, the Corporation concluded that, irrespective of whether the Tudor I's flying qualities could be rectified and its deficiency in performance could be fully recovered, there was no longer any justification for including the Tudor I in the Corporation's operating programme. 'Our handicap today is having to use obsolete and uncommercial aircraft,' B.O.A.C. told the Minister bluntly. 'The loss to the Corporation arising from the use of these aircraft is a restriction to the development of our Empire routes. It is at the moment forced upon us by circumstance, but if we acquiesce in further attempts to rectify the Tudor I, the continuance of this restriction will then have become our own choice.' B.S.A.A., on the other hand, reported after flight trials of the Tudor I that they considered it normal for a four-engined type with a tail wheel, and suitable for operation on their routes. In fact, however, they preferred an improved version with a longer fuselage, capable of carrying thirty-two passengers, and later in 1946 they took delivery of three of this version known as the Tudor IV, which was likewise given a certificate of airworthiness.

Then there was the ill-fated project known as 'Project X'. Peter Masefield's experience as Civil Air Attaché in Washington had led him to the conclusion that, at this date, the most economic aeroplane for long-haul operations on world routes during the next few years

would be a 'stretched' version of the Lockheed Constellation, provided that enough power could be put into it to make possible a
substantial increase in both fuel load and pay load. The 2,600 h.p.
Bristol Centaurus engine of British make appeared to combine the
possibility of increased power and, if fitted in a Constellation, a substantial British content in an American aeroplane which was ahead of
anything then flying in the United Kingdom. It also appeared to
offer prospects of sales of a British engine in an American air-
frame to long-distance airlines both in the United States and in the
Commonwealth.

In January, 1947, Masefield discussed this possibility with the
Minister and the Permanent Secretary. Both saw the attractions of
such a development to get B.O.A.C. commercially competitive
ahead of the arrival of the projected 'Brabazon 3' and 'Brabazon 4'
aircraft—later the Bristol Britannia and de Havilland Comet. Accordingly, armed with the Bristol Company's specifications of the
Centaurus and a letter from Lord Natham, Masefield flew off to
Burbank, California, early in February, 1947. Robert Gross and
Hall Hibberd, President and Chief Engineer of the Lockheed
Aircraft Corporation, immediately grasped the possibilities, and
after a week of intensive work Masefield returned to Ariel House
with an outline of a Centaurus-powered and stretched Constellation
for B.O.A.C. This was mutually designated as 'Project X'.

In his confirmatory letter, Lockheed's president wrote to
Masefield:

> I wish to reaffirm to you our sincere enthusiasm for this
> project, particularly with respect to the opportunity that it
> offers for a mutual effort between the estimable Bristol Com-
> pany of England and Lockheed. We are not only enthusiastic
> concerning the immediate prospects, but we believe that this
> example of teamwork between the British and American air-
> craft industry would hold great significance for the future, and
> we look forward gratefully for an opportunity to renew our
> association in a mutual project with the British Government,
> which we felt was so acceptable and successful in the early days
> of the last war.

We are particularly enthusiastic concerning 'Project X' because we are certain that the resultant aircraft, namely, the Constellation equipped with British Centaurus engines, a joint product of the British and American aircraft industries, will be an outstanding leader in its class for years to come, and we feel sure that your examination of the performance data will confirm such a conclusion on our part. We further believe that the project is technically sound, realistic and practical, and that the proposed time schedule can be accomplished.

Nathan was delighted. He saw the prospect of a valuable Anglo-American development which might lead to substantial sales of British aero engines and of putting B.O.A.C. on a profitable basis much earlier than had been previously contemplated. A Lockheed team was invited to England and arrived in March, 1947, under the leadership of Mr Kelly Johnson, the Chief Project Engineer. A complete plan was drawn up between Lockheed and Bristol, including a proposal under which Constellations might be built under licence at Filton for B.O.A.C., Quantas and other Commonwealth airlines.

Alas, when Nathan presented 'Project X' to the Cabinet in the middle of 1947, it was strenuously opposed by the Minister of Supply, Mr George Strauss, on the grounds that the development costs would be a severe drain on dollars, as also would be the initial purchase cost of nine aircraft for a total of $10·6 millions. The Supply Minister contended that B.O.A.C. should be told that they must not flirt any more with American designs but they must await the 'Brabazon 3' project (also powered by Centaurus engines), at that time contemplated as an Avro product. After a long discussion in the Cabinet room in Downing Street, the project was rejected.

Looking at 'Project X' with the advantage of hindsight, there is no doubt that it did provide possibilities of much more economic operations than in fact was attained for a number of years. The Constellations could have been delivered before the end of 1947 and could have been equipped with Centaurus engines during 1948. However, it was not to be. As things turned out, B.O.A.C. was eventually allowed to order the Canadair IV, a Canadian aircraft with Rolls Royce engines made by Lockheed in Montreal, which first flew in July, 1947, and was to become known as the Argonaut; it was initially developed when Nathan was Minister, as will be related below.

Other developments in British civil aviation were less controversial. One of Nathan's first innovations was the establishment of an Air Safety Board, in November, 1946, including the veteran flyer Lord Brabazon of Tara, to keep the question of safety in the air 'under continual review'. The Minister went on to divide the United Kingdom for air traffic purposes into four divisions—London and south-eastern England, southern England, northern England, and Northern Ireland and Scotland—each under a Divisional Controller, and each airfield having its own Aerodrome Commandant. Work at the new London Airport at Heathrow was hurried on—the existing passenger accommodation consisted of Nissen huts and there was not a single passenger bar for the supply of refreshments at Heathrow when Nathan took over—and similar work was put in hand elsewhere, notably in Belfast (Nutt's Corner) and Edinburgh (Turnhouse). Plans were also prepared with a view to make the fullest possible use of Prestwick as an international airport in addition to Heathrow. The latter was designed to cover more than six square miles, with nine runways, at a cost of at least £20 millions. Public access to airports 'under appropriate conditions' was another point to which the Minister gave attention. 'They should see for themselves what is going on in civil aviation,' he said at this time. 'I am most anxious to do everything to make the public have confidence in civil aviation and in the Ministry.'

He also laid it down that, unless security considerations were involved, the results of investigations into air accidents involving loss of life should be published, particularly if useful lessons could be learned from the causes of the accident. Furthermore, he caused radio and allied navigational aids to bad weather to be installed in all major British airports. Finally, he set up a National Civil Aviation Consultative Council, consisting of operators, personnel, manufacturers, users, and others, to review current developments and advise him accordingly.

Throughout his time at the Civil Aviation Ministry, Nathan's main concern was to work out the technique of the relationship between the Ministry and the three Corporations, now that civil aviation had become a nationalized industry. 'As I see it,' he said, 'the key is to leave the Corporations to work out their own salvation through the united wisdom of their Boards operating within the framework of the Statute. Ministerial and departmental contact with them should be close, but of an informal rather than a formal nature. I am available, to help them when they ask me in their troubles and anxieties.'

One of the most difficult things in the conduct of a great business—yet one of the most important—is to steel oneself to leave the people in charge to get on with the job, even if one feels that they are going to make mistakes. No business can prosper unless those with top responsibility can steel themselves in this way, for only by making mistakes and being left free to make them can any worthwhile business find the solution to its problems. But sometimes it's pretty hard for the Minister to keep quiet whilst, from his aloof position, he can sense something happening, or not happening, for which he knows that in due course he is going to be made answerable to Parliament. I assure you it needs a steady nerve, but I am certain it is worth it.*

5

The year 1947 was a particularly full one both for Nathan and his wife. In that year Lady Nathan was Chairman of the London County Council, which involved her in a great number of functions, including the honourable duty of receiving the King and Queen on their unique visit to County Hall. The Chairmanship of the Council was, of course, very much a full-time job, and it was a remarkable fact that Lady Nathan's year of office, which she was only the second woman in the Council's history to hold, should

* Speech to the Council of the Royal Aeronautical Society, May 27, 1948.

have coincided with her husband being Minister of Civil Aviation. Often during this crowded year, their official cars, with pennants flying from each bonnet, would be seen together outside the Nathans' flat in Park Lane. And on the occasion of his wife's formal installation in County Hall, Nathan, although he was a Privy Councillor and Minister of Cabinet rank, was present not in either of these capacities but merely as the Chairman's spouse. This was indeed a fitting climax to a unique husband-and-wife partnership in public affairs.

In addition to his normal departmental and parliamentary activities, Nathan undertook an extensive tour of Australasia and the Far East during the summer recess. This originated in a desire to traverse the 'Kangaroo Route' to Australia, when a convenient opportunity was forthcoming, since it appeared that here the problems for B.O.A.C. were most considerable. The opportunity was provided by a meeting of the South Pacific Air Transport Council in Canberra to which Nathan led the United Kingdom Delegation. Similar problems which emerged at the Colonial Civil Aviation Conference in London earlier in the year determined him to extend his tour to Hong Kong and Ceylon, and on learning of this the Chinese and Siamese Governments invited him to visit Nangking and Bangkok as their guest at the same time, since he would be so close to these centres. The Chinese were about to ratify a bilateral air transport agreement with Britian and similar negotiations were about to be opened with the Siamese. He was also asked by the Government to help with the distribution of rice in the Japanese occupied territories.

The tour was most strenuous, and only a man of Nathan's stamina, both physical and mental, could have withstood its rigours without falling sick. In ten weeks he and his party, who stood up to it equally well, covered 34,276 miles by air in 152 hours flying, mostly over the main trunk routes, besides 2,000 miles by road. During this period they slept in thirty-three places, not counting two in the air, while Nathan made twenty-two major speeches and three broadcasts, as well as attending fourteen Press conferences.

Besides Nathan, his wife and their son Roger, the party included Mr Peter Masefield, the Director-General of Long Term Planning and Projects at the Civil Aviation Ministry, and Mr R. D. Poland, Nathan's Private Secretary in Ariel House. They travelled in a Lancastrian belonging to B.O.A.C., and it said much for the efficiency of British aircraft that throughout the whole of the tour there was only one brief delay due to mechanical causes—1½ hours at Hong Kong—although they were held up for two days by bad weather. On the outward journey to Sydney, stops were made in Cairo, Karachi, Singapore and Darwin.

After their return to England, Nathan was strongly criticized by Conservative M.P.s in the House of Commons for not travelling by scheduled services, rather than in a specially chartered aircraft which, in a time of strict petrol rationing for the general public, had consumed 31,600 gallons of petrol on the journey at a cost to the Exchequer of over £20,100. George Lindgren, Nathan's loyal and trusted Parliamentary Secretary, had to reply to the critics, which he did effectively enough, pointing out that the Far Eastern part of the trip could not possibly have been undertaken except by charter aircraft, and so far as the remainder was concerned, particularly the flight to Australia, travelling by the scheduled services would have meant adding to the backlog of passengers waiting to be accommodated, since the Lancastrians were limited to five passengers on the 'Kangaroo' Service. The cementing of Commonwealth and international relations, which was largely the object of the tour, Lindgren added, could not be measured in terms of £ s d. Indeed, had the Conservatives been in office at this time, it is difficult to see how their Minister could have acted otherwise in the circumstances.*

Nathan and his party arrived in Sydney on August 6 and were met by the Australian Air Minister, the Hon. Arthur Drakeford, as well as by a large gathering of civil aviation officials, Press and Radio. In Sydney, they started the familiar routine of a civic

---

* *The Times*, November 6, 1947.

reception by the Lord Mayor, a luncheon with the Governor and a reception by the Empire Parliamentary Association, a routine followed in Melbourne, Adelaide, Brisbane and Hobart. At Canberra the Minister was fully occupied with the South Pacific Air Transport Council meeting. Nothing very spectacular emerged from this gathering. The most important results were agreement that the Tasman sea would continue to be operated by British flying boats of the Solent type and that the Transpacific service, which was then being operated by American aircraft (Douglas DC-4s), should eventually turn over either to British or Canadian aircraft.

One of the primary impressions, gained constantly during such a tour [wrote Nathan afterwards] is that, although Australasia is both practically and sentimentally anxious to use British equipment and methods wherever convenient, the Australasian market has been far too little studied or cultivated in the United Kingdom. As a result—on the aircraft side, for instance, the characteristics of the latest British products are largely unknown or insufficiently known. Australians are critical of the lack of British sales efforts in their country compared with the constant attention of the Americans. The result can be seen practically in the fact that new orders are at present all for American machines. . . .

A great effort by the British aircraft industry to gain orders in Australasia is needed. Indeed Australia is an ideal continent for the development of civil aviation. Its potentialities are probably second only to those of the United States. Half the population of Australia is grouped, conveniently, in six large cities distant, on the average, 450 miles from one another. Such a distance means a long journey by surface transport, particularly in view of the nature of the journey. But such a distance is ideal for air transport.

A long week-end was spent in Tasmania, where the party were the guests of the Governor, Admiral Sir Hugh Binney, and Lady Binney, at Government House, Hobart. According to Peter Masefield, Nathan enjoyed every minute of what was almost a 'last outpost of Empire' in those days. The Binneys maintained Vice-Regal style in the antiquated Victorian Government House, dinner jackets and long dresses being the order of the day, and the evening meal was endearingly preceded by His Excellency, his Lady, and their guests stiffening to attention round the dinner table as 'God Save the King' was played on an ancient gramophone. During this brief visit, the Minister and his Director-General of Long Term Planning renewed their light aeroplane flying together when they flew over Hobart and the surrounding sea and country in a Moth Minor which had been chartered from the local aerodrome, in Nathan's words, 'all of thirty stone suspended, presumably in an inverted position, "Down Under" on only 100 h.p. over one of the deepest of deep-water harbours in the Antipodes'.

At this stage, Masefield had to return to London for urgent meetings on the progress of the D.H. 6 (later the Comet), while the others continued the journey to New Zealand and the Far East.

In New Zealand, the hospitality was equally abundant, although there were on the whole fewer official engagements. At Wellington they were the guests of the Governor-General, General Freyberg, V.C., whom Nathan remembered from his Gallipoli days. ('It is not easy for a Governor-General to be accepted by the people as a whole—there is a natural apathy to be overcome. Freyberg, however, may well be one of those few whom they take to their hearts.') New Zealand's domestic civil aviation Nathan found still in an embryonic state, due to the lack of adequate airports as distinct from airstrips. Here their tour was confined to the North Island.

In most of the provincial towns through which we passed or in which we stayed, we met local Mayors, usually for a meal in the local hotels which are of an unexpectedly high standard. It was interesting to note, too, how many small towns had aerodromes and flying clubs. For the rest—it's a beautiful country, but New Zealand stalactites look much like those at home and one geyser is very much like another. It was, however, a new experience to be accorded a Maori reception at Rotorua. In such a showplace it is inevitable that Maori customs should be somewhat commercialized, but there is, nevertheless, a desire to maintain these customs and traditions. How far, with intermarriage and modern education, they can genuinely survive is open to doubt. Fascinating and, with the singing, beautiful as they are, it hardly seems conceivable that they can be preserved; they belong to the period when the Maori canoe and the great tradition of the Polynesian voyagers were real and vital factors in daily life. They are little so now; and so it is a real experience to have seen something in which, in however small a part, these traditions still survive.

In Hong Kong ('a beautiful and impressive place'), Nathan was taken round the island and the leased territories, where he was struck by 'the apparently bustling and healthy commercial life which has been restored so quickly' after the Japanese occupation. Here he considered the biggest civil aviation problem was the airport at Kai Tak, situated on the north shore of Kowloon Bay, which 'must be one of the most dangerous in the world and, if regular land-planes are to be operated there, must be replaced as soon as possible'. Unfortunately no effective alternative site was available, and Kai Tak has remained the Hong Kong airport, although the runway was to be extended to 8,350 feet and the dangers were to be further minimized by the provision of full night-flying facilities, precision approach radar, and an instrument landing system.

Lady Nathan had to leave the party at Hong Kong in order to return to her duties as L.C.C. Chairman in London, while her husband and the remainder of the party flew on to Nanking, a distance of 930 miles which they covered in four hours. The impression left upon him of the Nationalist capital was of 'an untidy, dirty, poverty-stricken town in which everything seems to be unfinished and undecided and where only its ancient and beautiful walls match its pretensions as the capital of a vast Empire'. He heard much of Peiping (Peking) as 'the true and suitable capital', but had not time to go there. At this time civil war was raging in the north, and Peiping was only accessible by air, the railway having been cut by the Communist forces of Mao Tse-tung. Inflation was also rampant, and it took 123 notes in denominations of $10.000 for Nathan to pay for £10 worth of goods. ('Nobody bothered to count; they just looked at the first and last serial numbers in a bundle of notes.')

Indeed the rule of the Kuomintang was fast disintegrating, and in little more than than a year Generalissimo Chiang Kai-shek was to resign and depart with the rump of his Government to Formosa. Nevertheless, in spite of their domestic preoccupations Chiang and his wife invited Nathan and his party to dinner at their home. Afterwards Nathan recorded some of the things Chiang had said to him.

'The Generalissimo told me that he watched the domestic policy of our Government with very great interest. He had observed that the Government had not lost any by-elections. He knew that this was unique in our political history for any Government after so long a period thus to have continued assurances of public support. He was himself sympathetic to the policies of nationalization adopted by the Government and he had been watching with great care the form which the various socialized organizations were taking. He also found himself in agreement with their social policy in general. He told me—and he was anxious that Mr Attlee, Mr Bevin and Sir Stafford Cripps should know—that he had not been unobservant of the new British policy towards India and Ceylon, and also our policy with regard to Egypt. All of this met with his warm approval and would make co-operation between China and the United Kingdom much easier. He himself would welcome closer co-operation.'

In the course of this dinner, Nathan remarked to his host and hostess, 'You must come to London,' adding that he would be happy to have an opportunity of returning their hospitality. Next morning he was intrigued to receive a message from Madame Chiang asking whether his remark was serious or 'was it just a conversational elegance?'

In both Siam and Ceylon the Minister and his suite had another warm welcome. At Bangkok, they were accommodated in the Rose Palace, the V.I.P. Guest-house. 'There we were looked after most hospitably, although it was somewhat embarrassing that every time one even lifted a finger one was brought a glass of soda water or a glass of beer, more frequently the latter. If one came in just to change, it was in an hour possible to collect a glass of beer immediately on arrival, a glass of beer on leaving the bathroom for one's bedroom, and a glass of beer on leaving one's bedroom to leave the house.' In Siam the party had to watch a prolonged display of native dancing, some of which Nathan found 'a little tedious', and this was repeated in Ceylon, where four Temple dancers in Kandy, 'having got themselves worked up, were stopped with very considerable difficulty'.

The last port of call, apart from refuelling, was at Karachi, which in common with the rest of Pakistan was enjoying the bitter fruits of independence. 'Inevitably we found everyone much preoccupied with the present troubles,' Nathan remarked. 'It was interesting to note that even the majority of the British population strongly supported Pakistan's case and the view that a determined effort was being made by the Indian Government to stifle Pakistan at birth. The general view seemed to be that there was a well-designed Sikh conspiracy, with the Maharajah of Patiala at its source, which had been received not without some enthusiasm by the Indian Government. On top of this, there seemed to be a concerted attempt to stifle communications between East and West Pakistan.' In this connection Nathan found the local authorities very grateful for the recent 'Operation Pakistan', in which at very short notice Nathan's Ministry, in conjunction with B.O.A.C., had brought in twenty-five aircraft to evacuate Pakistan officials from the old central government in New Delhi to Pakistan's temporary capital in Karachi.

While in Karachi, Nathan stayed at Government House with the Governor-General, 72-year-old Mahomed Ali Jinnah, who as the creater of Pakistan had been the natural choice as tenant of Government House on the declaration of independence a few weeks previously.

Mr Jinnah who was extremely dapper and obviously takes an interest in his own personal appearance, was an older man in years than I had realized, though he still retained the slimness and upright bearing of youth.

He was very doubtful whether, administratively, Pakistan could survive, anyhow without formidable assistance from British Civil Servants. He said that he had never had the chance of getting his administration into being before pressure was brought to bear upon Pakistan by India, and that India had behaved very badly both in the way of finance and arms. They had not let Pakistan have their fair share of either, and administration had been made all the more difficult by the fact that they have refused to allow files relating to Pakistan affairs to leave Delhi.

He expressed himself as convinced that the British association needed to be maintained and was anxious that Pakistan should be made an integral part of the Commonwealth. He was altogether very cordial. I did not get much chance of saying anything because he is a fluent speaker whose fluency is difficult to dam; he clearly likes the sound of his own voice.

Nathan had spent a day in Karachi on his outward journey to Australia, which was just before independence. The new Governor-General was thus conscious that he was the last British Minister who had been in Government House under the old regime and the first British Minister under the new regime. 'He therefore took me into the garden in order that our photograph might be taken together to commemorate this notable occasion,' Nathan noted afterwards, 'and he promised me, later fulfilling the promise, that he would send me an autographed photograph.'

The Minister arrived home on October 6. 'From my own point of view,' he said afterwards, 'I have certainly gained a most valuable insight into the operation of our trunk services and into local civil aviation problems, while from a broader point of view I am quite certain that personal contact between a British Minister and the people not only of the Commonwealth and Empire but particularly also of the Far Eastern countries, cannot but have a beneficial effect on our relations generally. . . . I am convinced that B.O.A.C., so far as their actual operations are concerned, will more than bear comparison with any other operator in the world. With a multiplicity of types of inadequate aircraft they are doing a wonderful job. They can scarcely be blamed for wanting adequate tools with which to do the job not only better but more economically than anyone in the world.'

6

For his first year as Civil Aviation Minister, all had gone well for Nathan, and the sailing had been relatively smooth. However, after his return from his Australian tour, he began to encounter rough weather, which increased in turbulence during the next few months. First, there was the parliamentary outburst over the cost of the trip, which has already been noticed. Here Nathan was unlukcy, for had not a serious economic crisis in Britain developed during his absence, there would probably have been no hostile questions in the House of Commons such as, 'Why is it that Socialist Ministers are such gluttons for privilege?' Personally he brushed aside the attacks. Called to the telephone while reading the newspaper reports over breakfast in his Park Lane flat, he told the *Evening Standard* that he was not surprised that the questions had been asked. 'People are taking a legitimate interest in what is being done,' he said. On the tour itself and its cost, he commented: 'There is nothing odd or unusual in it. I don't settle the figure, and I cannot personally tell you how it is made up. The airplane was hired in the usual way, just as you would hire a car to take you to Manchester.' On the subject of why he had taken his family with him, it had already been pointed out that his wife was included in the official invitations extended to him by the various overseas governments, so that her fare was a legitimate charge on public funds. So far as his son was concerned, the Minister had paid the cost of his transport from his own pocket. Roger Nathan had recently been released from the army, and his father thought that he had earned a break before going to work in his office in the City.

This irritating aftermath of the air trip was a minor worry compared with the file which the Minister found on his desk after his return to Ariel House. The file contained the certified accounts of the three state-owned airways corporations for the financial year ended March 31, 1947. The accounts, which were published as Government White Papers during the Christmas recess, disclosed a loss of approximately £8 millions for B.O.A.C. or £60 for every passenger carried in what was its first post-war operating year, and a loss of £2 millions for B.E.A. or £30 for every passenger carried in the first eight months of its working. British South American Airways, on the other hand, showed a profit over a similar period of £32,000, although this did not reflect the true position, since B.S.A.A. had been able to charter aircraft from the Government at exceptionally low rates, which in effect amounted to a hidden subsidy. So far as B.O.A.C. was concerned, its deficit was attributed to various causes including the multiplicity of types of aircraft which the Corporation had to use, the delay in the delivery of the Tudors, scattered and improvised maintenance bases, and flight schedules in which commercial considerations were often subordinate to the national interest and considerations of national prestige. The B.E.A. losses were mainly due to the high cost of spare parts for aircraft and engines, which like B.O.A.C. it was obliged to order through the Ministry of Supply, the uneconomic rates paid for the carriage of troop mails, and to some extent the small British tourist traffic to the Continent, since holiday travellers at that time were each restricted to £25 foreign currency.

Nevertheless, the fact that the two major Corporations had lost more than £10 millions between them inside twelve months was bound to provoke a public outcry since the taxpayer had to foot the bill, and this was reflected in a debate in the House of Lords on the reassembly of Parliament in January, 1948. The debate was initiated by Lord Swinton, a Conservative and former Minister of Civil Aviation. Nathan replied that the losses were inevitable in the circumstances and he preferred to dwell on what the Corporations had achieved. He said that the Government had 'accepted open-eyed' the consequences of their 'fly British aeroplanes' policy, which would involve continuing losses for the next few years until new British aircraft types, which it was hoped would lead the world, became available. 'But,' he went on, 'I am determined that there shall be no element in that loss which powerful management or ruthless economy control can obviate.' He admitted that the Government was not satisfied with the existing procedure for ordering planes and equipment, and said that it had decided to seek the aid of business men of wide experience to assist in reviewing that procedure.

The Minister had a further worry a few days later when the B.S.A.A.C.'s Tudor IV, *Star Tiger*, disappeared on a flight from the Azores to Bermuda. The aircraft carried a crew of six, and twenty-five passengers including Air Marshal Sir Arthur Cuningham. At 3.15 a.m. on January 30, 1948, a message was sent from the *Star Tiger* to Bermuda asking for a bearing. A radio bearing was given and acknowledged. This was the last message from the aircraft. No abnormal weather conditions were reported. 'What happened in this case will never be known,' reported the court of investigation later, 'and the fate of the *Star Tiger* must remain an unsolved mystery.'

On February 3 it was announced that the Minister had decided, 'in view of the lack of evidence as to the cause of the accident', to ground the three remaining Tudor IV's in service, 'as a measure of prudence' pending detailed investigation.* This caused an immediate outcry from A. V. Roe & Co., makers of the Tudor, and also from the chief executive of B.S.A.A.C., 37-year-old Australian Air Vice-Marshal Donald Bennett, pioneer of the famous Pathfinder force in R.A.F. Bomber Command during the war. 'I resent the implication that there is anything wrong with the Tudor,' Sir Roy Dobson, Avro's managing director, publicly protested. 'The aircraft is sound and will stand any amount of chucking about. No one will get me to believe that the *Star Tiger's* four engines failed unless there was a shortage of petrol. The pilot could have finished the journey comfortably on two engines.'

The Minister could not reasonably object to Sir Roy's protest. But it was otherwise with 'Pathfinder' Bennett, a Corporation

* The restriction was lifted three months later.

216

employee, who unwisely gave an interview to the *Daily Express*. 'Interference with management has now reached such a degree that it has become increasingly difficult for an airline executive to be held responsible for the results he achieves,' Bennett was reported as having said. 'It was with the deepest regret that I heard from Lord Nathan, the Minister of Civil Aviation, that he found it necessary to interfere with what I took to be a matter for my own decision, namely whether an aircraft which is fully certified as airworthy should be withdrawn from service without any evidence. I add at once that I would be the first to withdraw a plane from service given the faintest grounds of expectation of improved safety. But on the advice of all the authorities concerned, including the Accidents Investigation Branch of the Ministry of Civil Aviation and the Air Registration Board, I have been unable to find the slightest grounds for any suspicion of fault in the Tudor IV. None whatever. I very deeply regret, therefore, that I should have been ordered to withdraw the Tudor IV from service, thereby inferring a lack of confidence in this type of air-liner.'

There could be only one outcome of such flagrant insubordination. At its next meeting the Board of British South American Airways 'unanimously concluded' that Bennett's statements were 'in contradiction of the considered views of the Board of which the chief executive was aware. Moreover, this was not an isolated instance of its kind, and was the culmination of a series of differences between the Board and the chief executive. They had accordingly lost confidence in him and had decided that they had no option but to dispense with his services. He had refused the Board's suggestion that he should tender his resignation, and the Board were therefore obliged to dismiss him.' The pill was sweetened by 'a gratuitous payment' of £4,500, which the Board made and which Bennett accepted as compensation for loss of office.

'Today I have had the highest honour of my life conferred upon me,' said Bennett, who was a C.B., C.B.E. and D.S.O. 'I have been sacked for having spoken my own mind.' At the same time he announced that he was going to stand as a Liberal candidate in the by-election which was then pending in North Croydon. In the ensuing campaign the dismissed executive complained of 'a state of servitude, of restrictions, and a spiritual poverty unbelievable in this land of freedom' and declared that he would fight to the utmost against 'Socialist strangulation'. He might have saved his energies and his pocket, since, in spite of strong support from the Beaverbrook press, sometimes reckoned to be the kiss of death, he was returned at the bottom of the poll and forfeited his deposit. But in the attacks on Nathan, which he made during the campaign, unfortunately some of the mud stuck.

Bennett's dismissal was followed a week later by the resignation of another Air Vice-Marshal, Sir Conrad Collier, Controller of Technical and Operational Services (traffic control, navigational aids and telecommunications) at the Civil Aviation Ministry. Asked by one newspaper whether he had had any disagreements with 'the high-ups' at the Ministry on the policy of Britain's nationalized air lines, Sir Conrad replied: 'You will have to fathom that out for yourself. I am not resigning because of my health.'

On top of these worries, Nathan was being pressed by Herbert Oppenheimer to return to the City and resume his share of their law practice, since the senior partner was now over seventy and wished to take things more easily. At the next opportunity Nathan explained the position to the Prime Minister and asked to be released, but Attlee asked him to stay on at the Ministry as a personal favour for at least some months longer. The Whitsun recess was then agreed as a suitable time. The reason was that Attlee was anxious to bring back Hugh Dalton, who had been obliged to resign as Chancellor of the Exchequer following an inadvertent 'leak' as he was about to present his Budget in the previous November, and the Prime Minister felt he could not do this until at least six months had elapsed. In the event, the change came about at the end of May when Dalton returned to the Cabinet and Attlee formally accepted Nathan's resignation, with effect from June 1, at the same time announcing the appointment of Lord Pakenham (later Earl of Longford) as the new Minister of Civil Aviation.

Meanwhile Nathan had come to realize that Government policy must be modified in order to reduce the running losses of B.E.A. and B.O.A.C. A start was made with the first before he left the Ministry, when it was announced, on May 19, that certain private lines were to be allowed to operate some internal services which B.E.A. could not run economically. As regards B.O.A.C., he became convinced, in spite of opposition from the British aircraft industry, that the 'Fly British' policy must be abandoned and at least replaced by 'Fly Commonwealth' for a period of years. He therefore favoured the proposal that B.O.A.C. should buy a fleet of the powerful four-engined Canadian airliners (Canadair IV's), capable of accommodating 40 passengers on Transatlantic flights. Nathan was not to remain in Ariel House long enough to see this proposal through the Cabinet, which it fell to his successor to implement; but he did some useful preliminary work on it which Lord Pakenham was later to acknowledge. His last public appearance as Minister was to open the plenary session of the Commonwealth Air Transport Council in London on May 28, when he appealed to the delegates of ten Commonwealth countries to beware of the dangers of too many regulations. 'In our search for order in the air,' he said, 'let us avoid that over-regulation that can easily develop into strangling restrictionism.'

Nathan's departure from the Ministry was signalized by the customary exchange of letters with the Prime Minister. Nathan had already submitted the draft of his letter to Downing Street and at Attlee's suggestion dated the final version in the same week as the Prime Minister's reply 'in order to avoid any appearance of undue haste'.

Ministry of Civil Aviation,
Ariel House,
Strand,
London, W.C.2.
25th May 1948

My dear Prime Minister,

It is now some months since I advised you that I should be wishing, at a convenient moment about Whitsuntide, to relinquish my office. For it is essential that I should return to my professional practice after so long an absence, especially as my senior partner, now well on into the 70s and by no means in robust health, cannot continue to sustain the burden which my absence whilst holding Ministerial Office has thrown upon him.

I must express my very real regret at taking leave as a Minister of yourself, under whom I have been proud to serve during these difficult years, and of my other colleagues; all have throughout shown me unfailing co-operation and much personal kindness, which I shall always recall with pleasure.

Let me add that, though I must now make myself free to resume my profession, I shall nevertheless hope to participate in public activities where it is thought that my particular experience may be useful, as I did for so many years before I was appointed a Member of your Government.

Yours very sincerely,
NATHAN OF CHURT.

10 Downing Street,
Whitehall.
31st May, 1948

My dear Nathan,

As you say in your letter, you informed me some months ago that business reasons would necessitate your relinquishing your office before long. I am much obliged to you for your consideration, and I fully understand the compelling reasons which oblige you to offer your resignation. I must, therefore, accept with regret your departure from the Government.

I should like to express to you my warm appreciation of the good and loyal service which you have rendered both as Under Secretary of State for War and as Minister for Civil Aviation during a period when there were many difficult problems to be faced.

I am glad to know that I can count upon you in the future as in the past for service to the country and the Party. I hope, too, that you will be able from time to time to bring to the debates in the House of Lords the valuable experience which you have gained in office.

With all good wishes,
Yours sincerely,
C. R. ATTLEE

The Right Honourable Lady Nathan, Chairman of the London
County Council

Arriving at Sydney, August 8, 1947. Left to right: Lord Nathan, Hon. Roger Nathan, Lady Nathan

'The letters, the letters. It's all in the letters,' the ex-Minister protested, when he was asked by a staff correspondent on the *Manchester Guardian* about his future. In fact, he said, he had not given much thought to what lay ahead apart from his work as a solicitor. The newspaper man thought that the sceptics who doubted that there was no political significance about Nathan's departure from office should know that for an ex-Minister 'he was in a particularly happy mood'. On the other hand, it was plain that he was suffering from nervous strain and overwork. His anxieties were not lessened about the rumours which attributed his resignation to the action of Ernest Bevin, the Foreign Minister.

One version emanated from Russian sources. Two months previously there had been a collision over Berlin between a B.E.A. Viking and a Soviet Yak fighter, in which fifteen people were killed, including the pilot of the fighter. The official British report on the crash alleged that it was caused by the action of the Soviet fighter which disregarded the accepted rules of flying. The Foreign Office sent a Note to the Russians claiming compensation, but this was rejected by the Russians, who made a counter-claim. Later, *Taegliche Rundschau*, the official organ of the Soviet military administration in Berlin, claimed that Nathan had been forced to resign on account of his 'wrong handling' of the incident.

> Instead of waiting for full and objective reports of the catastrophe, Lord Nathan jumped to conclusions and put Mr Bevin and the British Prime Minister in a very difficult situation. The British investigation showed that the British plane had not observed the regulations between western Germany and Berlin. As a result of Lord Nathan's rash action, the British even claimed compensation. Lord Nathan's resignation is obviously an attempt to compensate for British mistakes in this scandalous affair.

The other rumour, equally without foundation, was more disturbing. It was expressed by a rich and influential Jewish client of Nathan's law firm, who telephoned him and said: 'You have resigned for reasons which you have given, but it is believed that the real reason may be that you have had trouble with Mr Ernest

Bevin about recognition of the State of Israel. Having regard to the fact that you have been a member of the Government for the last two and a half years and silent upon matters relating to Israel, we must ask you unequivocally to state your position.

A heated altercation followed on the telephone, in the course of which Nathan pointed out that he could not, within twenty-four hours of leaving the Government where he had a collective responsibility along with his colleagues, take a line contrary to Government policy, and it would be contrary to this policy to advocate the immediate recognition of Israel. Tackled about not sending Dr Weizmann a message of congratulation on his election as President of the new state, which had been proclaimed a fortnight previously, Nathan answered that he could not have done this for the same reason, but now that he was out of the Government he intended to write to the President privately as an old friend.

Oppenheimer, to whom Nathan reported these exchanges, was not unnaturally annoyed. He wrote frankly to the client:

> You were very wrong in upsetting H.L.N. the other evening on the telephone. He is in a very unsettled condition anyhow and has to undergo a cure, and my one anxiety is that he shall be fit again as soon as possible and take his full share of a double burden which I have carried too long at my time of life.
>
> As regards the cause you have at heart, everyone knows *where* N. has stood for a quarter of a century. Had he been so stupid as to try and push his views on the subject whilst he was in the Government, it would obviously have done incalculable harm, and if he agitated now the effect would be very similar and create the quite false impression that events in Palestine were the reason for his resignation. It would gravely injure the cause if ill-disposed people could spread the lie that one of the Jewish members of the Government had put Zionism before loyalty and service to his own country.*

* This view was indicated by the diplomatic correspondent of the Palestine *Jewish Herald*, who wrote under a London date-line (June 3, 1948): 'Although Lord Nathan's resignation from the British Cabinet [*sic*] is ascribed to "personal business reasons" it is widely believed that his Zionist outlook rendered it impossible for him to remain in the Government.'

Nathan's nineteen months as Minister of Civil Aviation had been one of the stormiest periods in air transport history. Although he had many problems and troubles he also had some constructive achievements in his record, particularly in the field of air safety. 'Lord Nathan has discharged an unenviable task with some credit,' wrote the aviation journal *Flight* on his resignation. 'He had innumerable difficulties to face. And it can be said that he was always willing to listen to the views of all concerned. If, afterwards, he did not always act upon the advice given him, that may often have been due to the obtuseness of some of his colleagues in the Government, and to the imperviousness to persuasion of the Treasury.'*

Later his successor at Ariel House was to pay him an equally warm tribute. 'If he had continued in office a few weeks longer,' wrote Lord Pakenham in his autobiography, 'it would have been he, not I, who would have fought and won the Cabinet battle for the re-equipment of B.O.A.C. with modern Canadair aircraft. He had done the indispensable spadework in this as in many other ways.'† One of these 'other ways' was the appointment of a lawyer, Lord Macmillan, to head the Court of Inquiry into the loss of the *Star Tiger*, in the face of opposition from the technicians. The report was issued after Nathan had left the Ministry. In sending him a copy of it, Lord Pakenham wrote: 'I think that the persons appointed have done a brilliant job and that your decision to set up an official Court of Inquiry has been completely justified. I might incidentally remark that this Report does finally demolish the old argument that such Courts are incapable of assessing adequately the highly technical and scientific issues involved.'

The final word may be left with Nathan's Private Secretary at the Ministry, Dick Poland. 'Rather to my surprise,' wrote Poland to his former chief three weeks after Nathan had left Ariel House, 'I have not heard one single person express any disbelief in the official and (unusual combination) true reason for your resignation. Several people—that is all those who have commented on your

* *Flight*, June 10, 1948.
† *Born to Believe* (1953), at p. 202.

resignation—have said they were sorry to lose a Minister who, even though he had not succeeded in getting anything out of the Treasury, had tried to do what he could for the [flying] clubs, etc. I am sure that is genuine. I have not recently had much to do with the Corporations or charter firms, etc., but insofar as I have I have not heard anyone in those circles repeating any of the rumours we both expected. I have a rather incredible vision of Truth pointing at your case with an air of surprised gratification as proof that she is indeed in the end triumphant.'

CHAPTER SEVEN

Last Years

NATHAN'S DEPARTURE FROM THE GOVERNMENT IN 1948 ENABLED him to resume his law practice and so relieve Herbert Oppenheimer of the burden he had been carrying for the past two and a half years in Copthall Avenue. It also made it possible for him to devote more time to the many voluntary charitable and communal organizations in which he had come to take an interest over the years. Fortunately, he was a man of immense vitality, both physical and mental, and his energies found fulfilment in public service. He proved to be the ideal committee man, shrewd, good-humoured and imperturbable, and the number of public bodies and institutions, whose deliberations he guided as Chairman or President for most of the remainder of his life, was evidence of his skill as well as his popularity in this field. These ranged from the Westminster Hospital, the Wolfson Foundation, the Maccabiah (Jewish Olympic Games), the Council of the Weizmann Institute Foundation, and the Old Pauline Club, to the Royal Geographical Society, the Mount Everest Expedition, the Royal Society of Arts, the Faculty of Royal Designers for Industry, the Association of Technical Institutions, and the London and Middlesex Archaeological Society. He was also active in the City of London, where he served as Master of two Worshipful Companies, the Pattenmakers and the Gardeners. Nor did he neglect his interest in Freemasonry. He was a member of nine lodges, of which he became Worshipful Master of three; finally he was appointed Grand Warden of the United Grand Lodge of England. He was the first English Jew to be an Associate Knight of the Order of St John of Jerusalem. Fortunate, too, was any organization—and there was about a score of these— who could secure his presence on its committee of management.

If there was one particular field of activity into which he put more work than any other, this was undoubtedly the medical. From 1948 until the year of his death, fifteen years later, he was Chairman of the Westminster Hospital, having been a Governor since 1935 and Vice-Chairman from 1943 to 1948. He had previously been Chairman of the Westminster Children's Hospital (The Infants Hospital) for fourteen years. After the National Health Services Act became law, he was appointed Crown representative on the British Medical Council, being the first layman to sit on the Council. He was also Chairman of the Executive Committee of the British Empire Cancer Campaign; he served on the Council of King Edward's Hospital Fund for London and the Fleming Memorial Fund for Medical Research, as well as the research committee of the College of General Practitioners and the advisory committee of the Royal Society of Medicine; and he was a founder member and Vice-President of the British Society for International Health Education. Finally, when Queen Mary's Hospital, Roehampton, was integrated with the Westminster Hospital, he became Chairman of its House Committee and a Trustee.

The Westminster, known as 'Parliament's Own Hospital', was the oldest of the voluntary hospitals in the metropolis, having been founded following the meeting of four philanthropists in a London coffee house in 1716 called to discuss a 'Charitable Proposal for Relieving the Sick and Needy and other Distressed Persons'. The outcome of their discussion was the establishment three years later of an 'Infirmary for the Sick and Needy' in a small house in Petty France, later to become known as the Westminster Hospital. During the next two centuries the hospital was located in three other premises, until it finally settled in the present commodious buildings occupying an acre and a half in St John's Gardens shortly before the last war. The then Chairman was Sir Bernard Docker 'whose services and munificence,' in his successor's words, 'might well be held to entitle him to be known as a Second Founder of the Hospital.' On July 5, 1948, the hospitals of the country passed under the jurisdiction of the Minister of Health, and, as with the others, the Governors of the Westminster, which had for generations been an independent body elected by the subscribers, became the agents of the Minister, appointed by him.

Some members of the old board resigned because they did not approve of what Nathan euphemistically called 'the new order of things'. They included the Chairman, Sir Bernard Docker, who was consequently succeeded in the chair by the Vice-Chairman. However, although there were a few new faces, the majority of the new Board, like Nathan himself, was the same as before—'men and women long actively associated with the Westminster as a voluntary hospital, who welcomed the opportunity of continuing to serve it in the difficult transition from the old dispensation to the new'.

From the outset the new Chairman and his colleagues, old and new, were 'determined that the links with the past should not be broken, but that there should be continuity of tradition, applied with respect for the past coupled with recognition of the changing and increasing needs of the times'. For that reason, at the opening of the first meeting of the new Board of Governors on that memorable July afternoon in 1948, Nathan instituted a practice, which has since continued, that 'the first Minute Book of the First Founders should be placed upon the Table and attention drawn to the opening Minute, dating back almost two and a half centuries, as a reminder that we are charged with present responsibility for the wise conduct and good government of a hospital with a long and respectable history'.

It was a great feather in the Westminster's cap, in which the Chairman took much pride, that the hospital should have been called upon to provide the surgeon and the medical and nursing staff for the lung operation which King George VI underwent in

September, 1951. A preliminary bronchoscopy had revealed that the King was suffering from cancer, and this necessitated the removal of the whole of the left lung. The operation which was a complete success, in spite of the risk of cardiac complications, was carried out by Sir Clement Price Thomas, the specialist and house surgeon, with the aid of a team of assistants, anaesthetists and nursing staff from the Westminster, whose present buildings incidentally had been opened by the King in 1939. Certainly His Majesty appreciated everything that was done for him. 'I have been most beautifully looked after from the surgeon to the nurses and doctors,' he wrote to Queen Mary while he was convalescing. 'They have all done their best to make me as comfortable as possible.' That the accompanying administrative work also went smoothly and was performed with 'appropriate discretion' was a further source of satisfaction to the Chairman. 'It is right to record,' he wrote afterwards, 'that the setting up of an operating theatre in Buckingham Palace and the other arrangements connected with the operation upon and the tending of the King called for administrative abilities of a high order.'

It is only right to add, too, that throughout his term as the Hospital Chairman Nathan was thoroughly well liked by the whole staff, medical, nursing and administrative—as well as the patients, of whom from time to time he himself was one, due to the increasing bouts of illness from which he suffered during this period. Even as a Governor he was no stranger to the wards. On Christmas Day he made a point of going round and carving the turkey, a practice which he never missed and which incidentally resulted in his own family having their Christmas dinner in the evening.

Nathan's association with hospitals and their staffs, in conjunction with his practice as a solicitor, stimulated an interest in the law relating to the liability of medical practitioners and medical institutions for professional negligence. A little research led him to the discovery that there was no comprehensive and detailed statement of the law on the subject, and he decided to produce a book about it. He was struck by the fact that, so long as the hospitals were voluntary and the medical staff honorary, an action brought against a hospital or a medical practitioner was something quite out of the way; yet, since the National Health Service Act had come into force, there was a remarkable and in some instances an alarming flood of such cases. Nathan concluded that this increase was attributable to three main factors; first, the introduction of the Health Service, which effected a subtle change in the relationship between the doctor or institution and the patient; secondly, the introduction of the Legal Aid Act, which made it possible for impecunious plaintiffs to litigate where before their lack of means would have prevented it; and thirdly, certain modifications in the law as to the liability of hospitals for the acts of their staffs, which made the plaintiff's task much easier. Until 1942, it had been generally accepted that a hospital could not be held liable for the acts or omissions of its staff in professional as distinct from administrative medical matters; the hospital's duty was simply to provide a competent professional staff and by doing so discharged its obligations to the patient. After 1942, and more particularly after 1948, the conception of a hospital's obligations to its patients underwent profound changes, and the area of a hospital's personal liability was progressively extended by decisions of the Courts, until the position was reached within a few years that a hospital was liable for the negligence of any member of its professional staff—even, it was thought, for the negligence of a part-time visiting surgeon.

'It is enough for me to say in this connection,' wrote Nathan in 1956, 'that I have become very conscious, as a Hospital Chairman, of the effect on medical men and hospital administrators (particularly the former, and more especially the junior among them in standing) of the apprehension of litigation.' Hence the publication in 1957 of *Nathan on Medical Negligence*, which he wrote with the assistance of a barrister named Anthony Barrowclough, who had previously helped him with his contribution on Civil Aviation to the new edition of *Halsbury's Laws of England*.

'I trust that the result may be considered useful and worthwhile by my fellows of the legal profession,' was the author's wish, 'and by the members of the medical and nursing professions and hospital administrators, so many of whom I have known so long as colleagues and friends.'

Certainly in an age of increasing complaints by patients against the medical profession and hospital authorities in respect of treatment received under the National Health service, it is an advantage to have in compact and easily readable form the answers to such questions as to who is responsible when a hypodermic needle breaks, when a lethal dose of procaine is administered in mistake for a harmless injection of cocaine, when a theatre sister leaves a swab inside a patient during an operation, and when a surgeon does not explain to a patient the risks of the operation he is about to perform. All the answers can be found in *Nathan on Medical Negligence.*

2

Nathan made one outstanding contribution to English law reform. His original inspiration came from Lord Beveridge, the chief architect of the welfare state, who had undertaken a survey of voluntary social service shortly after the war. 'Opportunity and encouragement must be kept for voluntary action,' Beveridge had urged. 'There is a need for political invention to find new ways of fruitful co-operation between public authorities and voluntary agencies.' In considering what needed to be done to enable the voluntary or charitable movement to give of its best, Beveridge advocated, among other points, 'an exhaustive survey of the charitable trusts already established in this country and of the means of making them most beneficial to the community.' What he had particularly in mind was the existence of idle millions in the funds of obsolete charities, which had long ago ceased to serve their purpose, and how best these funds might be made available for new and creative ventures. The publication of Beveridge's *Voluntary Action* was followed, two years later, by a debate in the House of Lords on a motion brought forward by Lord Samuel on 'the need for the encouragement of voluntary action to promote social progress' (June 22, 1949). From this historic debate there emerged unanimity on the continuing value of charity in the welfare state.

Samuel began by pointing out that voluntary organizations had found that the question of finance was becoming steadily more difficult. Formerly, they depended largely on the patronage of wealthy people and subscriptions, but high taxation had now left such people in the position of Rabelais, who said in his will: 'I have nothing. I owe much. The rest I give to the poor.' On the other hand, there were millions of pounds lying derelict and unused in banks, in the Court of Chancery, and in moribund charities. As a first step Samuel suggested the appointment of a Royal Commission or some other form of inquiry into the whole matter.

Samuel was followed, among others, by Nathan, who said his experience as chairman of the Westminster Group of Hospitals had proved that 'there was nothing incompatible between a health service organized under a Government department and the voluntary work which did so much to humanize what otherwise might become somewhat rigid'. He, too, thought that there should be an inquiry into a subject about which very little was known. 'Those concerned in it,' he added, 'should have an assurance that the Government looked with sympathy on their aspirations and ideals.'

Beveridge, who also spoke in the debate, related an example of an obsolete charity discovered by the Royal Commission of 1878. In 1491, a man left money to produce 5s a year for an annual 'love feast' at St Clement's, Eastcheap, each Maundy Thursday. The churchwardens were to call together all citizens who had quarrelled and give them a dinner to reconcile them. By 1878 the 'love feast' had grown into a dinner at Richmond, costing £70 a year, for sixty or seventy of the richer ratepayers of the district whether they had quarrelled or not. 'What we want is to get money out of dead hands into living hands,' said Beveridge, 'and into the living hands of private citizens,' adding amid laughter, since he was a Liberal, 'not His Majesty's Government.'

Lord Pakenham, replying for the Government, said that the Government's view was that the voluntary spirit was the lifeblood of democracy, and it was quite wrong to imagine that the nationalization of any social service excluded the volunteer. 'We are convinced that voluntary associations have rendered, are rendering, and must be encouraged to continue to render, great and indispensable service to the community.' At the same time, the Government was sure that the purposes which Beveridge particularly had in mind, namely an inquiry into the state of charitable trusts, would not be well served by the establishment of a Royal Commission. 'The famous Royal Commission of Lord Brougham sat for nineteen years,' Lord Pakenham went on, 'and while we might hope for speedier progress in this age of movement and crisis thinking, there is no doubt that an elaborate investigation of the kind suggested in Lord Beveridge's book, poking its nose, inevitably as of duty bound, into every individual trust, would take far too long to deal with what the noble Lord rightly claims is a pressing problem.' On the other hand, the Minister assured the House that the Government agreed that something needed doing and doing without delay. Hence they would undertake to 'inquire forthwith into the steps appropriate and necessary to remedy the situation that is admitted on all sides to contain elements of waste, anachronism and anomaly'.

The result was that, six months later, in January, 1950, the Prime Minister appointed a committee of twelve consisting of ten men and two women, under Nathan's chairmanship, to report on the changes in the law and practice relating to charitable trusts in England and Wales which would be necessary 'to enable the maximum benefit to the community to be derived from them'.

Behind the public pressure for this inquiry there were two motive forces: first, the appreciation of the importance, particularly in the circumstances of the times, of putting to the best possible use the country's voluntary agencies, including charitable trusts; and secondly, and more specifically, the importance of providing for voluntary action what it was hoped would be considerable additional

LAST YEARS

finance from private, as opposed to public, funds, by the re-
allocation of the endowments of charitable trusts which were
thought to be 'moribund' or 'dormant'. How far this re-allocation
would prove possible or be justified was not known at the time
the committee was appointed, but Nathan realized that little or
nothing could be achieved without revising what was known as
the *cy-près* doctrine then governing changes in the purpose of a
trust, that is to say, that it was necessary to keep 'as near as possible'
(*cy-près*) to the original purpose of the founder, and that no change
could be made unless it was impossible at the outset or subsequently
to carry out the founder's wishes, or funds became surplus to
needs.

The Nathan Committee, as it became known, proceeded more
rapidly than Lord Brougham's Royal Commission, completing its
work and publishing a 250-page Report within three years, during
which period it held thirty-one meetings besides nine of a drafting
Sub-Committee and received evidence from seventeen individuals
and seventy-five bodies. The Committee's principal recommendation was that the *cy-près* doctrine should be relaxed so as to admit
of trust instruments being altered, even though the carrying out of
their objects had not become impracticable. The Committee's other
recommendations, which like the relaxation of the *cy-près* doctrine
the Government subsequently accepted, included the reconstitution
of the Charity Commission with the introduction of a non-legal
element, the removal of the remaining restrictions on the accumula-
tion of land in the 'dead hand' (*mortmain*) of charitable corporations, and the establishment of a system of central, classified records
of trusts, with the obligation of trustees to register with the relevant
central authority prescribed details of their trusts. Apart from
30,000 educational trusts, there were no accessible and up-to-date
statistics of the remainder, upwards of 80,000, religious and otherwise, with estimated assets of £200,000,000 and vast holdings of
land.*

* *Report of the Committee on the Law and Practice relating to Charitable
Trusts* (1952). Cmd. 8710.

The most typical and numerous of these non-educational trusts were parochial charities, the benefits of which were confined to a single parish or small group of parishes. Many of these were anomalous or obsolete, like the example quoted by Lord Beveridge. At Biddenden in Kent, to take another example, seventy people were entitled to receive loaves annually from a charity founded by Siamese twins in 1100. But for many years few had availed themselves of the privilege. Similarly, at Weston Turville in Buckinghamshire, a widow died in 1736 and left her property to provide bread for the poor of the parish. The income could purchase 1,000 loaves a year, but even if the bread were to be baked it would have been impossible to distribute it under the definition of poverty laid down in the widow's will. Similarly, a fund started at Bitteswell in Leicestershire at the time of the Spanish Armada 'to provide an armed man in time of war', and estimated to yield £30 a year, had amounted to over £11,000 in the bank and could not be touched under the *cy-près* doctrine. So rigid was the doctrine that the churchwardens of another parish, who were the trustees of a fund established 'for the advancement of prayer', could not use it for the purpose of providing prayer-stools, which were badly needed in the church. Then there were many thousands of pounds locked up in trust funds to provide red flannel nightgowns for widows and spinsters. 'What self-respecting woman,' asked Nathan, 'would dare to claim money for a red flannel night dress today?' Yet this was at a time when many women were in desperate need of warm clothing for their families.

The Nathan Committee had drawn attention to the 'tangle' of statutes with which trustees had to contend and had pleaded that the law, with the changes they proposed, should be simplified and re-enacted as a 'single, short, intelligible statute'. So great proved the task of revision and of drafting that it was not until February, 1960, that the Charities Bill was introduced by the Lord Chancellor, Lord Kilmuir, in the House of Lords. The measure had its second reading on March 1, when Nathan spoke in the debate. Among those who congratulated him was Professor A. L. Goodhart,

Master of University College, Oxford, and former Professor of Jurisprudence in the University.

University College, Oxford. 3 March 1960.

Yesterday evening Raymond [Lord] Evershed [Master of the Rolls] dined with me in London and he told me that you had made a magnificent speech on the Charities Bill. My heartiest congratulations on the wonderful work you have done in creating an orderly system where chaos reigned in the past.

There is an interesting article on American charities in the last number of the *Harvard Law Review*. In an introductory footnote the author points out how sound was the work of the Nathan Committee.

You must feel great satisfaction at the successful outcome of your labours. It is a pity that the old practice of naming the Act after its progenitor has gone out of fashion; it would have been pleasant to refer to the Nathan Act.

The Bill naturally followed closely the Nathan Committee's recommendations, all the most important of which were embodied in it. As *The Times* remarked in a leading article on the day the Bill received the Royal Assent (29 July 1960): 'It is at least as much a tribute to the soundness of the principles and draftsmanship as of governmental intransigence that it has emerged from Parliament virtually intact.'

The four main aims of the Charities Act, 1960, were expressed by the Lord Chancellor in the second reading debate on the measure as follows:

1) to modernize the machinery of administration of charity law, by replacing the complex series of eleven earlier Acts, passed between 1853 and 1939 and containing 186 sections in all, with new provisions amounting to 49 sections;
2) to establish a statutory foundation for voluntary co-operation between charity and the statutory welfare services on a basis of equality and partnership, by authorizing a local authority to maintain an index of local charities, open to public inspection, to carry out a review of the working of local charities, and to make arrangements for co-ordin-

ating the activities of the authority with those of one or
more charities providing similar services;

3) to establish a central register of charities, so that the particulars of charitable institutions available to meet any
particular need can be more easily discovered and made
available to the public, especially to social workers;

4) to extend and specify the conditions which must be satisfied before the purposes of a charitable trust can be altered
thus relaxing the *cy-près* doctrine.

In addition the opportunity was taken to repeal the law of *mortmain*, an anachronism dating from feudal times whose original
purpose had been lost. The trustees of a charity further benefited
from registration, since so long as an institution is on the register
it is conclusively presumed to be a charity and so is automatically
entitled to income tax relief.

The following private letters were exchanged between Nathan
and the Home Secretary, then Mr R. A. Butler, after the Act had
received the Royal Assent.

Nathan to Home Secretary

July 31, 1960. I'm clucking like an old hen, and so should
you be: or perhaps more appropriately I should say you must
be clucking, and so am I. For it cannot but be a real satisfaction to both of us that the Charities Bill is now off the stocks
and on the Statute Book. We shall be at one in hoping that it
may have for the future the results for which it is designed.

If, with my Committee, I laid the foundations, you certainly built firmly and squarely on them. I write to express
my own feeling, which I am sure is shared by all concerned
with this particular area of activity, that your effort and
achievement will be proved, as the years go by, to have been
well worth while. It is a matter of much gratification to me to
have been in some degree associated with you in all this, and
I much appreciate the confidence and goodwill you have
shown to me in discussing at various stages the problems
requiring solution.

With H. E. Mohamed
Ali Jinnah, Governor-
General of Pakistan, at
Government House,
Karachi, October, 1947

Greeting
Chaim Weizmann,
President of Israel

At Dr Weizmann's 75th Birthday Dinner, November 9, 1949. Left to right: Lord Nathan, Lady Nathan, Field Marshal J. C. Smuts, Viscount Samuel

The Second Generation
Left to right: Jenny, the Hon. Mrs Roger Nathan, Rupert, Nicola

Home Secretary to Nathan

August 15, 1960. It has been an arduous session; but one of the compensations is to receive a letter like yours and to feel that all the work that has gone into framing the Charities Bill and carrying it through both Houses has not only achieved its end, but has been appreciated by those best qualified to judge. Everyone concerned with this subject knows that you and your colleagues performed a most signal service in clarifying issues and clearing the ground on which we have been able to erect the new structure; and I can only repeat to you privately what the Government has said publicly, that the country owes you a great debt of gratitude: and I am sure that your work will long be remembered.

It was most helpful also to have your views in confidence during the preparation of the Bill, and your support in the House of Lords. I myself regarded it as an important item in my programme of social reforms; but it was not a Bill with a popular appeal; and the general acceptance of its main features perhaps gave undue prominence to a number of small Committee points which took up a lot of time and left us with all too little room for the final stages. But I have noticed with pleasure the welcome given by organized charity and informed opinion to the passage of the Act, and like you I have every hope that its massive benefits will become more and more apparent as time goes on.

At this time, charity trustees had no power, in the absence of any special provision in the trusts of the charity or of a scheme regulating it, to invest the charity's funds outside a limited range of fixed interest securities, commonly known as the Trustee List. Safety of income and capital was the prime consideration, but this theory had been upset by inflation and the fall in the purchasing power of money, a process accelerated by two world wars in a little more than twenty years. The Nathan Committee had therefore recommended that, subject to certain safeguards, trustees should be empowered to invest a proportion of their trust funds in equity stocks and shares of leading financial, industrial and commercial companies quoted on the Stock Exchange. The Committee regarded this as essential to the safety of the trust fund for two reasons; first, because equities represent the right, not to a fixed money income and a fixed capital sum, but to a share in the companies' profits and assets, and are thus ultimately associated with real values and not with money values; and secondly, because equities contain the possibility of growth, owing to the practice adopted by most companies of retaining in the business a considerable part of the profits and so adding to the value of the equity.

The Nathan Committee's recommendations under this head were accepted in general by the Government and were embodied in the Trustee Investments Act, 1961, which in this respect supplements the Charities Act. The Trustee Investments Act empowers all trustees, in the absence of any contrary intention, to invest up to one-half of their trust funds in a wide range of investments, including ordinary stocks and shares in substantial public companies, and, moreover, it imposes a duty on trustees to have regard to the need for diversification of investments of the trust, in so far as is appropriate to the circumstances of the trust. Since a great many charities had very small trust funds—the Nathan Committee estimated that at least 35,000 had a gross annual income of less than £25—the Act confers on the Court and the Charity Commissioners a general power to make schemes for the establishment of common investment funds, for instance, by investing in a unit trust which itself holds a widespread portfolio of equities. The Trustee Investments Act also requires the trustees to take expert financial advice before investing in any investment other than Defence Bonds, Savings Certificates and certain bank deposits, and to take similar advice at regular intervals.

Among the charitable trusts to be registered under the new Charities Act was one in which Nathan was particularly interested, since he had been chairman of the trustees since its inception in 1955. This was the Wolfson Foundation created by the industrialist Sir Isaac Wolfson, Bart., in the founder's words, 'mainly for the advancement of health, education and youth activities in the United Kingdom and Commonwealth'. For the first three years of its existence Nathan did all the administrative work himself in an honorary capacity, but with the gradual extension of the Foundation's activities it was necessary to appoint an officer who would combine the duties of Director of the Foundation and Secretary to the trustees. At this time, Lieutenant-General Sir Harold Redman had just retired as Governor of Gibraltar, and Nathan was able to enlist his services.

When Nathan died, *The Times* in its obituary notice omitted to mention his work for the Foundation. Sir Harold Redman supplied the omission.*

With his great knowledge of the law and practice relating to charities, he was of the greatest possible help at the outset in framing with the founder members of the Wolfson family the trust deed and the policy to be adopted for the important first years of its existence.

Later, in 1958, he was largely instrumental in widening the basis of the Foundation and in the inclusion on its Board of Trustees of such distinguished members as the late Lord Birkett, the late Lord Evans, Sir Stanford Cade, Professor Goodhart, Sir John Cockroft and Lord Kilmuir.

Probably the greatest contribution that Lord Nathan made to the Foundation was to lend the creative imagination, which was one of his great attributes, to the development of the policy of the trustees, the effect of which has been the adoption of substantial projects in new fields.

During the first seven years of its existence, while Nathan was its chairman, the Foundation disbursed £4½ millions, all out of income from the capital fund. 'Nearly all our money goes for health and educational purposes,' said Nathan at the end of the first seven years. 'Only in two cases have we made grants to individuals. Both were doctors, and in each case the results have been brilliant.' One institutional grant in which Nathan took an especial interest made possible the establishment of a chair and an Institute of Criminology in Cambridge. Hitherto criminology had received little attention in

---

* *The Times*, October 30, 1963.

academic circles in England, and there was no chair in the subject at any British University. The gap was filled through the generosity of the Foundation. In 1959 Dr Leon Radzinowicz, a leading expert, was appointed first Wolfson Professor of Criminology in Cambridge, and in the following year Director of the Institute of Criminology. This facilitated the adoption of criminology in the curriculum of the University School of Law and the promotion of a postgraduate course in the subject, as well as the production under Professor Radzinowicz's general editorship of the well known series of *Cambridge Studies in Criminology*, of which upwards of thirty volumes have already appeared.

Another project which Nathan fathered with the Foundation was the donation of the greater part of the £140,000 which the National Gallery required to purchase Goya's famous portrait of the Duke of Wellington from a private owner. Unfortunately the picture was stolen shortly after it had been put on exhibition in the Gallery in 1961. The Prime Minister, then Mr Harold Macmillan, wrote to Nathan after appointing a committee to inquire into the theft and the security arrangements at the Gallery.

November 3, 1961. I hope that you will not have thought that my silence since the theft of Goya's 'Wellington' implied any lack of appreciation on my part either of the gravity of the loss which the nation has sustained by the theft or of the sense of frustration which you and your fellow Trustees must have experienced at the apparently nugatory effect of the Foundation's extreme generosity in this case. I and my colleagues have of course been keenly awaiting news of the picture's recovery, and it is really because we have been sincerely hoping for this as each day has passed that I have not written to you earlier. Although we must all go on trusting that sooner or later the picture will come to be restored to its place in the National Gallery—and it has to be remembered that the Mona Lisa was missing from the Louvre for no less than two years—it now seems clear that we can no longer rely on its early recovery.

In fact, more than four years were to elapse before the Goya was recovered, virtually undamaged. By this time Nathan was dead, but the Gallery immediately took steps to inform his family before the news was generally released. 'To me it was very seemly that the National Gallery's first reaction was to let your son know,' wrote Sir Harold Redman to Lady Nathan on May 26, 1965, 'for your husband's was the inspiration behind the Foundation grant. But for him it would not have gone through.'

3

Some mention has already been made of Nathan's long-standing interest in the affairs of Anglo-Jewry, dating back to his management of the Brady Boys Club in the East End of London before the First World War. Further details of his activities in this field may conveniently be given here. From 1921 to 1945, he was a Member of the Board of Deputies of British Jews, and from 1937 until the year of his death he was a Trustee. Other Anglo-Jewish organizations with which he was associated as Chairman or President included the Association for Jewish Youth, of which he was a founder and first chairman, the British Maccabi, the Hillel Foundation, the Jewish Association for Backward Children, the Jewish Hospitality Committee for British and Allied Forces during the Second World War, the Friends of Jewish Servicemen, the London Jewish Postgraduates Society, and the Jewish Museum. Particularly notable was his work for the Maccabi movement, the international Jewish youth organization which derives its inspiration from Yehuda Ha'Maccabi (Judas Maccabaeus) and his small but courageous band of Maccabees who raised the standard of revolt in 170 B.C. against Antiochus IV, King of Syria, and his attempt to force Hellenism upon Judaea, preferring death to surrender in their determination to preserve their freedom of worship.

The Maccabi movement, in its modern form, emerged in the last decade of the nineteenth century as the direct result of the persecution of Jewish communities in various European countries, particularly the terrible pogroms in Russia and Poland, which made the

Jewish communal leaders realize the urgent necessity for rendering Jewish youth fit and capable of physical self-defence. The movement aimed specifically at the promotion of good health, physical strength and friendly co-existence with non-Jewish neighbours through sports and games; the fearless and vigorous upholding and, if necessary, fighting for the cause of tolerance, social justice and freedom; the inculcation in both young and old of a sense of belonging to and a will to serve the community; and assisting, actively and morally, in the building up of Palestine as the Jewish National Home.

In 1909, during the Zionist Congress in Hamburg, an impressive display of physical exercises was staged by 300 Jewish youths from all over Europe. 'We are witnessing an unprecedented phenomenon in the development of Jewry,' said Max Nordau, one of the early Zionist leaders, on this occasion. 'I can see the birth of a generation of muscular Jews.'

The movement spread rapidly after the First World War, and by 1923 there were Maccabi Associations in twenty-two European countries, with a collective membership of 100,000. In 1932, the First 'Maccabiah', or Jewish Olympic Games, took place in Prague, to be followed three years later by the second function of this kind and the first to be held in Palestine. The Third Maccabiah, which was to have been held in 1939, had to be postponed owing to the outbreak of the war. It eventually took place in 1950 in the free and independent state of Israel. The first two Games had been confined to Maccabi members, but the organizers of the Third Maccabiah decided to throw open the Games to Jewish athletes of every nationality, irrespective of whether they belonged to Maccabi Clubs or not. In all twenty-two nations competed in the Ramat Gan Stadium near Tel-Aviv, including the United States, Canada, Argentina, India and South Africa, besides various European countries. Nathan, who occupied a seat of honour as President of the European Organizing Committee, was deeply moved by the opening ceremony, which began with the roll of drums and the firing of a cannon, when an Israeli athlete ran into the arena, holding aloft the lighted torch which had been carried by relays of runners from Modin, the scene of the heroic resistance of the Maccabees of Biblical times.

What impressed Nathan most of all at this opening ceremony was the smart appearance and bearing of the British team. 'Their reception was terrific,' he remarked afterwards. 'I never felt prouder of being a Briton or prouder of being a Jew. And I knew—and everything that has passed since has confirmed it—that in a moment, as in a flash, old unhappy acerbities had become lost in the past and friendships were remembered and renewed again. In a moment the young Jews of Britain had put Britain on the map again in Israel. All unknowingly, perhaps, these young Jews, drawn from London and the provinces, had done what statesmanship had thus far not achieved, and Britain and Israel were at one again. That, to me at least, was the highlight of this memorable Maccabiah.'

Equally impressive at the closing ceremony was the display given by the Israeli Defence Forces, which included commando drill, the dropping of parachute troops, and sword combat by the women's branch. 'It is clear beyond peradventure that the Defence Forces of Israel are a body to be reckoned with,' Nathan noted. 'I do not doubt that they are the most formidable, the best trained and the most resolute in the Middle East. What I saw was a revelation to me, and, I do not doubt, to others too. It is a tribute to the Chief of the General Staff and to his coadjutors that in so short a time they should have turned out so fine a force. It is a fine tribute to the Israelis, bearing in mind that Jews are not believed to be among the most susceptible of people to discipline, that they have voluntarily accepted a discipline which has enabled them to develop into the formidable body which it is apparent even to the least observant that they are now becoming.'

Three more Games were to take place in Israel during Nathan's lifetime. On the occasion of the Sixth Maccabiah in 1961, the last which he attended, athletes from twenty-seven countries participated. They were accommodated in the Maccabiah village, specially constructed beside the National Park at Ramat Gan. 'I can assure you that it did my heart good to watch them, to be with them and to applaud them,' Nathan wrote to a friend at the time. 'It is not an exaggeration to suggest that this coming together of so many young people, with all the energies and enthusiasms of youth, meeting together thus in Israel for the common purpose of clean sport, and a fine spirit of good sportsmanship, is not merely good for Israel, but is a worthwhile contribution to international good feeling among the peoples of so many countries, and thus a real contribution to the peace of the world.'

Although the British mandate in Palestine had ended in May, 1948, and the Jewish National Council had proclaimed the new State, Palestine had been immediately invaded by the forces of the neighbouring Arab countries—Egypt, Syria and Jordan—and hostilities did not cease until eight months later when armistice agreements were signed under United Nations auspices. On January 30, 1949, the date on which Great Britain officially recognized Israel, Nathan sent telegrams to Dr Chaim Weizmann, the President, and Mr Ben Gurion, the Prime Minister. To the President he said:

> Of all men you indeed should be the happiest on this memorable day which we may fervently hope and believe marks the opening of a new era of long-lasting friendship so necessary to both between Britain and Israel, for which as I know well you have always striven with such devotion and in which I am ever anxious to help. Let the recent quarrels be forgotten and only the old friendship be remembered. You now see your dreams come true and the work of the long years fulfilled.

Later in the same year, Nathan promoted the presentation of a forest of 750,000 trees in Israel as a tribute to President Weizmann from British Jewry—10,000 trees for every year of his life. Thus Nathan repeated the action he had taken over the Balfour Forest twenty-one years earlier. The occasion was marked by a dinner in the Savoy Hotel on November 22, Weizmann's seventy-fifth birthday, at which General Smuts, an old friend of the President's, was the guest of honour, having made his journey from South Africa

specially for this function. 'Let Israel never forget that it was
Britain that first took Weizmann by the hand,' said Smuts, speaking
at this dinner. 'Let the Weizmann Forest be the memorial of the
great planter, who replanted his people in their ancient homeland.'
As Chairman of the Weizmann Forest Committee, Nathan and a
small British delegation, including Lord Samuel, visited Weizmann
at his home in Rehovat in April, 1951, after the initial planting
ceremony in the Hills of Judeaa, when he was presented with a Gift
Scroll. Nathan and Weizmann had long been friends, their friendship covering most of the thirty years in which the Russian-born
Israeli President had held a British passport. It was the last time they
met, since he died just over eighteen months later. Nathan, who
had also been the President's legal adviser during his years in
England, flew to Israel with other prominent members of Anglo-
Jewry for the funeral and saw the remains of the President laid to
rest in the grounds of his home in a spot specified in his will, where
beyond the orange groves and cultivated slopes the stark outlines of
the Judean Hills were visible in the distance. Nathan and the others
with him on this solemn occasion were very conscious that, in
spite of much suffering and bloodshed, the first President of Israel
had achieved his ambition. Asked by Lloyd George during the
First World War what he desired as a reward for his vital dis-
coveries for the Government as a research chemist, Weizmann had
answered simply, 'A country for my people.'

At this point perhaps it may be most conveniently added that
Nathan was associated with a third forest project in Israel. This was
the Queen Elizabeth Coronation Forest, subscribed by the Anglo-
Jewish community in Great Britain. The suggestion was made by
Nathan, who became Chairman of the Forest Committee, and the
scheme was launched in the coronation year at a dinner in the
Guildhall, which the Duke of Edinburgh attended and at which
His Royal Highness accepted on the Queen's behalf a book from
the Chairman commemorating the gift from her Jewish subjects.
Nathan later presented the Queen personally with a volume of
photographs taken on the occasion of the inauguration of the

Forest. 'This Coronation Forest,' remarked the *Jewish Chronicle* at
the time, 'will provide living evidence not only of Anglo-Jewry's
allegiance to the Throne, but also of their ties with the ancient
homeland of their faith and race. For future generations of Jewry it
will provide the most appropriate and significant memorial that
could be possibly devised of this year's historic event. It also carries
forward a notable tradition, fostered in the past by Royal and civic
patronage and by the endeavours of several of its distinguished
sponsors, including Viscount Samuel, the Honorary President, and
Lord Nathan, the Chairman.'*

4

Nathan's activities in the field of physical endeavour were not
confined to exclusively Jewish organizations. For some years he
served as a Fellow on the Council of the Royal Geographical
Society and on the Management Committee of the Mount Everest
Foundation, becoming President of the former in 1958 and Chairman of the latter in 1959, having previously been President of the
Geographical Association. As the subject of his Presidential Address
to the Geographical Association in 1956, he chose 'World Aviation
and Geography', which he illustrated with examples of the different
fields in which aviation may be usefully applied, notably agricultural
production, exploration and surveys, and the transformation of
regional geography. He prefaced his discourse with what he recalled
as the strongest reminder he had ever had of the connection between
aviation and geography. This was once when he received an agitated
telephone call as Minister of Civil Aviation. 'B.O.A.C. had flown a
Tudor to Nairobi for testing, but the operators found that the aircraft could not take off once it had touched down. Their calculations had completely neglected the fact that Nairobi is 5,500 feet up
and that, in the thin air at this height, the Tudor needed a longer
runway than the local airfield possessed.'

Nathan was President of the Royal Geographical Society for the

* *Jewish Chronicle*, May 15, 1953.

customary three-year term, in his case from 1958 to 1961. The work of the Society is so well known, both domestically and internationally, that it is unnecessary to dwell upon it in any detail here. Little more need be said than that Nathan took an especial pride in the presidency, following as he did in the wake of so many distinguished men who had held the office since its establishment in 1830. 'He had, for one thing, a high regard for its prestige, for its traditional role and status in the intellectual life of the nation,' the Society's Director and Secretary, Mr L. P. Kirwan, has writ ten 'This was reflected in his attitude to the post. He saw the presidency as it had been seen in more aristocratic days, as an office appropriately held by a man whose own distinction in public life could give him easy access to the highest in the land, enabling him in the influential circles in which he was accustomed to move, to promote the Society's cause.'

There were two aspects of the Society's work to which he devoted special attention. The first was medical geography, a subject which had hitherto been pursued more intensively in the United States than in Great Britain, but which thanks to Nathan's interest has now become firmly established in the Society's programme of research. In 1959, a Medical Geography Committee was formed, consisting of doctors and representatives of allied sciences, such as anthropology, in addition to geographers and cartographers. It met under Nathan's chairmanship, and gave priority to the preparation of a national atlas of disease mortality. This pioneer project was entrusted to Dr Melvin Howe, Senior Lecturer in the Department of Geography and Anthropology in the University College of Wales, Aberystwyth. Dr Howe had already conducted some useful research into the distribution of deaths from cancer in Wales. The project was also attractive, because the cartographic work could be based on mortality statistics a good deal more reliable than those from most other parts of the world. The resultant *National Atlas of Disease Mortality in the United Kingdom* was published in 1963, actually on the day before Nathan's death.

The other aspects of the Society's work which especially attracted

Nathan and which, in many ways he made the central theme of his presidency, was the fostering of interest in geographical adventure and exploration in the young. It was this for which, in the opinion of his successor in office, Sir Raymond Priestley, Nathan would most like to be remembered in the field of geography. Under his presidency the Society not only greatly increased its support of undergraduate expeditions but extended its aid to expeditions of schoolboys and young apprentices from industry. As Mr Kirwan has put it, 'this extended support of youth expeditions, like the new work in medical geography, was made possible by generous grants from the Wolfson Foundation of which Lord Nathan was chairman, and no doubt in this his own enthusiasm and his firm belief in their value played a very important part'.*

The Society's Director and Secretary has also recorded some personal recollections.

Working at over seventy years of age far harder than most younger men, and seldom able to resist the temptation to add yet one more to a lengthy list of voluntary labours, Lord Nathan found it difficult to find, in addition to formal meetings, leisure for the Society's routine business which at times had to be done over breakfast at Brown's Hotel or travelling with him in his car between his flat and the City. . . .

Restless, immensely industrious to the last, Lord Nathan continued to strive on the Society's behalf after his presidency came to an end. As a man, he had unsuspected sides to his character. The genial, exuberant chairman, displaying the presidential badge of office which he had personally presented to the Society, had also more than a touch of shyness and reserve. The sophisticated and ambitious man of affairs inured to battle in a highly competitive world could also—in an environment not previously familiar—display a simplicity, a wistfulness, which had particular appeal. Certainly determination and exceptional courage were among his qualities, as those who had seen him fight his way through critical illness knew. So too were his generosity and kindness, as was illustrated by his constant care for the welfare of the Society's staff.

* The Geographical Journal, December, 1963, at p. 584; March, 1964, at p. 22.

In this context Nathan was also a member since its inception of the Committee of Management of the Mount Everest Foundation, a charitable trust created to encourage and support mountaineering and mountain exploration and research. Membership of the Committee was drawn equally from the Alpine Club and the Royal Geographical Society, and the expeditions which received grants from the Foundation were expected to make available the results of their labours to the journals of the Club and Society respectively.

During Nathan's year of office as Chairman (1959–60), grants amounting to over £13,500 were made to thirty-two applicants, ranging from Sir John Hunt's Greenland Expedition, the British–Indian–Nepalese Himalayan Expedition, and the Anglo-American Karakorum Expedition, which each received £1,500, to the New Zealand Antarctic Alpine Club Expedition, the Patagonia Party led by Mr E. E. Shipton, and expeditions from Cambridge University to the Congo and Northern Norway, which received lesser amounts. In addition to his work for the Mount Everest Foundation, Nathan took an active interest in the Public Schools Exploration Society, of which he was a Patron.

In the tribute he paid Nathan on the first meeting of the Royal Geographical Society held after his death, Sir Raymond Priestley, who was also a former Vice-Chancellor of Birmingham University, said:

> There never has been a time in the history of this country when the nation's spiritual health was in greater danger than it is today through the high level of material prosperity we have achieved for the great majority of our people, and our consequent preoccupation with physical welfare and pleasure. One answer—and the key one—to this very real menace is to foster in youth a spirit of adventure, and Lord Nathan, through his influence with the Wolfson Foundation and through his activity in this Society in general, was able to do more than anyone else possibly could.

In preparing his various speeches and addresses, most of which were subsequently published, Nathan went to considerable trouble. Nor did he object to going as far afield as the United States of

America to deliver them. When he crossed the Atlantic, his principal host was the well-known New York lawyer and inveterate opponent of censorship in all its forms, Morris Ernst, who had served as Special Assistant to President Roosevelt during the Second World War, and whose law firm of Greenbaum, Wolff and Ernst was one of the correspondents of Nathan's London office on legal matters. In 1951, at Ernst's invitation, Nathan spoke to the New York Bar Association on 'English Law and the Nationalized Industries'. He again visited America in 1957 and 1958, in which latter year he delivered the Charles Evans Hughes Memorial Lecture to the New York County Lawyers Association on 'The Changing Concept of Domicile'. During the same visit he also addressed the Law Medicine Research Institute of Boston University on 'Medical Negligence', and the Harvard University Law School on 'The *Cy-près* Doctrine and the Problem of its Reform'. Particularly appreciated was the address which he gave in 1957 on 'Eavesdropping' to the Lawyers' Division of the Federation of the Jewish Philanthropies of New York.*

By eavesdropping Nathan meant the interception by the authorities and recording of human speech through the use of various mechanical devices unknown to the speakers.

> Eavesdropping, in the sense in which we are considering it, is an invasion of privacy by stealth for the purpose of gaining information which will, or may, incriminate the man or woman being eavesdropped upon.
> We are here face to face with a new facet of the fundamental problem of all human society: the problem of balancing the claims of the state against those of the individual: the problem of power. The telephone—and the tape-recorder—the microphone—in short, all devices for recording the sound of the human voice is a new weapon which can and does immensely strengthen the hand of the state.
> It is a horrid weapon, a poisonous weapon, and it has a gruesome record. . . . It is a highly effective weapon; there is

---

* The address on 'Eavesdropping' was subsequently published in *The Law Times*, March 7, 13, 21, 1958.

no defence against it; and, in the hands of the unscrupulous, it can lead to corruption, to desolation and to slavery. Police states have not hesitated to use it, pleading, if by chance they felt obliged to make a pretence of defending their action, the 'inescapable' claims of 'security'—the claims of necessity. And necessity, as has been truly said, is 'the plea of every infringement of human freedom'. It is the argument of tyrants. William Pitt said that in the House of Commons in 1783—nearly two hundred years ago.

But police states were not alone in resorting to this kind of eavesdropping, as Nathan proceeded to point out. In regard to the telephone, where interception was known in America as 'wire tapping', this could only be legally undertaken by law enforcement officers and only subject to special authorization of the courts. In Great Britain the corresponding authority was the Home Secretary, who granted it comparatively rarely and then for the detection of serious crime such as espionage. However, the practice had recently come into the limelight in England, when the responsible Minister had authorized the interception of telephone conversations between a barrister and his lay client, and the consequent outcry in Parliament had led the Prime Minister to appoint a committee of three Privy Councillors under the chairmanship of Lord Birkett to look into the whole question. While the committee described as 'mistaken' the Home Secretary's decision to make the transcripts of the conversations available to the Bar Council, a private body, in this particular case, it had nevertheless recommended that the exercise of the power should be allowed to continue under the strictest rules and safeguards and never without the considered approval of the Home Secretary.*

Nathan summarized his conclusions as follows:

> In the last analysis, both our Home Secretary and your judges are answerable to the people. The kind of Home Secretary we get and the kind of judges you will get will depend

---

* *Report of the Committee of Privy Councillors appointed to inquire into the Interception of Communications.* Cmd. 283 (1957).

on what kind of Home Secretary and what kind of judges the people want. And if it is true to say that every nation has the government it deserves, it is also true to say that it will get the eavesdropping it deserves. 'As states are, so men are; they grow out of human characters.' That is very true, I think you will agree; though, I hope, not because I said it. I didn't. Socrates did!

Nor did Nathan forget his old school. He had kept in touch with St Paul's over the years and, as we have seen, the mural plaque recording Lord Montgomery's war-time association with the school was the result of his generosity. In 1957 he became President of the Old Pauline Club, an office which he filled for three years. 'The Club prospered under his guidance,' another distinguished Old Pauline, Lord Justice Pearson, recalled when Nathan died. 'It was fortunate and fitting that he was holding this office at the time of the 450th anniversary of the School's foundation and so presided at the Commemoration Banquet at the Mansion House on June 22, 1959, which was the acme of the Club's activities. At that banquet Nathan's speech on the debt that English education owes to the City of London exactly matched the occasion, combining a tribute to the City with a moving encomium of Colet's foundation and the broadmindedness which inspired it. I think a similar broadmindedness was shown by Nathan himself when he read the Old Testament Lesson in the Feast Services in St Paul's Cathedral. . . . He was a good friend to the Club and a great Pauline.'

5

The Second World War had brought about changes in Nathan's way of living, as they did with many other people. In war-time conditions he had found it impossible to maintain a large town house, and so he had taken a flat at 55 Park Lane, having no difficulty in securing the top apartment in this building, since it was shunned by other tenants on account of air raids. After the war the house in Wilton Crescent was sold, and also his property at Churt,

Relaxing at Churt House, Rotherfield

Sir Bernard and Lady Waley-Cohen with their children. Left to right: Joanna, Stephen, Robert, Rosalind

which was not capable of accommodating the overflow of belongings from London, particularly his collection of prints and rare books relating to London. Accordingly, in 1947, he bought a place at Rotherfield in East Sussex, consisting of a dwelling, which he renamed Churt House, and about one hundred acres of land, which for the next dozen years he assiduously farmed. Besides cattle, he kept horses for riding and hunting, for he continued to derive great pleasure from a day in the saddle and regularly went out with the Eridge Hounds.

The Eridge country is largely woodland, and there is not much open country for fast runs without frequent checks. But it was not devoid of risks, and in January, 1953, he had a serious accident. He was coming home at the end of the day, when his horse took fright at a passing train and bolted. To avoid crashing into a wall on a bend of the road and probably being killed, he flung himself off— always a courageous thing to do as every horseman knows—and came down heavily on a heap of stones at the roadside. He was taken to hospital in Tunbridge Wells, with a fractured pelvis and multiple bruises, and thence to the Westminster, where he spent the next six weeks. 'I have had the nastiest smash I have ever hand,' he wrote to his nephew Peter from the Westminster. 'But I am being well looked after here—as why should I not be, in the Hospital of which I am Chairman? I am told that I am making good progress, though it is all a frightful bore, and I hope to get out of here before too long and then to go away for a period of convalescence.' His injuries were more serious than at first supposed, and he had to endure a long and painful period of convalescence before he could resume his normal routine of work. What particularly worried him was that he might miss the Coronation of Queen Elizabeth II in June, to which he was determined to go, as he said, 'even if it kills me'. He did go to the Abbey, helped by two sticks. But the accident put an end to his riding for good.

However, as a hobby and a recreation he still had one of the finest collections of its kind of prints and books on old London, which he had formed over many years. When he was a young man

an eminent K.C. had told him, 'Everyone ought to collect something.' And so he had begun collecting books and prints of old
London, adding to it from time to time as well as displaying it to
visitors to Rotherfield, in which he took a great delight. It included
such rare items as the first edition of Stowe's *Survey of London*
(1595) and Westell and Owen's *Picturesque Tour of the Thames*
(1828), illustrated by twenty-four exceptionally fine aquatints.
Churt House was eventually given up in 1959, when Nathan and
his wife decided to base themselves permanently on London.
Accordingly, they moved into a larger flat in Park Street, Mayfair,
but it was not large enough to take the library and prints, which in
due course went up for auction at Sotheby's, where the sale occupied two days in 1962, and fetched a total of over £19,000. It may
be asked, why did Nathan not present the collection to a public
library or similar institution? The answer may well be a view
which his biographer shares, namely that instead of immobilizing
the collection, which would be the case if it went to an institution, it
was better to put it on the market and so let other private collectors
have the chance of enriching their own collections from its contents.

He also delighted in the progress of the younger generation,
notably his seven grandchildren and their parents, besides his
nephews Michael and Peter. By this time his daughter Joyce had
two sons and two daughters, while his son Roger, who had married
Philippa, daughter of Major J. B. Solomon, M.C., in 1950, had a
son and two daughters. His son-in-law Bernard Waley-Cohen had
been knighted in 1957 after serving as Sheriff in the city; three years
later Sir Bernard was elected Lord Mayor of London, and in 1961 he
was made a baronet, in accordance with custom, on the conclusion
of his year of office in the Mansion House.

Nathan was attached, too, to his two nephews. Like his own son
Roger, Peter became a solicitor on coming down from Oxford and
joined the firm of Herbert Oppenheimer, Nathan & Vandyk. He
encouraged Peter Nathan to form what was to become a remarkable
collection of celebrities' autographs. He also took an interest in
Peter's spiritual welfare, and was interested to learn that he had

made contact with the Moral Rearmament movement. 'I am all in favour of morals,' he warned him at this time, 'and under stress of necessity I am in favour of rearmament, but I do not know that I much care for the conjunction of the two.'

Like his father had been before him, Nathan had the reputation for abundant hospitality, and he and his wife entertained on a generous scale. Indeed, he might be called a free spender, for he was always ready to put his hand in his pocket to help any deserving individual, or at least individual who he thought to be deserving. More than once he lent considerable sums of money to friends who were in financial difficulties. One of these friends he obliged in this way at very short notice. Nathan wrote to him afterwards:

> I am glad, indeed, to have been able to do you a friendly service, which I hope will be effective for its purpose, and think it quite natural that you should have turned to me, though I must frankly say that I was rather taken aback to receive a request asking for such an immediate reply. I could scarcely help wondering what would have happened, in view of the urgency you expressed, if I had not happened to be available at that time, after 5 o'clock on a Friday afternoon.

This particular loan was promptly repaid within the time agreed. But Nathan was not so fortunate with other borrowers, such as a certain ex-Cabinet Minister, for whom he also acted professionally. Nathan made him an interest-free loan of £4,500 during the war. 'To lend money to a friend is a proverbially first-class patent for losing a friend,' he wrote to the individual in question when the latter showed some reluctance to repay the loan, 'but in this instance the proverb shall be falsified.' The individual pleaded as an excuse the 'serious juncture of history', which Nathan noted with wry amusement. 'It is the "serious juncture of history" which has created the new situation,' Nathan bluntly told the borrower; 'had it not been for a "serious juncture of history", you would no doubt still be a popular Minister and I still a prosperous solicitor, whereas you unfortunately are out in the cold as a Minister, whilst I am not merely now running at a loss as a solicitor, but have since the beginning of the war, as you know, been giving practically my whole time to public service in a purely voluntary capacity.' The loan was eventually repaid after considerable delay, the repayment being spread over three years. But relations between the two men were never the same afterwards.

Indeed, Nathan was most scrupulous in all his business and professional dealings. One client, for whom he had been able to render very considerable service, wished to show his appreciation. He was a very wealthy industrialist and the shares in his company were quoted on the Stock Exchange. He was aware that the forth-coming publication of the company's annual report and accounts, among other factors, was bound to have a considerable effect upon the market and that the shares would rise rapidly. He therefore offered Nathan an option on a large block of the shares, which Nathan would be free to take up any time within the next six months. Had Nathan done so and sold the shares immediately afterwards, he could have netted a substantial tax-free capital gain for himself. But he declined the offer with thanks, not wishing to take advantage of advance information unknown at the time to the general public.

A personal memento from a valued client was a different matter, such as the one which came from the Dowager Lady Londonderry, widow of Nathan's friend, the former Conservative Air Minister and colliery owner. The latter had died in 1949, leaving an estate of over a million pounds and under his will had appointed Nathan as principal trustee. This brought Nathan into touch with the various members of the Londonderry family, whose relations with each other were not always harmonious and called for the exercise of much tact on his part. After one family conference which he attended at Londonderry House, the Marchioness Dowager vrote to him:

> You don't really know, I am quite sure, how much I appre-
> ciate *all*, and I repeat *all*, that you have done for me and mine.
> As soon as I return to Mount Stewart next Monday, I am send-
> ing you a little token, which I have kept for you for a long time,

to show you how much I value all your deep and real kindness since Charley's death.

It is a little souvenir that I have always valued very much and my very own, given to me by dear Queen Mary. At my age I would rather give it to you myself than wait until after I am 'in my box'!

Nathan's business experience owed something to the fact of his long association with Gestetner Limited, manufacturers of duplicator machines. He had known Sigmund Gestetner, the son of the company's founder and 'a very exceptional man', since 1919, and when the company 'went public' ten years later, Nathan joined the board and remained on it until he became a Minister. When he went back to his solicitor's practice in 1948, he had not immediately rejoined the Gestetner company. They had decided to carry on with a 'purely functional' board; and it was not until after the death in 1956 of Sigmund Gestetner, who combined the offices of chairman and managing director, that Nathan returned to the company, this time as chairman. His experience with this company, coupled with the 'inside knowledge' of the working of other companies he had gained as a solicitor, no doubt contributed to his strongly held views on the ideal composition of a board of directors. He believed, for instance, that a wholly executive board was 'a psychological mistake', since it was apt to lead to 'a good deal of back-scratching' between technical directors. Above all, in his view, they needed an outside chairman. 'Gestetner have it in me,' he used to say. 'I'm not technical; but I have a good working knowledge of the world of affairs and the world of business. The outside chairman is in much the same position as a Minister—it's his job to assess the advice of the experts and give a hand in forming policy.'

Ideally, he believed that a large firm, particularly if it was horizontally diversified (which incidentally Gestetner was not), should have a two-tier direction—a 'management board to conduct the business,' grouping the managing director, finance director and heads of the various operating companies, and 'a top board', i.e. the board of the holding company, including the managing director, a finance man and a number of outside directors. 'This board should be small, and should not as a routine meet frequently, though available to be called together for special consultations.' But the outside director on it who was prepared to accept £250 a year for his services was, in Nathan's opinion, not worth having. ('If he's a man worth having, the outside director these days ought to command a four-figure salary.')

Nor did he have any use for the outside chairman who never went near the factory. 'The great function of the chairman is to walk about, and be seen on the factory floor,' he would say. 'Most people in employment are like young puppies that like to sniff round anyone who comes along to decide whether you're "all right". If they feel you are, eventually somebody will come and speak to you. Then you know you have succeeded.'

He felt strongly that large companies should be conscious of their public responsibilities, and though he acknowledged that many of them were, he believed nevertheless that there should be some statutory authority to see that they did not forget them—'a Consumer's Council, to supplement the Restrictive Practices Court and the Monopolies Commission, and to deal with individual products'. This and other views were later to be implemented by legislation, although Nathan was not to live to witness it. For instance, he also felt that there should be far less secrecy about interlocking industrial holdings. Subsidiary companies should be required to display their owners' names on their writing paper, and parent companies should be required to reveal holdings of 40 per cent or over in other companies.

But Nathan's attitude towards capitalism was very far from that of a dedicated Marxist. ('I have no feeling against profits—I like 'em very much!') Asked in 1962 by *The Director*, the official journal of the Institute of Directors, whether he still called himself a Socialist, he replied that he never had, though other people had called him so 'as a term of abuse'. He also rebuffed the suggestion that his membership of the Institute of Directors was looked upon with suspicion by the Labour Party. 'I've never myself heard anyone mention it within the Party,' he recalled. 'The only quarrel I ever had with the Institute was that I didn't think it should have got involved in party politics.'

On the return of the Conservatives to power after the General Election of 1951, Lord Jowitt, the ex-Lord Chancellor and a Law Lord, then acting Leader of the Labour Party in the House of Lords, formally invited Nathan to sit with him on the Front Opposition Bench and to co-operate with him fully in the work of the Front Bench in the Lords Chamber. 'I need not say that I value the co-operation that I know I shall receive from you,' Jowitt added. 'It is unnecessary to say that I shall require the very full assistance of all my colleagues, because, as I have made clear, I must give a part of my time to judicial work. This I know you fully understand and will therefore respond as far as may be possible.'

Nathan did respond in this sense, although at this time he was carrying a considerable burden of non-party political work, since in addition to being Chairman of the Committee on Charitable Trusts, he was Deputy Chairman of a similar Committee on the Consolidation and Amendment of the Law of Customs and Excise. On the whole, however, when he rose from his place on the Opposition Front Bench he tended to speak in a non-party political controversial sense on subjects on which he had a specialized knowledge, such as defence, army welfare, the Territorial Army, hospitals, the criminal law, and the like. But he did attend the Lords' debates regularly, if he was not such a frequent speaker as in the past. He was nearly always available to show visitors round the Palace of Westminster; indeed, his knowledge of the Parliament buildings and their history, which he displayed on these occasions, was the envy of the official guides. He knew every corner of the historic pile, which he loved as everyone who has served in either House cannot fail to do. His conducted tours were greatly in demand, although the visitors' reactions were sometimes unexpected. Once, when he took his eleven-year-old grandson Stephen Waley-Cohen round the buildings, he asked the boy what he had found most interesting. He was surprised to learn that what had struck young

Stephen most was not the Woolsack or the Speaker's Chair or Westminster Hall, but 'the place where they keep the fire hose'. This was something that the usual guide could hardly be expected to point out, but Nathan had done his stint of fire-watching in the war and he was only too familiar with it.

6

The year 1963 opened for Nathan with seemingly as much work as ever, although in fact he was preparing to shed some of his responsibilities. A journalist who interviewed him at the end of January, a few days before his 74th birthday, found him 'as spry and active as many men twenty years his junior'.* He had always managed with three or four hours sleep a night, and he still rose punctually at 6.30 a.m., being wakened by a telephone alarm call. He seldom went to bed before one o'clock in the morning; indeed, he would often work as late as three and would occasionally go on throughout the night at his desk in his Mayfair flat. 'That is so that I can have all Saturday off,' he would explain. Asked if he did not keep dozing off on the Friday following such an all-night session, he would reply, 'On the contrary, I feel exhilarated after accomplishing my work free of interruption—even by the telephone.' Three or four mornings a week he would have people in to breakfast ('It's a habit I learned from Lloyd George'), or sometimes he and his guests would meet for breakfast in Brown's Hotel, which was one of his favourite places for entertaining all-male company.

Early in the New Year, it was officially announced that he would be retiring from the Board of the Westminster Hospital at the end of March, and that he would be succeeded as Chairman by Sir John Vaughan-Morgan, M.P., a former Parliamentary Secretary to the Ministry of Health. He took the chair for the last time on March 28, when he reminded the Board of the tradition he had established on becoming Chairman by which the first Minute Book was displayed,

* Tudor Jenkins. *Evening Standard*, January 29, 1963.

Welcoming Sir John and Lady Hunt at Royal Artillery Dinner, Woolwich,
May, 1963

With the Matron, Miss Lavinia Young, and the nursing staff of the Westminster Hospital. The Chairman's farewell visit with Lady Nathan, 1962

and he expressed the hope that his successor would maintain the practice at future meetings of the Board. Then, to quote from the current Minutes,

> Lord Nathan said that it was difficult to find appropriate words to express his feelings at this, his last meeting as Chairman of the Board. He had been closely associated with Westminster and Westminster Children's Hospital for the past thirty-five years and he had been appointed a Governor on the same day as the late Lord Wigram had been elected President. He said that it had given him great gratification that in all discussions at the Board there had been agreeable harmony amongst the members. On no occasion had there been ill feeling, and the Board had worked together as a whole with a single-minded aim in the welfare and progress of the Hospital. He deeply appreciated the complete support he had received from the Board as a whole.

He went on to express his appreciation to the members of the staff of all grades, and had a particular word for the Matron, Miss Lavinia Young, for her care of the patients, and to the Deputy Matron and nursing staff. Finally he commended the Hospital to the new Chairman, thanking him for his co-operation and friendly attitude and wishing him well. His last act as Chairman was to invest Sir John Vaughan-Morgan with the badge of his new office.

The appreciation was mutual. At the next monthly meeting of the Board of Governors, it was unanimously agreed that a special resolution expressing 'deep appreciation' of Lord Nathan's 'outstanding services' should be incorporated in the Minutes.

> The Board wished to place on record their gratitude for the sound judgement, tireless energy and administrative practice of a high order which Lord Nathan gave to the problems of immense complexity which have faced the Hospital since 1948.

Accordingly the Board resolved that their late Chairman should be appointed a Vice-Patron of the Hospital, and further that he should be asked to lay the foundation of a new extension to the Hospital buildings in Page Street. He accepted this latter invitation, but unfortunately he was not to live to perform the ceremony.* Also to mark his service to the Hospital the Board of Governors gave a dinner in his honour in the Merchant Taylors' Hall, and later a reception in the Queen Mary Nurses Home in Page Street so that the hospital staff might bid him an affectionate farewell.

The same month in which Nathan relinquished the Chairmanship of the Westminster completed his fiftieth year as a solicitor. His private secretary, Miss Marjorie Dyce, who had served him with exemplary ability and devotion for thirty years, had recently retired, and he too began to think of giving up practice. However, he decided to carry on until after he had reached his half-century as a partner. Nor was there any slackening in his other activities. ('It's all so frightfully interesting.') He was busy, too, entertaining as usual and being entertained. Among others, he was host on separate occasions to the Israeli, Swiss and Polish Ambassadors. In April, the Royal Regiment of Artillery, of which he was senior Honorary Colonel ('Sir Winston Churchill comes immediately below me'), gave a dinner in his honour in the R.A. Mess at Woolwich, to which officers' ladies were also invited, an unusual innovation.

On July 31, the day Parliament rose for the long summer recess, there was a debate in the Lords on the proposed reorganization of the Ministry of Defence, in which Nathan intervened. It was to be the last time on which he addressed that assembly. The House was due to meet again on October 24 to hear the Queen's Speech proroguing Parliament. But on that morning Nathan's usual place on the Opposition Front Bench was empty.

The new defence scheme was designed to absorb the three service ministries in the Defence Ministry. But there had been ten Defence Ministers since 1947, and, as Lord Montgomery put it in the same debate, if that sort of musical chairs went on the new organization could not possibly succeed. Nathan, who agreed with his old schoolmate, also wondered whether there was likely to be in the Ministry of Defence anyone with 'the same unusual qualifications'

* It was performed by Lady Nathan on November 2, 1964.

as the then Chief of Defence Staff (Admiral Lord Mountbatten), who was competent to present an opinion to the Minister where differences might arise between the Chiefs of Staff of the three services. Unlike the Permanent Under-Secretary and the Chief Scientific Adviser, who were permanent civil servants, the Chief of Defence Staff and the Chiefs of Staff were only there for three or four years. 'Those who are there permanently, when the Minister, the Chief of Defence Staff and the Chiefs of Staff of the various services are all birds of passage,' he emphasized, 'come to occupy a position of the greatest possible responsibility and authority. The question is whether in an office so complex as this, and covering so wide a range of responsibilities, that is altogether a sound position.'

National Defence had been Nathan's greatest interest ever since the days he had drilled and marched with the school cadet corps at St Paul's sixty years before. He had given abundant proof of it in two world wars, in his ministerial service and in his peace-time work for the Territorial Army. It was fitting therefore that he should refer to this in his political swansong.

My Lords, I think that I personally am in a pretty good position to speak on this question because I have spent a great deal of my time and interest in connection with it—in a very minor way, it is true—but one cannot do more than give one's interest and activities to the matter which interest one. . . .

I think that in all this post-war period the Labour Party have a record which is entitled to respect. They have in every way played their part in seeking to secure the defence of the country in all the ways that were open to them. And I may say, on behalf of my noble friends, that we hold the defence and honour of the country as high and as warmly as do any Members of your Lordships' House.

The day after the defence debate marked the fiftieth anniversary of his joining Herbert Oppenheimer in Finsbury Square, and it made him happy to receive a note from the former senior partner in his retirement (then 87) which showed that he had not forgotten the occasion. 'Do you realize that today it is fifty years since we became partners?' Oppenheimer wrote. 'And it is nice to recollect that during that half-century there has not been one unfriendly word between us—not even when you messed up the lawn mower at Loddon Acre during your reconvalescence after Gallipoli?'

In September, Nathan and his wife went off to Italy for a holiday. He had always wanted to stay in the Villa d'Este, the luxurious hotel with its superb gardens and scenic views on the shore of Lake Como, once the home of Princess Caroline, the estranged wife of the English King George IV. In these serene and beautiful surroundings, the Nathans spent their last happy month together. He returned to the office at the beginning of October seemingly refreshed and buoyant. But in reality things were far from well with him physically. One day, shortly after they had got back, he came into their flat and told his wife that he felt so poorly that he had had to leave a meeting and come home. He complained of severe internal pains. His doctor, on examining him, suspected appendicitis and recommended his immediate admission to Westminster Hospital. There the diagnosis was confirmed.

The last time Nathan had been in the hospital as a patient was eight years previously, when he had been operated on by Mr Stanley Lee, the hospital surgeon and Director of Surgical Studies at the Westminster Medical School. After that experience he had written to the Israeli Ambassador: 'I have had a pretty rough time with three technically major, though not normally dangerous, operations, which is more than the human frame was made to sustain within so short a time. Indeed, I have marvelled at how the human body can resist the assaults upon it.'

Mr Lee, who was thus familiar with Nathan's clinical history, was reluctant to operate again. But the patient's condition made this imperative. The appendectomy was successfully performed, but the operation unfortunately revealed that there were serious complications due primarily to an acute kidney ailment. It also appeared that

Nathan was suffering from diabetes. This combination proved too much for the patient to withstand. Although he recovered consciousness, his post-operative condition rapidly deteriorated through kidney failure. As a final resort, he was placed in the hospital's kidney machine. To the last he showed his usual consideration for the doctors and nurses. 'I'm feeling really awfully ill,' he said just before the end. 'I do hope nobody thinks I'm making a fuss.' When his system failed to respond to the kidney machine, it was evident that there was no further hope. He died quite peacefully in the hospital a few hours later, during the night of October 23, 1963.

'It is sad that a life full of vigour and devoted to public service has come to an end,' so wrote his fellow Old Pauline, Lord Justice Pearson, when he heard the news. 'Harry Nathan will be remembered with respect and gratitude in many walks of life.' No doubt it would have gratified him to know—for there was an endearing streak of vanity in his character—that *The Times* rated him a full column in its obituary notice and also published tributes from its readers on six successive days.

The respect and gratitude, and indeed affection, in which he was widely held may be judged from the fact that Lady Nathan received 1,400 letters of sympathy. Hundreds of old friends and colleagues crowded into the West London Synagogue, which amongst others was attended by representatives of the Duke of Edinburgh and the Lord Mayor of London, as well as the many branches of the public service, welfare and other organizations with which he had been identified. Here the service was conducted by Rabbi Leslie Edgar. The Rabbi included in his address a touching tribute from 'an old personal friend', who preferred to remain anonymous but was in fact Nathan's cousin and lifelong friend Leonard Stein.

If I were asked to single out Harry Nathan's most distinctive qualities, my answer would be—loyalty, warm-hearted humanity and creative imagination.

He possessed in an unusual degree the power to fertilize any activity in which he might be engaged with fresh thinking and new ideas. Those who worked with him know how often some flash of inspiration would enable him to perceive something which had escaped less constructive minds. That is what I mean by creative imagination.

It was that same gift of imagination which, in another aspect, was reflected in his warm-hearted concern for all of those, high and low, with whom he had any personal contact, whether in his professional life or in the Army or in the many public bodies on which he served or among the members, far or near, of his own family circle. With his sympathetic understanding of other people's problems and difficulties, he saw each of them as an individual human being, entitled at all times, irrespective of rank and station, to consideration and respect and in trouble to all the help he could give.

Lastly (it might be that I should have spoken of it first, for of all his qualities this, perhaps, shines out most brightly), his loyalty—loyalty to his friends, to the institutions with which he had at any time been associated, and to the community into which he was born. For him a friendship once made was a friendship for life, to be kept bright and burnished to the end. As it was with individuals, so it was with institutions—his synagogue, his school, his regiment, the Boys' Club for which he had worked so hard long years ago—the list could be extended indefinitely, for attachments once formed were never broken. All these ties he cherished as long as he lived with a fidelity and a warmth of feeling for which he will long be affectionately remembered.

A smaller and more intimate service was arranged by the Governors of Westminster Hospital and took place in the new Wolfson School of Nursing in Vincent Square. Here there was a fitting division of duties between the hospital staff, the Church of England chaplain (the Rev. D. C. Francis) officiating, the Jewish chaplain (Rabbi R. Unterman) reciting the memorial prayers, the Matron (Miss Young) reading the lesson and the Senior Consulting Surgeon (Sir Clement Price Thomas) delivering the address. More than one pair of eyes was dimmed with tears that day, for Lord Nathan was greatly beloved at the Westminster.

His remains were laid to rest in the family burying ground in the

Jewish Cemetery in Golder's Green. A quotation from the Old Testament prophet Ecclesiastes was later inscribed on the headstone of his grave. It aptly expresses the characteristic pattern of his life.

Whatsoever thy hand findeth to do, do it with thy might.

Index

Bennett, Air Vice-Marshal Donald, 216–18
Bernays, Robert, 86
Bernhard, Prince of the Netherlands, 133
Beveridge, Lord, 230–2, 234
 Voluntary Action, 230, 232
Bevin, Ernest, 136, 151, 179, 181, 183–4, 189, 191, 211, 221
Bibergeil, Abraham, 3
Bibergeil, Adolph, 3
Bibergeil, Hirsch (Henry), 3
Bibergeil, Louis—*see* Beaver, Louis
Binney, Sir Hugh, 208–9
Birdwood, General, 59, 62, 64
Birkenhead, Lord (F. E. Smith), 88, 95–6
Birkett, Lord, 239, 251
Birmingham University, 249
Blake, William, 86
 Preface to *Milton*, 86
Board of Trade, 17, 118
Bolitho, Hector, 76
Bolter, Arthur, 14, 21–2, 25, 42
Bonaparte, Napoleon, 1, 167
Booth, John, 197n
Booth Shipping Lines, 197n
Bossom, Alfred (Lord), 179
Boston University, 250
Bowhill, Sir Frederick, 198
Brabazon of Tara, Lord, 201, 204
Bracken, Brendan, 177
Brady Street Club for Working Lads, 30–1, 38, 79, 241, 266
Bristol Engine Co., 202
British Airways Authority, 199
British Army, 137, 197n
 World War I regiments:
  1st Volunteer Battalion, Royal Fusiliers (City of London Regiment), 31–3, 35–6, 44, 50, 52, 55, 59, 63–70, 116, 266
  2nd South Middlesex Volunteers, 21, 31
 3rd Army, 56

8th Army Corps, 69–70
19th County of London Regiment, 66
29th Division, Reserve Brigade, 47–8, 59, 62, 65, 67, 69
Australian and New Zealand (Anzac) Corps, 59
Rifle Brigade, 66
World War II regiments:
 17th/21st Lancers, 148
 21st Army Group, 21
 33rd (St Pancras) T.A. Anti-Aircraft Battalion, Royal Engineers, 128–9
 300th Royal Regiment of Artillery (T.A.), 128
 Durham Light Infantry, 187–8
 Royal Artillery, 187, 262
 see also Auxiliary Territorial Service, British Expeditionary Forces, Mediterranean Expeditionary Forces, Rhine Army, Territorial Army
British Broadcasting Corporation (B.B.C.), 170
British Empire Cancer Campaign, 226
British European Airways (B.E.A.), 197, 215, 219, 221
British Expeditionary Forces, 145
British Medical Association (B.M.A.), 125
British Medical Council, 226
British Overseas Airways Corporation (B.O.A.C.), 197, 200–4, 206–7, 212–15, 219, 223, 246
British Society for International Health Education, 226
British South American Airways Corporation (B.S.A.A.C.), 197, 214–16
Brougham, Lord, 232–3
Brown, Ernest, 182
Brown, Sir John, 142

s* 269

INDEX